Al 'I'tibaa'a

AL 'I'TIBAA'A

AND THE PRINCIPLES OF FIQH OF THE RIGHTEOUS PREDECESSORS

SHEIKH WASIULLAH MUHAMMAD ABBAAS

PROFESSOR OF HADEETH AND TEACHER

IN THE MASJID AL HARAAM IN MAKKAH SAUDIA ARABIA

TRANSLATED BY

ABU ABDUR RAHMAN FARUQ POST

DAR UL ITIBAA'A PUBLISHING

2013/1434

Al 'I'tibaa'a

Al 'I'tibaa'a

Table of Contents

Translators Note 8

About the Author 9

Introduction 26

Chapter One: Definition of al It'ibaa'a 41

Part One: Creation of Mankind and the Reason for their Creation 43

Part Two: The Sending of the Messengers 44

Part Three: What is obligatory upon the nations with regards to the Messengers 51

Part Four: The time period between the Prophet Muhammad and the Prophet who preceded him 55

Part Five: The condition of the world when the Prophet Muhammad was sent to mankind 57

Part Six: How The Companions learned and acquired the religion from the Prophet Muhammad 72

Part Seven: Allah and His Messenger ordered with the imitation and following of the Prophet 76

Part Eight: Methodology of the Companions when differing, after the time of the Prophet 98

Part Nine: The changing of affairs after the best of generations 114

Chapter Two: Learning the Religion and the 'fiqh' of the Salaf 137

Part One: Obligation of learning the religion 138

Part Two: 'Fiqh' in the religion 148

Part Three: Subsidiary Divisions of 'fiqh' 152

Part Four: Fundamentals and principles of 'fiqh' of the Companions 159

Part Five: The Fundamentals which the scholars of 'fiqh' used to base their rulings upon 165

Al 'I'tibaa'a

Part Six: Seeking and giving religious verdicts and opinions..193

Part Seven: That which is obligatory upon the one seeking a religious verdict............196

Part Eight: Mufti's obligation to give verdicts with the strongest and most preponderant view..207

Part Nine: The Mufti's knowledge of the different opinions..212

Part Ten: The actions of the Mufti regarding the affairs which the religious opinions differ..215

Part Eleven: The Manners of the Mufti..221

Closing Statements..222

Bibliography..223

Glossary of Terms..229

Al 'I'tibaa'a

Al 'I'tibaa'a

A note from the author of the book-Sheikh Wasiullah Abbaas, may Allah preserve him:

In the name of Allah the Most Merciful the Bestower of Mercy

All praises are due to Allah the Lord of all creation and may the Prophet Muhammad, his family, and all of the righteous and noble companions be mentioned amongst the heavens. As to what proceeds:

Indeed the American brother Faruq Post mentioned to me that he translated the book 'Al'Iti'baa'a and the Principles of Fiqh of the Righteous Predecessors' into the English Language.

I have known the brother Faruq for many years. I have known him to have sound aqeedah and upright conduct. He has graduated from the College of Da'wah, department of (Quran and Sunnah) and he is currently studying his Masters Degree in the department of the Sunnah (Hadeeth) in the University of Umm al-Qura. By the grace of Allah he is well-acquainted with understanding of the Arabic Language as well as understanding his native language which is English, according to what the American brothers have mentioned to me.

Verily, I have given him permission to translate this book while expressing my thanks and gratitude to him and making supplication for him to be successful and be guided.

Written by:

Wasiullah ibn Muhammad Abbaas
1432/2/12 (January 6, 2012)
Teacher in the Masjid al Haraam and Ustaadth in the University of Umm al Qura

Al 'I'tibaa'a

Translators Note

All praises are due to Allah and may the Prophet Muhammad's name be mentioned within the heavens and may peace and blessings be sent upon him, his companions, his wives and all those who follow them in righteousness until the Day of Resurrection.

This book is an English translation of the book (الاتباع و أصول فقه السلف) **'Al It'ibaa'a and the Principles of 'Fiqh' of the Righteous Predecessors'** by the great noble scholar, muhaddith, faqeeh, professor sheikh Wasiullah ibn Muhammad Abaas, may Allah preserve him and raise his status in this world and the next. I depended upon the first (2010/1431h) 'Dar ul Istiqaamah' printing of this book while translating.

I thank Allah, then sheikh Wasiullah for granting me the opportunity to translate this great treatise into the English Language and we ask Allah to make it beneficial for all who read it and act upon it.

While translating this work I referred back to the sheikh numerous times in which the sheikh clarified some important points and made some slight additions and comments which are not found in the first edition of the Arabic version, but which I included in the English translation.

Sheikh Wasiullah did the referencing for the majority of the prophetic narrations and narrations of the companions and also mentioned the authenticity of these narrations. Some of these refrences were moved to the footnotes for easier reading. I also consulted the Sheikh and requested to do biographies for some of the narrators, scholars and authors which were mentioned in the treatise, which the sheikh pleasantly obliged, may Allah reward him greatly. I also commented on some of the resources used in this treatise. Any comments added by the translator are indicated by **(TN)** within the footnotes.

I also included a glossary of some of the terminology used in the treatise which can be found at the end of this work. In addition I also added on a brief biography of the sheikh which will enlighten readers as to who the sheikh is and what are some of his works.

I ask Allah to accept this translation from me and place it on my scale of good deeds on the day when no wealth, children, friends nor spouse can aid me. Whatever the translation contains of truth is from Allah and whatever it contains of mistakes in the translation than verily it is from myself and the shaytaan and verily Allah, His Messenger, Islam and Sheikh Wasiullah are free from them and I seek Allah's forgiveness.

One in dire need of Allah's guidance and forgiveness:

Abu AbdurRahman Faruq Post

About the Author

Name: He is Shaykh al-Allaamah Wasiullah ibn Muhammad Abbaas ibn Ahmad Abbaas

Date/Place of Birth: Shaykh Wasiullah was born in this town of "Bherabhoj" on the first day of Jumaadaa al-Oolaa, 1367H (1948ce). His father's name was Muhammad Abbaas Khaan, his grandfather's name was Ahmad Khaan, and great grandfather's name was Khush-Haal Khaan.

Family: The grandfather of Shaykh Wasiullah, Ahmad Khaan, was the chief of his town, "Bherabhoj", for a period of forty years. The internal affairs of this town were under his control.
In other words, he was the interior minister of this town. Baytul-Maal was established, with which those in need were helped. In accordance to necessity, some people would be given cloth, some would be given food, and some would be given money. It was forbidden for any person to be out on the streets after midnight without due cause. The residents of this town would resolve their internal disputes amongst themselves rather than going to the central courts. If a dispute occurred, the elders would visit the town chief. The chief would hear from both sides and end the dispute between them. Shaykh Wasiullah's ancestors are from a town close to the municipality of "Basti", which falls under the district of "Basti" in the northern state of India, Uttar Pradesh. The municipality of "Basti" is approximately two hundred kilometers north of the famous capital of the state of Uttar Pradesh, Lucknow.

Approximately four hundred years ago, in 1600ce, five brothers of the Shaykh's ancestral family migrated from this town to another town by the name of "Bherabhoj". At the time, this town was an abandoned rain forest which spread over numerous kilometers. These five brothers worked day and night cutting the trees, bushes, and scrubs of this forest, and built houses on this cleared land. The names of these five brothers, in sequence of age, were: Bhoj Baba, Satgarle Billa, Sa'adullah Billa, Zor-Aawar, and Jahar Babbu Baba. This town is named after the oldest of these five brothers, Bhoj Baba, and is famously identified by this name until today.

Al 'I'tibaa'a

It is narrated that after arriving in this town and clearing the land for residence and agriculture,
the eldest brother of these five, Bhoj Baba, first established the foundation of a Masjid on the cleared land. However, one of the brothers died after the establishment of the foundation of this Masjid, and hence, the construction of the Masjid was halted. It is narrated that the construction was abandoned for a period of twelve years. After this long period, the desire to do goodness increased in their hearts, and they started completing the construction of this Masjid. In accordance to those times, a vast and outstanding Masjid was built, which consisted
of three large pillars and wide walls. Old-fashioned bricks, exceptional-quality wood, and other
building material were utilized in the construction.

This Masjid is still present in its original state, and is a testimony of the glorious Islaamic constructional history of India. This Masjid is also proof of the religious efforts of Shaykh Wasiullah's ancestors and grandfathers, as well as being as-Sadaqah al-Jaariyah (continuous charity) for them. May Allaah accept it from them and make it heavy on their scale of good deeds on the Day of Resurrection.

Education: The Shaykh gained primary education in this town from Shaykh Muhammad Saleem who was a well-respected personality from a religious family of this town. Shaykh Muhammad Saleem was a student in "Madrasah (school) Rehmaaniyyah" in Delhi in August of 1947ce. He travelled to his resident town in Ramadaan of that year during the annual holidays. This was an extremely dangerous time period in the history of India, as on one hand, the mutiny against the British rulership was in its peak stages, and on the other hand, Pakistan was in its foundational stages and numerous Muslims were displaced as migrants. Shaykh Muhammad Saleem had to fight for his life whilst travelling to his resident town during this time period. Eventually, some peace was restored, and Shaykh Muhammad Saleem returned to "Madrasah Rehmaaniyyah" for further studies a few days after Ramadaan of that year. However, "Madrasah Rehmaaniyyah" was now destroyed in the mutiny, and the exemplary sounds of "Allaah said…" and "the Messenger of Allaah said…" which had been heard for ages in the Madrasah had gone silent. Consequently, Shaykh Muhammad Saleem travelled to "Madrasah Riyaadil-Uloom, Delhi", which was established by Shaykh al-Allaamah Abdus-Salaam al-Bastawee, and he himself was its director, "Shaykhul-Hadeeth", and teacher during his entire life. Shaykh Muhammad Saleem completed his studies under him in his Madrasah.

Al 'I'tibaa'a

After completing his primary studies in his resident town, Shaykh Wasiullah travelled to the town of "Yusufpoor", which is three miles from the Shaykh's resident town. Shaykh Wasiullah enrolled in "Madrasah Daaril-Hudaa" in this town, where three elderly honorary graduated students of now destroyed "Madrasah Rehmaaniyyah" of Delhi were teaching. These three were: Shaykh Abdur-Rahmaan ar-Rehmaanee, Shaykh Muhammad Ibraaheem ar-Rehmaanee, and Shaykh Jalaal-ud-Deen ar-Rehmaanee. Additionally, Shaykh Abdul-Ahad al-Kaanpooree and Shaykh Muhammad Idrees al-Qaasimee were also responsible for educational activities. These five scholars were extremely famous for teaching and lecturing amongst the people. Shaykh Wasiullah benefitted tremendously from these five in accordance to his ability.

The year in which Shaykh Wasiullah completed the third grade, a large conference of the major Salafee scholars was held in this Madrasah in the month of Sha'baan, the last month of the academic year for Arabic schools in India. From the scholars who participated in this conference was Shaykh al-Allaamah Nadheer Ahmad al-Amlawee ar-Rehmaanee who was the director and "Shaykhul-Hadeeth" of "Jaami'ah Rehmaaniyyah" in the city of Banaras at the time. Shaykh Wasiullah was from the brilliant students of his Madrasah, and would pass with top ranking amongst his classmates in the yearly examinations.

In the third grade, the Shaykh attained the highest marks amongst all of the students at his level in the Madrasah. This with the fact that the Shaykh was fourteen years old, and those at his level from his classmates and otherwise were older than him. His honorable teacher, Shaykh Jalaal-ud-Deen ar-Rehmaanee, introduced Shaykh Wasiullah to Shaykh al-Allaamah Nadheer Ahmad al-Amlawee ar-Rehmaanee, and informed him of the Shaykh's brilliance and excellence in his studies in relation to his peers and classmates, and the Shaykh's zeal for gaining knowledge. He requested from Shaykh al-Allaamah Nadheer Ahmad ar-Rehmaanee to grant admission to Shaykh Wasiullah in "Jaami'ah Rehmaaniyyah" in the city of Banaras, and informed him that Shaykh Wasiullah would swiftly pass through the various incremental levels of seeking knowledge under his tutelage.

Shaykh al-Allaamah Nadheer Ahmad ar-Rehmaanee informed Shaykh Jalaal-ud-Deen ar-Rehmaanee that Shaykh Wasiullah was small in age, and that he should remain at "Madrasah Daaril-Hudaa" for a few more years. However, Shaykh Jalaal-ud-Deen ar- Rehmaanee was adamant in his request and urged Shaykh al-

Al 'I'tibaa'a

Allaamah Nadheer Ahmad ar- Rehmaanee to test the knowledge of Shaykh Wasiullah, and informed him that he would find the Shaykh ahead of his age in terms of knowledge. Accordingly, Shaykh al- Allaamah Nadheer Ahmad ar-Rehmaanee asked Shaykh Wasiullah a few questions and was surprised at the Shaykh's brilliance and deemed him to be in accordance of the academic standard of "Jaami'ah Rehmaaniyyah". Thereafter, he ordered Shaykh Wasiullah to arrive in the city of Banaras at a future date.

Shaykh Wasiullah enrolled in "Jaami'ah Rehmaaniyyah" in 1963ce and continued with his studies at this Madrasah until 1966ce. Various scholars would teach at this Madrasah, from them was Shaykh al-Allaamah Nadheer Ahmad ar-Rehmaanee himself, as he would teach students in their last years of studies.

Shaykh al-Allaamah Nadheer Ahmad ar-Rehmaanee enlisted Shaykh Wasiullah amongst his circle of students, and began teaching him the famous foundational book in Mustalah al-Hadeeth (terminologies of Hadeeth sciences), "Nuzhatun-Nadhar". However, Shaykh Wasiullah informs with sadness that he could not complete this book with him, as Shaykh al-Allaamah Nadheer Ahmad ar-Rehmaanee became sick and had to be admitted in a hospital, and on the 30th day of the month of May, 1965ce, Shaykh al-Allaamah Nadheer Ahmad ar-Rehmaanee passed away.

Whilst a student in "Jaami'ah Rehmaaniyyah", Shaykh Wasiullah also gained knowledge from Shaykh Muhammad Idrees Aazaad ar-Rehmaanee, Shaykh Abdul-Waahid ar-Rehmaanee, Shaykh Muhammad Yoosuf al-Bahraa'ichee, and Shaykh Muhammad Aabid ar-Rehmaanee During the Shaykh's time as a student in "Jaami'ah Rehmaaniyyah" in the city of Banaras, an invitational program came to form in relation to the establishment, commencement, and inauguration of "Jaami'ah Salafiyyah" in the same city of Banaras. A large conference was held for this event, in which various scholars from all parts of India participated. Additionally, numerous representatives of various Islaamic countries also took part in this event. The director of the Islaamic University of Madinah, Shaykh al-Allaamah Abdul-Azeez ibn Abdullaah ibn Baaz was also extended an invitation for attendance in this program. Shaykh al-Allaamah Abdul-Azeez ibn Abdullaah ibn Baaz appointed Shaykh al-Allaamah Abdul-Qaadir Shaybah al-Hamd
as his representative and sent him to Banaras. The Ambassador of Saudi Arabia to India at the
time was Muhammad al-Hamd ash-Shubaylee, and he accompanied Shaykh al-Allaamah Abdul-Qaadir Shaybah al-Hamd to Banaras.

Al 'I'tibaa'a

Shaykh al-Allaamah Abdul-Azeez ibn Abdullaah ibn Baaz particularly directed his representative at the conference, Shaykh al-Allaamah Abdul-Qaadir Shaybah al-Hamd, that he presents to the administrative committee of "Jaami'ah Salafiyyah Banaras" the proposal of sending some students of "Jaami'ah Salafiyyah Banaras" to the Islaamic University of Madinah for further studies. Accordingly, Shaykh al-Allaamah Abdul-Qaadir Shaybah al-Hamd presented this proposal to the administrative body of both "Jaami'ah Salafiyyah Banaras" and "Jaami'ah Rehmaaniyyah". Consequently, the administrative committee of "Jaami'ah Rehmaaniyyah" selected four students for further studies in the Islaamic University of Madinah. These four students were: Shaykh al-Allaamah Wasiullah Abbaas, Shaykh al- Allaamah Abdul-Hameed ar-Rehmaanee (hafidhahullaah), Shaykh Abdus-Salaam al- Madanee, and Shaykh Abdur-Rahmaan al-Bastawee. These four students were taken to the guesthouse of Shaykh al-Allaamah Abdul-Qaadir Shaybah al-Hamd, where they were interviewed by him, and were given promise of their acceptance to the Islaamic University of Madinah. In this way, Allaah (subhaanahu wa ta'aalaa) made easy for the Shaykh to travel to Madinah, Saudi Arabia in his quest for further Islaamic knowledge.

Shaykh Wasiullah attained a High school certificate in the year 1387-1388H from the Islaamic University of Madinah. He attainted his Bachelors degree in the year 1391-1392H from the Faculty of Da'wah and Usool ad-Deen (Principles of the Religion), department of Tafseer and Hadeeth, the Islaamic University of Madinah.

From the scholars who were teachers at the Islaamic University of Madinah at that time were: Shaykh al-Allaamah Abdul-Ghaffaar Hasan ar-Rehmaanee [d.2007ce], Shaykh al-Allaamah Abdul-Muhsin ibn Hamad al-Abbaad al-Badr, Shaykh al-Allaamah Saalih al-Araaqee, Shaykh Aboo Bakr al-Jazaa'iree, Shaykh al-Allaamah Hammaad al-Ansaaree [d.1418H], and Shaykh al-Allaamah Abdul-Lateef (rahimahullaah). In 1967ce, Shaykh al-Allaamah Taqee-ud-Deen al-Hilaalee (rahimahullaah) [d.1407H] was alsoappointed a teacher in the University.

Shaykh Wasiullah tremendously benefitted from the scholars who were teachers at the University as previously mentioned. These scholars also deemed Shaykh Wasiullah to be from their honorable students. Specifically, the Shaykh remained extremely close to Shaykh al-Allaamah Hammaad al-Ansaaree. The Shaykh would often visit Shaykh al- Allaamah Hammaad al-Ansaaree's house after the

Asr prayer with his classmates and peers. Numerous respectable teachers at the Islaamic University of Madinah would also visit Shaykh al-Allaamah Hammaad al-Ansaaree in his house during this time frame. Those in attendance would greatly benefit from the knowledgeable dialogue which would occur in these sittings with Shaykh al-Allaamah Hammaad al-Ansaaree.

The Islaamic University of Madinah allocated the work of Takhreej (authentication) of the Ahaadeeth in the renowned book, "Bidaayatul-Mujtahid", to Shaykh al-Allaamah Hammaad al-Ansaaree and Shaykh al-Allaamah Abdul-Lateef. Shaykh al-Allaamah Hammaad al- Ansaaree appointed some of the students who would visit him with regularity in his house, amongst them Shaykh Wasiullah, with completion of this task. Shaykh Wasiullaah and those students with him benefitted greatly from this work of Takhreej, as they would research the Ahaadeeth in this book in great length in the various books and manuscripts. This exertion also increased their zeal for the work of Tahqeeq (verification) and Takhreej. Shaykh Wasiullah acknowledges the immense benefit he gained from the direction of Shaykh al-Allaamah Hammaad al-Ansaaree.

The Shaykh also immensely benefitted from Shaykh al-Allaamah Saalih al-Araaqee, from the teachers at the Islaamic University of Madinah and from the close companions of ash- Shaykh al-Allaamah Abdul-Azeez ibn Abdullaah ibn Baaz. He was also a teacher at "Jaami'ah Salafiyyah Banaras" for some time, and had special concern about the affairs of the Salafee Ahlul-Hadeeth students at the Islaamic University of Madinah. He had desired from Shaykh Wasiullah that he arrives at his house after the Asr prayer, and consequently, the Shaykh would consistently visit Shaykh al-Allaamah Saalih al-Araaqee in his house after the Asr prayer and benefit from his knowledge.

Shaykh Wasiullah immensely benefitted from his knowledge. He had allowed for the students to visit his house after the University would close daily in order to benefit from his knowledge and direction. Accordingly, Shaykh Wasiullah and some of his peers and classmates would visit his house after the Asr prayer, where Shaykh al-Allaamah Taqee-ud-Deen al-Hilaalee would make some students read a book, others would be directed to write a letter to a scholar from the major scholars, and some others would be given the responsibility of composing an article. The students of knowledge would benefit tremendously from these activities.

Al 'I'tibaa'a

Shaykh Wasiullah was blessed with the opportunity of residing with Shaykh al-Allaamah Taqee-ud-Deen al-Hilaalee in his house for a complete year. The Shaykh would go to the University and return home with Shaykh al-Allaamah Taqee-ud-Deen al-Hilaalee. Additionally, the Shaykh would buy necessary items for the house of Shaykh al-Allaamah Taqee-ud-Deen al-Hilaalee from the market. Consequently, Shaykh al-Allaamah Taqee-ud- Deen al-Hilaalee was extremely pleased with Shaykh Wasiullah. Shaykh al-Allaamah Taqee-ud-Deen al-Hilaalee was also in close contact with the scholars in Egypt. This was due to the fact that he had spent much time in Egypt previously calling to the Da'wah of the Ahlul-Hadeeth and Salafiyyah. Due to his efforts, the Salafee Da'wah spread in numerous towns in Egypt and the people initiated action upon it. During histime as a teacher in the Islaamic University of Madinah, he visited Egypt and brought Shaykh Wasiullah along with him. He visited various areas in Egypt upon receiving requests by the people of knowledge in those areas. Shaykh Wasiullah was his partner during these trips.

From the scholars who were teachers at the Islaamic University of Madinah at that time was Shaykh al-Allaamah Rabee ibn Hadee Umayr al-Madkhalee. Shaykh Wasiullah remained close to him and continues to keep relationship and contact with him. The Shaykh's relationship with Shaykh Rabee ibn Hadee Umayr al-Madkhalee has been continuous since the time when Shaykh Rabee ibn Hadee Umayr al-Madkhalee was a teacher in "Jaami'ah Salafiyyah Banaras" in India almost half a century ago. Shaykh Wasiullah also remained close to and benefitted from Shaykh al-Allaamah Muhammad al-Ameen ash-Shanqeetee (rahimahullaah) [d.1393H], Shaykh al-Allaamah Abdul-Muhsin ibn Hamad al-Abbaad al-Badr, and numerous Egyptian Salafee scholars in the Islaamic University of Madinah.

After successfully completing the bachelors (undergraduate) program at the Islaamic University of Madinah, the Shaykh travelled to Makkah, Saudi Arabia for the purposes of higher (post-graduate) studies. This was the first year of granting acceptance to non-Saudi students for higher post-graduate studies. He entered the higher studies examinations and successful passed through the selection and interview processes. Thereafter, he completed his Masters and PhD (doctorate) programs in Makkah, with specialization in Hadeeth sciences. He completed his PhD (doctorate) program in the year 1981ce, which was the year in which Umm al-Quraa University was established in Makkah. Before this, structured study in Makkah – "ad- Dirasaat al-Ulyaa" (the higher studies programs), the Faculty of Sharee'ah, and the Faculty of Tarbiyyah – were under the administration of King Abdul-Azeez University of Jeddah.

Al 'I'tibaa'a

His Higher Educational History and Academic Achievements Whilst a Student of Higher Studies in Makkah:

• Masters degree attained on the 19th day of Jumaadaa ath-Thaaniyah, 1397H from King Abdul-Azeez University in Makkah, the Faculty of Sharee'ah and Islaamic Studies, deparment of Tafseer and Hadeeth.

• PhD (doctorate) degree attained on the 29th day of Rajab, 1401H from Umm al-Quraa University in Makkah, the Faculty of Sharee'ah and Islaamic Studies, with specialization in the field of the Qur'aan and the Sunnah and its sciences.

During his time as a PhD (doctorate) student, he was appointed as a teacher at the "Ma'had" in al-Masjid al-Haraam (the Grand Mosque in Makkah). After attaining his PhD (doctorate) degree, he continued with this teaching position for numerous years. Thereafter, he was selected as a professor in Umm al-Quraa University in Makkah, where he continues to hold a teaching position in the department of "al-Kitaab (the Qur'aan) and the Sunnah" in the Faculty of Da'wah and Usool-ud-Deen, lecturing on numerous subjects related to the science of Hadeeth.

His Teaching Positions:
• Appointed as a teacher at the "Ma'had" in al-Masjid al-Haraam from 1 Safar, 1399H to 15 Muharram, 1409H.
• Then as an "Ustaadh Musaa'id" (Assistant Professor) in Umm al-Quraa University in Makkah from 16 Muharram, 1409H, the Faculty of Da'wah and Usool ad-Deen, department of "al- Kitaab and the Sunnah".
• Promoted as an "Utaadh Mushaarik" (Senior Lecturer and Professor) by Umm al-Quraa University on 1 Ramadaan, 1413H.
• At present, a senior lecturer and professor in the department of "al-Kitaab and the Sunnah" in the Faculty of Da'wah and Usool-ud-Deen.

Teaching Chair in al-Masjid al-Haraam (the Grand Mosque in Makkah) and Books Taught: The Shaykh also holds a teaching chair in al-Masjid al-Haraam, with authorization attained from the "General Director of the Affairs of the Grand Mosque in Makkah and the Prophet's Mosque in Madinah", based upon the agreement of the Royal Court, since 1419H. His chair is located in the "Mutaaf" (the area of Tawaaf around the Ka'bah), between the doors of "Baab al- Malik Fahd" and "Baab al-Umrah", where he continues to teach five days a week between the Maghrib and Ishaa prayers. From the books Shaykh Wasiullah has completed teaching in the Arabic language in al-Masjid al-Haraam are:

• "Fathul-Baree Sharh Saheeh al-Bukhaaree" of al-Imaam al-Haafidh Shihaab-ud-Deen Aboo al-Fadal Ahmad ibn Alee ibn Hajar al-Kunaanee al-Asqalaaanee (rahimahullaah) [d. 852H], which is an explanation of "al-Jaami' as-Saheeh as-Musnad min Hadeeth Rasoolillaah wa Sunanihee wa Ayyaamih" [well-known as "Saheeh al-Bukhaaree"] of al-Imaam Ameerul- Mu'mineen fil-Hadeeth Aboo Abdullaah Muhammad ibn Ismaa'eel ibn Ibraaheem ibnul- Mugheerah al-Ju'fee al-Bukhaaree (rahimahullaah) [d. 256H]. The Shaykh recently completed the explanation of this magnificent book "Fathul-Baree" before Hajj of the year 2009ce, continuously teaching it for a period of eleven years in al-Masjid al-Haraam.

• "Naylul-Awtaar min Asraar Muntaqaa al-Akhbaar" of al-Imaam Muhammad ibn Alee ash- Shawkaanee (rahimahullaah) [d. 1355H], which is an explanation of "Muntaqaa min Ahaadeeth al-Ahkaam" of al-Imaam Majd-ud-Deen Aboo al-Barakaat Abdul-Salaam ibn Abdullaah ibn Taymiyyah al-Harraanee (rahimahullaah) [d. 652H]

• "Nuzhatun-Nadhar fee Tawdeeh Nukhbatil-Fikr", which is an explanation of "Nukhbatul- Fikr fee Mustalah Ahlil-Athar", both by al-Imaam al-Haafidh Shihaab-ud-Deen Aboo al-Fadal Ahmad ibn Alee ibn Hajar al-Kunaanee al-Asqalaaanee (rahimahullaah) [d. 852H].

• "Buloogh al-Maraam min Adillatil-Ahkaam" of al-Imaam al-Haafidh Shihaab-ud-Deen Aboo al-Fadal Ahmad ibn Alee ibn Hajar al-Kunaanee al-Asqalaaanee (rahimahullaah) [d.852H]

• "Zaad al-Ma'aad fee Hadee Khayril-Ibaad" of al-Imaam Shams-ud-Deen Aboo Abdullaah Muhammad ibn Aboo Bakr ibn Ayyoob ibn Sa'ad az-Zar'ee ad-Dimishqee, well-known as Ibn Qayyim al-Jawziyyah (rahimahullaah) [d. 751H].

• "Tadreeb ar-Raawee fee Sharh Taqreeb an-Nawawee" of al-Imaam Jalaal-ud-Deen Abdur- Rahmaan ibn Aboo Bakr as-Suyootee (rahimahullaah) [d. 911H], which is an explanation of "at-Taqreeb wat-Tayseer fee Ma'rifah Sunan al-Basheer an-Nadheer" of al-Imaam Muhee-ud-Deen Aboo Zakariyyaa Yahyaa ibn Sharaf an-Nawawee ad-Dimishqee (rahimahullaah) [d.676H].

Al 'I'tibaa'a

- "ar-Rawd al-Mubrabbi' bee-Sharh Zaad al-Mustaqni'" of al-Imaam Mansoor ibn Yoonus ibn Salaah-ud-Deen ibn Hasan al-Bhootee (rahimahullaah) [d. 1051H], which is an explanation of the book "Zaad al-Mustaqni' fee Ikhtisaar al-Muqni'" of al-Imaam Sharaf-ud-Deen Aboo an-Najaa Moosaa ibn Ahmad ibn Moosaa ibn Saalim al-Maqdisee al-Hajaawee thummaa as- Saalihee ad-Dimishqee (rahimahullaah) [d. 960H]

- "Muqaddimah Ibnus-Salaah" of al-Imaam Aboo 'Amr Uthmaan ibn Abdur-Rahmaan ash- Shaharzooree (rahimahullaah) [d. 643H]

- "Kitaab at-Tawheed alladhee huwaa Haqqullaahi alal-Ibaad" of Shaykhul-Islaam Muhammad ibn Abdul-Wahhaab ibn Sulaymaan at-Tameemee (rahimahullaah) [d. 1206H]

- "Sharh Ilal at-Tirmidhee" of al-Imaam al-Haafidh Zayn-ud-Deen Aboo al-Faraj Abdur- Rahmaan ibn Ahmad ibn Abdur-Rahmaan as-Salaamee al-Baghdaadee thummaa ad- Dimishqee, well-known as Ibn Rajab al-Hanbalee (rahimahullaah) [d.795H]

- "Umdatul-Ahkaam min Kalaam Khayril-Anaam" of al-Imaam Taqee-ud-Deen Aboo Muhammad Abdul-Ghanee ibn Abdul-Waahid al-Maqdisee (rahimahullaah) [d. 600H]

- "as-Salsabeel fee Ma'rifatid-Daleel Haashiyah alaa Zaad al-Mustaqni'" of Shaykh al- Allaamah Saalih ibn Ibraaheem al-Baleehee (rahimahullaah) [d. 1410H], which are explanatory notes on the book "Zaad al-Mustaqni' fee Ikhtisaar al-Muqni'" of al-Imaam Sharaf-ud-Deen Aboo an-Najaa Moosaa ibn Ahmad ibn Moosaa ibn Saalim al-Maqdisee al- Hajaawee thummaa as-Saalihee ad-Dimishqee (rahimahullaah) [d. 960H]

- "al-Jaami' as-Saheehayn bi-Hadhfil-Ma'aad wat-Turuq" of al-Imaam Aboo Nu'eem al- Haddaad Ubaydullaah ibnul-Hasan ibn Ahmad al-Asbahaanee (rahimahullaah) [d.517H].

From the books which Shaykh Wasiullah has completed teaching in the Urdu language in al-Masjid al-Haraam are:

- "Fathul-Majeed Sharh Kitaab at-Tawheed" of al-Imaam Abdur-Rahmaan ibn Hasan ibn Shaykhil-Islaam Muhammad ibn Abdul-Wahhaab (rahimahullaah) [d.

1285H], which is an explanation of the book "Kitaab at-Tawheed" of his grandfather, Shaykhul-Islaam Muhammad ibn Abdul-Wahhaab ibn Sulaymaan at-Tameemee (rahimahullaah) [d. 1206H]

• "Subul as-Salaam Sharh Bulooghil-Maraam min Adillatil-Ahkaam" of al-Imaam al-Ameer Muhammad ibn Ismaa'eel as-San'aanee (rahimahullaah) [d.1182], which is an explanation of the book "Buloogh al-Maraam min Adillatil-Ahkaam" of al-Imaam al-Haafidh Shihaab-ud- Deen Aboo al-Fadal Ahmad ibn Alee ibn Hajar al-Kunaanee al-Asqalaaanee (rahimahullaah) [d. 852H]

• "al-Usool ath-Thalaathah wa Adillatuhaa" of Shaykhul-Islaam Muhammad ibn Abdul- Wahhaab ibn Sulaymaan at-Tameemee (rahimahullaah) [d. 1206H]

• "Kashf ash-Shubuhaat" of Shaykhul-Islaam Muhammad ibn Abdul-Wahhaab ibn Sulaymaan at-Tameemee (rahimahullaah) [d. 1206H]

• "Aqeedatut-Tawheed" of Shaykh al-Allaamah Saalih ibn Fawzaan ibn Abdullaah Aal Fawzaan (hafidhahullaah)

• "Tafseer al-Qur'aanil-Adheem" [well-known as "Tafseer Ibn Katheer"] of al-Imaam Imaadud-
Deen Aboo al-Fadaa' Ismaa'eel ibn Umar ibn Katheer al-Basree al-Dimishqee (rahimahullaah) [d. 774H]
• "Masaa'il al-Jaahiliyyah" of Shaykhul-Islaam Muhammad ibn Abdul-Wahhaab ibn Sulaymaan at-Tameemee (rahimahullaah) [d. 1206H]

Presently, the Shaykh is teaching "Sunan Abee Daawood" of al-Imaam Aboo Daawood Sulaymaan ibnul-Ash'ath as-Sijistaanee (rahimahullaah) [d. 675H] in the Arabic language three
days a week, and "Tafseer Ibn Katheer" al-Imaam Imaad-ud-Deen Aboo al-Fadaa' Ismaa'eel ibn Umar ibn Katheer al-Basree al-Dimishqee (rahimahullaah) [d. 774H] two days a week in the Urdu language.

His Scholastic Positions:
• Supervisor of various Masters and PhD (doctorate) treatises in Umm al-Quraa University in
Makkah.

- Debated and continuous to debate various Masters and PhD (doctorate) treatises in Makkah, Madinah, Riyadh, Dammam, and in Jordan, India, Pakistan, and Britain.

His Academic Activities Other than Teaching in Umm al-Quraa University in Makkah: Within the University:
- Appointed as a member of the "Academic Board" in Umm al-Quraa University for a period of two years.
- Appointed as a member of the "Committee for Amendment of the Bachelors Degree Curriculum" in the department of "al-Kitaab and the Sunnah", the Faculty of Da'wah and Usool-ud-Deen.
- Appointed as a member of the "Committee for Implementation of a New Curriculum for the PhD (Doctorate) Program" in the department of "al-Kitaab and the Sunnah", the Faculty of Da'wah and Usool-ud-Deen.
- Appointed as a member of the "Council for Composing the Magazine of Umm al-Quraa University for Islaamic Studies and the Arabic Language and its Guidelines". Outside the University:
- Participated in numerous conferences in Jordan, India, and Britian, France.
- Participated in numerous academic retreats in various cities of Saudi Arabia, such as Makkah, Jizan, and Ha'il, and in India and Britain.
- Conducts various lectures within the Kingdom of Saudi Arabia and outside of it, such as Britain and America, by way of tele-link conferences. Similarly, conducts various lectures in the Da'wah Centers in Makkah, Jeddah, and other than these cities.
- Participated in the "Symposium on the Sunnah and the Seerah (Biography of the Prophet Muhammad (sallallaahu alayhi wa sallam))" in Madinah, Saudi Arabia.
- Appointed as a consultant to the "General Director of the Affairs of the Grand Mosque in Makkah and the Prophet's Mosque in Madinah", Shaykh al-Allaamah Muhammad ibn Abdullaah ibn Muhammad ibn Abdul-Azeez as-Subayyal (hafidhahullaah), for more than two years.
- Appointed as a member of the "Committee of the Signs [Landmarks] of Makkah" under the presidency of the "General Director of the Affairs of the Grand Mosque in Makkah and the Prophet's Mosque in Madinah", Shaykh al-Allaamah Muhammad ibn Abdullaah as- Subayyal, and membership of the noble Shaykh al-Allaamah Abdullaah ibn Sulaymaan ibn Muhammad ibn Munee' (hafidhahumallaah) and the noble Shaykh al-Allaamah Abdullaah ibn Abdur-Rahmaan ibn Saalih al-Bassaam (rahimahullaah) [d.1423H], along with some other people of expertise.

- Appointed as a verifier of some of the meanings of the noble Qur'aan translated into the Urdu language upon request of the "King Fahd Qur'aan Printing Complex" in Madinah, Saudi Arabia.
- Corrected and reviewed the translation of the meanings of the noble Qur'aan of Shaykh al-Allaamah Muhammad al-Joonaagardhee, and the explanation of Shaykh Salaah-ud- Deen Yoosuf (hafidhahullaah), upon the request of the "King Fahd Qur'aan Printing Complex" in Madinah. This Urdu translation and explanation is published and distributed worldwide by the "King Fahd Qur'aan Printing Complex" since numerous years.
- Member of the "Academic Boards" of some of the Universities in India and supervisor of some of the religious schools, especially in India.

Authorship and Research:

1. "ad-Du'afaa' wal-Matrookoon wal-Majhooloon fee Sunanin-Nasaa'ee" (The Weak, Abandoned, and Unknown [Narrators of the Ahaadeeth] in Sunan an-Nasaa'ee). This was the Shaykh's Masters Degree thesis.

2. Tahqeeq (Verification) of the book "Fadaa'il as-Sahaabah" (Virtues of the Companions [of the Prophet Muhammad (sallallaahu alayhi wa sallam)] of al-Imaam Aboo Abdullaah Ahmad ibn Muhammad ibn Hanbal ash-Shaybaanee (rahimahullaah) [d.241H]. This was the Shaykh's PhD (doctorate) thesis.

3. Tahqeeq of the book "al-'Ilal wa Ma'rifatur-Rijaal" ([The Science of] Defects [in the Asaaneed of the Ahaadeeth] and [the Science] of Narrators [of the Ahaadeeth]) as narrated by al-Imaam Aboo Abdur-Rahmaan Abdullaah ibn al-Imaam Ahmad ibn Hanbal (rahimahumallaah) [d.290H].

4. Tahqeeq of the book "Bahrid-Dam feeman Takallama feehi al-Imaam Ahmad bi-Madh aw
Dham" (The one [i.e. Narrators of Ahaadeeth] al-Imaam Ahmad [ibn Hanbal (rahimahullaah)] Spoke about with Commendation or Disparagement) of al-Imaam Jamaalud- Deen Yoosuf ibn Hasan ibn Ahmad ibn Hasan ibn Abdul-Haadee as-Saalihee, well-known as Ibnul-Mibrad al-Hanbalee (rahimahullaah) [d.909H].

5. Tahqeeq of the book "al-'Ilal wa Ma'rifatur-Rijaal" ([The Science of] Defects [in the Asaaneed of the Ahaadeeth] and [the Science] of Narrators [of the

Ahaadeeth]) as narrated by al-Imaam Aboo al-Fadal Saalih ibn al-Imaam Ahmad ibn Hanbal (rahimahumallaah) [d.266H].

6. Tahqeeq of the twelfth volume of the book "Ittihaaf al-Mahrah bil-Fawaa'id al-Mubtakarah min Atraaf al-Ashrah" of al-Imaam al-Haafidh Shihaab-ud-Deen Aboo al-Fadal Ahmad ibn Alee ibn Hajar al-Kunaanee al-Asqalaaanee (rahimahullaah) [d. 852H], upon request from "Markaz Khidmatis-Sunnah was-Seerah an-Nabawiyyah" of Madinah, Saudi Arabia.

7. Tahqeeq of the fifth volume of the book "Lisaan al-Meezaan" of al-Imaam al-Haafidh Shihaab-ud-Deen Aboo al-Fadal Ahmad ibn Alee ibn Hajar al-Kunaanee al-Asqalaaanee (rahimahullaah) [d. 852H], upon request from "Markaz Khidmatis-Sunnah was-Seerah an- Nabawiyyah" of Madinah, Saudi Arabia.

8. "al-Masjid al-Haraam: Taareekhuhu wa Ahkaamuh" (The Grand Mosque in Makkah: Its History and Its Rulings).

9. "Ilal al-Hadeeth wa Dawruhu fee Hifdhis-Sunnah" ([The Science of] Defects [in the Asaaneed of the Ahaadeeth] and its Role in Protecting the Sunnah).

10. "Tahqeeq al-Kalaam fee Wujoobil-Qiraa'ah Khalf al-Imaam" (Verification of the Speech Regarding the Obligation of Reciting [Sooratul-Faatihah] Behind the Imaam [in the Salaah]) of Shaykh al-Allaamah al-Muhaddith Abdur-Rahmaan al-Mubaarakpooree (rahimahullaah) [d.1353H]. This book has been translated from Urdu into Arabic by the Shaykh and he has added his annotations upon it.

11. "Khuluq al-Muslim fee Daw'il-Kitaab was-Sunnah" (Manners of the Muslim in Light of the Qur'aan and the Sunnah).

12. "al-Musaafahah bil-Yadil-Yumnaa" (Greeting with the Right Hand [Upon Saying Salaam]) of Shaykh al-Allaamah al-Muhaddith Abdur-Rahmaan al-Mubaarakpooree (rahimahullaah) [d.1353H]. This book has been translated from Urdu into Arabic by the Shaykh and he has added his annotations upon it.

13. "Fiqh Ahlil-Hadeeth: Khasaa'isuhu wa Mumayyizaatuhu" ('fiqh' of the People of the Hadeeth: Its Unique and Exclusive Aspects).

14. "at-Ta'reef bi-Kutub Taraajimir-Ruwaat" (The Introduction to the Books [which Contain] Biographies of the Narrators [of Ahaadeeth]).

15. "al It'ibaa'a w Usoolul Fiqhis Salaf" (Following the Quran and Sunnah and the 'fiqh' Principles of the righteous predecessors).

16. "at Taqleed wa Hukmuhu fi Dowil Kitaab was Sunnah wal Aathaar as Salafiyyah" (Blind Following, it's ruling from the Quran, Sunnah and narrations of the righteous predecessors)

17.'al Fidyah fi al Khula' (Paying of ransom for the woman who seeks divorce) Other general research and study.

Personal Life:
The Shaykh is married and has been blessed with four sons and five daughters. His sons, in sequence of age, are:
1. Usaamah
2. Muhammad
3. Abdullaah
4. Anas

His eldest son, Usaamah, is a student of higher studies in Umm al-Quraa University in Makkah, presently completing his Masters degree, in the Faculty of Da'wah and Usool ad-Deen, department of "al-Kitaab and the Sunnah". Usaamah is also an appointed teacher at the "Ma'had" in al-Masjid al-Haraam, Imam and gives the Jum'ah khutbah in their neighborhood masjid.

May Allaah preserve him and reward him with the best of rewards in this life and the hereafter for the efforts he has put forth in spreading the knowledge of the Qur'aan and the Sunnah. May Allaah protect him from all sorts of evil and continue to make him a benefit for the Ummah of Muhammad.[1]

---

[1]-(taken from The Shaykh's introductory page on the official Umm al-Quraa University website, http://uqu.edu.sa/wmabbas, "Qaafilah-e-Hadeeth" of Muhammad Ishaaq Bhattee [Urdu], refer to http://www.asliahlesunnet.com.

Scholars praise of Sheikh Wasiullah Abbaas:

Sheikh al Alaamah Muhammad Naasirud Deen al Albaani said: "Verily, our companion Wasiullah ibn Muhammad ibn Abbaas has spoken in his annotation upon [the book] "al-Fadaa'il" with good speech regarding [this] Hadeeth.1

He says in another place:
"As narrated by the virtuous brother Wasiullah in his annotation upon "al-Fadaa'il."2

He says in another place:
"I have mentioned a short while ago that [al-Imaam Muhammad ibn Ismaa'eel ibn Ibraaheem ibnul-Mugheerah al-Ju'fee] al-Bukhaaree [d.256H] has narrated [this] Hadeeth in [his book] "at-Taareekh", and the virtuous brother Wasiullah has preceded me in corroborating [theHadeeth] upon the authority of al-Bukhaaree in his annotation upon "al-Fadaa'il."3

He says also:
"I say: This is a grave error! [This error] has been elucidated by [al-Haafidh Jalaal-ud-Deen Abdur-Rahmaan ibn Aboo Bakr ibn Muhammad ibn Saabiq-ud-Deen] as-Suyootee [d.911H] in [his book] "al-La'aalee," and Ibn Iraaq in [his book] "Tanzeeh ash-Sharee'ah," and my companion, the one who has annotated upon [the book] "Fadaa'il as-Sahaabah": Wasiullah ibn Muhammad Abbaas, and other than them."4

Sheikh Muhammad Omar Bazmool said: For verily, our Shaykh Wasiullah Abbaas, may [Allaah], the Guardian, preserve him and assist him with health and wellbeing, is from the major scholars of Hadeeth in Makkah al-Mukarramah, and he is the one to whom belongs the virtue , after Allaah, the Most Magnificent, in spreading the Madhhab of the Ahlul-Hadeeth, and subduing the enemies of the Sunnah. And before him was our Shaykh in acquaintance, Shaykh Haafidh Fathee [al-Paakistaanee al-Makkee], may Allaah have mercy upon him, who used to circulate the Salafee books of Hadeeth, and dispense them amongst the students

---

[1]-See ("Fadaa'il as-Sahaabah" of al-Imaam Aboo Abdullaah Ahmad ibn Muhammad ibn Hanbal ash-Shaybaanee) and ("Silsilah al-Ahaadeeth as-Saheehah", no. 2295, volume 5, page 374.)

[2]-("Silsilah al-Ahaadeeth as-Saheehah", no. 3318, volume 8, page 941.)

[3]-("Silsilah al-Ahaadeeth as-Saheehah", no. 3437, volume 8, page 1290.)

[4]-(Silsilah al-Ahaadeeth as-Da'eefah", no. 5590, volume 12, page 187.)

of knowledge. And from these books was the book "at-Talkhees al-Habeer," and he had a large library which included many of the books of Hadeeth. I have heard that some of the judges have purchased it.

In any case, for verily our Shaykh Wasiullah, and I say with comprehensive knowledge about him, is from the Ahlul-Hadeeth, and is a person who strives in knowledge and action, and I do not praise anyone above Allaah. And the one who derides him or diminishes his status, then accuse him [in his claim of] holding on to the Sunnah. And the right of the Shaykh, and his virtue, and his striving, and his waging war against innovation and its people and his subduing of them, [then] this is known by the ones who know the Shaykh and are familiar with him."[1]

Sheikh Rabee ibn Haadee al Madkhalee said: 'We encourage the brothers to make I'tikaaf, because it a legislated affair [in the Islaamic Sharee'ah], and the Salaf used to halt their lessons for the purpose of becoming free for I'tikaaf, worship, and reciting the Qur'aan. And if you were to make I'tikaaf, then there are scholars, and to Allaah belongs the praise, in al-Masjid al-Haraam, who suffice [you] from attending this gathering, such as Shaykh al-Luhaydaan, Shaykh Wasiullah, Shaykh Uthmaan, and other than them. Attend the [circles] of knowledge, may Allaah bless you with Barakah, and benefit [yourselves]. And this will not conflict with the I'tikaaf, it will not conflict with the I'tikaaf, if Allaah so wills..."[2]

---

[1]-http://www.asliahlesunnet.com
[2]-http://www.asliahlesunnet.com

Al 'I'tibaa'a

Introduction

All praises are due to Allah, we praise Him we seek His assistance and we seek His forgiveness. We seek refuge in Allah from the evil of ourselves and from our evil deeds. Whomever Allah guides there is none who can misguide him, and whomever Allah misguides there is none who can guide him. I testify that there is no deity worthy of worship except Allah alone without any partners, and I testify that Muhammad ﷺ is Allah's slave and Messenger. Allah says:

﴿ يَٰٓأَيُّهَا ٱلَّذِينَ ءَامَنُوا۟ ٱتَّقُوا۟ ٱللَّهَ حَقَّ تُقَاتِهِۦ وَلَا تَمُوتُنَّ إِلَّا وَأَنتُم مُّسْلِمُونَ ﴾

"O you who believe! Fear Allah as He should be feared, and do not die except in a state of Islam (as Muslims) with complete submission to Allah." (Ali Imran 3:102) Allah says:

﴿ يَٰٓأَيُّهَا ٱلنَّاسُ ٱتَّقُوا۟ رَبَّكُمُ ٱلَّذِى خَلَقَكُم مِّن نَّفْسٍ وَٰحِدَةٍ وَخَلَقَ مِنْهَا زَوْجَهَا وَبَثَّ مِنْهُمَا رِجَالًا كَثِيرًا وَنِسَآءً ۚ وَٱتَّقُوا۟ ٱللَّهَ ٱلَّذِى تَسَآءَلُونَ بِهِۦ وَٱلْأَرْحَامَ ۚ إِنَّ ٱللَّهَ كَانَ عَلَيْكُمْ رَقِيبًا ﴾

"O mankind! Be dutiful to your Lord, Who created you from a single person (Adam) and from him (Adam) He created his wife (Eve) and from them both He created many men and women and fear Allah through Whom you demand your mutual rights, and do not cut off the relations of the wombs (kinship). Surely, Allah is Ever an All-Watcher over you. (an Nisaa' 4:1) Allah also says:

﴿ يَٰٓأَيُّهَا ٱلَّذِينَ ءَامَنُوا۟ ٱتَّقُوا۟ ٱللَّهَ وَقُولُوا۟ قَوْلًا سَدِيدًا ۝ يُصْلِحْ لَكُمْ أَعْمَٰلَكُمْ وَيَغْفِرْ لَكُمْ ذُنُوبَكُمْ ۗ وَمَن يُطِعِ ٱللَّهَ وَرَسُولَهُۥ فَقَدْ فَازَ فَوْزًا عَظِيمًا ۝ ﴾

"O you who believe! Keep your duty to Allah and fear Him, and always speak the truth. He will direct you to do righteous good deeds and will forgive you your sins. And whosoever obeys Allah and His Messenger, he has indeed achieved a great achievement (saved from the Hell fire and enter Paradise) (Ahzaab 33:70-71)

As to what proceeds: Verily the best of speech is the Book of Allah and the best of guidance is the guidance of Muhammad ﷺ.

Al 'I'tibaa'a

The worst of affairs are the newly-invented affairs in the religion and every newly invented affair in the religion is an innovation and every innovation is misguidance and all misguidance is in the Hellfire. As to what proceeds... Reasons for compiling this book:

1-When I was in India during the months of Rajab and Sha'baan some students of knowledge requested that I write a treatise pertaining to 'al I'tibaa'a'[1] and 'at Taqleed'[2]. An incident took place in some of the suburbs of the city of Haydaraabad (India) where some bigoted individuals to some of the 'madhaa'hib' destroyed one of the Masaajid of Ahlul Hadeeth (People of Hadeeth). The reason this took place was because their scholar gave them a religious verdict stating that the masjid was a masjid of the Jews and Christians and a place of mischief.

The destruction of the masjid has been confirmed as I saw pictures of the demolished masjid in some of the newspapers. I was overtaken by pity and grief and said to myself: 'What is happening to the great Muslim Nation of Muhammad', while we went on discussing this incident with some of the brothers. Then some of the brothers suggested that I should write something pertaining to the subject of 'al-I'tibaa'a and 'at Taqleed' their meanings, limits and the legality of them.

2-I have noticed that promoting the Quran and the Sunnah and calling the people to implementing it into their beliefs and actions is looked upon as something strange in some countries. Rather, it is considered by some of the Muslims as being a deficiency, defect, or drawback amongst some of the 'du'aat'. Unfortunately, it is something which we find many people disregard and show little importance to. The one who calls to the Quran and Sunnah is given nicknames such as: 'la madh'habee' non religious, not a follower, he follows no school of thought' and many other degrading nicknames which repel the people from him. However, I have found that the students of knowledge and especially in our modern day and time, understand the meaning of 'al-I'tibaa'a' more than those who were raised and taught in one of the religious schools when being

---

[1]-**(TN)**al-I'tibaa'a:This Arabic word has several meanings in English such as: observance, adherence to, imitation, copying, following the example of. What is intended in this compilation is clarifying how to follow, imitate and strictly adhere to the Prophet's Sunnah as done by the noble companions and the earlier scholars of 'fiqh'.

[2]-**(TN)** 'at Taqleed: This Arabic word is similar in meaning to al-I'tibaa'a, as it means: imitation, copying, mimicry. Technically it means: acting upon a saying or action from someone whose sayings and actions are not authoritative sources or evidences in the religion.

addressed and called to the Quran and the Sunnah. These are the people who are the fastest in understanding that the 'sincere religion', in beliefs and actions, is what is contained in the Quran and Sunnah. They understand that the scholars of 'fiqh'[1] are agents and intermediaries to understand the religion and not people to be blindly followed. For verily I have realized this is the case in India, Britain, and America.

3-Numerous times it has occurred to me during lectures and lessons that someone asks me: 'What 'madth'hab'[2] do you follow?', or 'what sect do you ascribe yourself to?' I reply to the questioner by saying: 'Verily, I don't follow any 'madth'hab', rather I follow and adhere to all of the 'madthaa'hib' in what is in accordance with the Quran and the Sunnah. I don't ascribe myself to any one of the scholars of 'fiqh' and I also don't ascribe myself to any sect except to the sect that represents the 'sincere religion'. This is the one and only Islam that was completed and perfected in the time of the Prophet ﷺ in beliefs and actions. After answering the questioner, I reaized that he was not convinced with this answer, and he replied: 'How can it be possible that someone is Muslim and he doesn't adhere or follow any of the four scholars of 'fiqh'?, and then this person is called 'la madth'habee' (someone who doesn't follow a specific madthaab).

> **A)** I have observed that there is a large number, rather the majority of the Muslims blindly follow and strictly adhere to one of the four 'madthaa'hib', and they consider it impermissible to abandon or leave off following one of the 'madthaa'hib'.
>
> **B)** Showing bigotry and fanaticism to the 'madthaa'hib' whether it is in matters of creed or 'fiqh', leads and causes separation and dissension amongst the Muslims and splits them up into group and sects. This is something dispraised and disliked in the Religion of Allah. This in turn leads to Muslims transgressing against other Muslims regarding their honor, blood and money. This is an ancient disease and ailment which has been inherited from the preceeding generations.
>
> **C)** Showing bigotry and fanaticism to a particular 'madth'hab' has led some people to contradict, deny and disagree with the outright authentic

---

[1]-**(TN)** The Four Imams of the schools of 'fiqh' are Abu Haneefah, Malik ibn Anas, ash Shafee'ee, Ahmed ibn Hanbal

[2]-**(TN)** School of 'fiqh', also the word may be used to refer to a certain way, belief or ideology which is followed.

texts which have been mentioned within the Sunnah of the Prophet Muhammad ﷺ.

Furthermore, I heard an audio cassette from one of the scholars of India in which he delivered a lecture attacking those who call to the correct creed of 'as Salafiyyah' and call to the implementation of the Quran and Sunnah while this man called them 'Sulfiyeen' (ones who take loans). From amongst the things that this 'scholar' said- who is extremely bigoted to his 'madth'hab'-: 'Whoever wants to look at the beauty of women from Ahlul Hadeeth then he should stand at the doors of their masaajid, for verily their women go to the masaajid especially the Friday (Jumu'ah) and the two yearly festivals (Eid). This man is a strict follower of the 'Hanafee' madth'hab and the followers of the Hanafee school of thought hold the opinion that it is impermissible for the women to go to the masaajid and they pay no attention to what has been transmitted to us from the Prophet Muhammad ﷺ -The Best Example for us-regarding the permissibility of the women attending and going to the masaajid. Abu Dawud[1], Imam Ahmed, Al Bayhaqi[2] and others narrated on the authority of Abu Hurairah that the Prophet Muhammad ﷺ said:

عَنْ أَبِي هُرَيْرَةَ، عَنِ النَّبِيِّ صَلَّى اللهُ عَلَيْهِ وَسَلَّمَ قَالَ: " لَا تَمْنَعُوا إِمَاءَ اللهِ مَسَاجِدَ اللهِ، وَلَكِنْ لِيَخْرُجْنَ و هُنَّ تَفِلَاتٌ "

"Do not prohibit Allah's female servants from the Allah's masaajid, however they should go out of their residences without wearing perfume."[3]

---

[1]-(TN)His name was Sulaymaan ibn al Ash'ath Ibn Shaddaad as Sijistaani. He is the author of one of the six reliable books of hadeeth. He was born in 202 hijri. He traveled to Baghdaad where he met Imam Ahmed ibn Hanbal. He also traveled to Makkah, Iraq, Syria, Egypt and other places. His book 'Sunan' contains over 5300 ahadeeth. He remained in Basrah until he died 275 hijri.

[2]-(TN)He is Abu Bakr Ahmed ibn Husein al Bayhaqi, he was born in 384 hijri in a small town of Khusraugird in Khurasaan. He authored many books the most popular of them being 'as Sunan al Kubraa'. He studied under al Haakim an Naysaaboori and was from his foremost students. He was well known for his adherence and advocation of the Shafi'ee madth'hab. He died in 458 hijri.

[3]-This is the wording of Abee Dawud, Book of Prayer, Chapter:What was narrated mentioning the women leaving their houses to the masjid #565, 566 pg. 94, see Musnad Imam Ahmed #9645,10144, 10835 and Sunan al Kubra by al Bayhaqi , Chapter: The woman going to the Masjid for the prayer #5377, Vol. 3/134.The narration is authentic.

Al 'I'tibaa'a

Imam Muslim, Abu Dawud, Imam Ahmed, Al Hakim and others also narrated this hadeeth on the authority of ibn Umar, similar to this narration.[1]

I also recall delivering a lesson in Masjid ul Haraam in the Urdu language (language native to India and Pakistan) which many people from different 'madthaa'hib' always attend. They ask many different questions for general knowledge and informational reasons. Such as questions related to creed, methodology and 'fiqh' mostly. It just so happened that some of them asked me a question regarding this issue (women attending and going to the mosques for prayer) in particular.

Responding to him I mentioned a hadeeth- as is my custom when reading the narrations of the Prophet Muhammad ﷺ in issues which I recall the proofs- the Messenger of Allah ﷺ said:

عَنِ ابْنِ عُمَرَ قَالَ قَالَ رَسُولُ اللَّهِ -صلى الله عليه وسلم- " لاَ تَمْنَعُوا نِسَاءَكُمُ الْمَسَاجِدَ (إماء الله مساجد الله) وَبُيُوتُهُنَّ خَيْرٌ لَهُنَّ"

"Do not prohibit your women from going to the masaajid (Allah's female servants from Allah's masaajid), and their houses are better for them."[2]

It has also been narrated that Ibn Umar reviled and cursed his son and became angry with him regarding this issue.

قَالَ عَبْدُ اللَّهِ بْنُ عُمَرَ قَالَ النَّبِيُّ -صلى الله عليه وسلم- « ائْذَنُوا لِلنِّسَاءِ إِلَى الْمَسَاجِدِ بِاللَّيْلِ ». فَقَالَ ابْنٌ لَهُ :"وَاللَّهِ لاَ نَأْذَنُ لَهُنَّ فَيَتَّخِذْنَهُ دَغَلاً وَاللَّهِ لاَ نَأْذَنُ لَهُنَّ". قَالَ: فَسَبَّهُ وَغَضِبَ وَقَالَ: "أَقُولُ قَالَ رَسُولُ اللَّهِ -صلى الله عليه وسلم- « ائْذَنُوا لَهُنَّ ». وَتَقُولُ لاَ نَأْذَنُ لَهُنَّ؟!

When Ibn Umar mentioned the Prophet's ﷺ saying: **"Give permission to the women to go to the masaajid in the night, so his son said to him: I swear by Allah, we will not permit them to go because they will use it to cause mischief, I swear by Allah we will not permit them. The narrator mentioned: Ibn Umar**

---

[1]-Saheeh Muslim, The book of Prayer, Chapter: Women exiting their houses to the masjid if it causes not fitnah and she doesn't leave out while wearing perfume, #134-142, vol. 1/327 with many chains of narration, Sunan Abee Dawud, Musnad Imam Ahmed-see previous footnote- and Mustradak al Hakim vol. 1/209

[2]-Sunan Abee Dawud, The Book of prayer, chapter: What was narrated regarding the women going to the masjid pg. 94 #567

then cursed and reviled him and became angry with his son, and Ibn Umar said: "I say: The Prophet Muhammad ﷺ says: 'Give permission to the women', and you say: We will not permit them.?!"[1] Imam Muslim also narrated this hadeeth stating:

فَقَالَ ابْنٌ لَهُ: يُقَالُ لَهُ وَاقِدٌ: إِذَنْ يَتَّخِذْنَهُ دَغَلًا. قَالَ: فَضَرَبَ فِي صَدْرِهِ وَقَالَ: "أُحَدِّثُكَ عَنْ رَسُولِ اللهِ صَلَّى اللهُ عَلَيْهِ وَسَلَّمَ، وَتَقُولُ: لَا؟!

'Then Ibn Umar's son said to him, (his name is Waaqid): 'the women will use this opportunity to cause mischief', so then Ibn Umar hit him in his chest and said to him: 'I relate to you from the Messenger of Allah ﷺ and you say no, I will not allow them'!!!. In another narration: Bilal (Ibn Umar's son) said:

فَقَالَ بِلَالٌ (يعني ابنه): وَاللهِ، لَنَمْنَعُهُنَّ. فَقَالَ لَهُ عَبْدُ اللهِ: "أَقُولُ: قَالَ رَسُولُ اللهِ صَلَّى اللهُ عَلَيْهِ وَسَلَّمَ وَتَقُولُ أَنْتَ: لَنَمْنَعُهُنَّ؟!

"I swear by Allah we will prohibit them', so Ibn Umar said to him: I say: the Messenger of Allah ﷺ said and you say: We will verily prohibit them!."

In another narration:

قَالَ فَزَبَرَهُ ابْنُ عُمَرَ وَقَالَ: "أَقُولُ: قَالَ رَسُولُ اللهِ صَلَّى اللهُ عَلَيْهِ وَسَلَّمَ. وَتَقُولُ: لَا نَدَعُهُنَّ؟!

So Ibn Umar rebuked him and he said: "I say: 'The Messenger of Allah ﷺ says..." and you say: We won't allow the women to go..!?"[2]

I don't know if the man who questioned me was satisfied or convinced with the narration of the Prophet Muhammad ﷺ however he was silent and didn't speak nor respond to my answer.

Then after the 'adthaan' for the Ishaa'a prayer and the 'iqamah', a rich man from the city of Banglore India, I think his name is Haj Qasim, mentioned to me saying: 'I built a large masjid in the city of Banglore and within this masjid is a prayer area for the women which can capacitate at least 500 women. The women's

---

[1] -Sunan Abee Dawud, in the same Book and Chapter as the previous narration and they are both authentic #568
[2] -The three previous narrations are mentioned in Saheeh Muslim, The Book of Prayer, Chapter: Women going out to the masaajid #138-142, Vol. 1/327-328

prayer area has its own separate walkway and bathrooms which are separate from the men. The masjid was opened in Ramadan so the men and women prayed Ramadan there and the women even came for the 'Taraweeh' prayer, an action which made the Muslims very delighted and pleased. However the scholars of the Hanefee school of thought gathered together and decided to close down the women's masjid stating that: "It is not permissible for the woman to pray in the masjid according to the Hanafee school of thought."

I replied to him: 'You built the masjid, so what was your position regarding this type of behavior and conduct??? He said: 'I built the masjid and turned it over to them and I have nothing to do with it."

Allah is my witness, on another occasion I recall one day while I was making 'tawaf' around the Ka'bah after Asr Prayer while a man who was a strict follower of the Hanafee school of thought from Pakistan was making tawaf with me. When we finished making the tawaf and we started proceeding to the station of Ibrahim to pray two 'rak'at' (units of prayer) which proceed the tawaf, the man grabbed my hand and said: 'Don't pray at this time, this time for praying is 'makrooh' (disliked), it is not permissible to pray after Asr. I replied to him: Verily a narration from the Prophet Muhammad ﷺ has come to us on the authority of Jubayr ibn Mutim that the Prophet Muhammad ﷺ said:

عَنْ جُبَيْرِ بْنِ مُطْعِمٍ أن النَّبِيَّ -صلى الله عليه وسلم- قَالَ « لاَ تَمْنَعُوا أَحَدًا يَطُوفُ بِهَذَا الْبَيْتِ وَيُصَلِّى أَىَّ سَاعَةٍ شَاءَ مِنْ لَيْلٍ أَوْ نَهَارٍ

"O Bani Abdu Manaf, do not prohibit anyone from making tawaf around this house (Ka'bah) and do not prohibit anyone from praying any time of the night or day."[1]

Then the man replied to me: 'Is this Abu Haneefah's 'hadeeth' (narration)?!

I then said to him: 'If it is said: 'hadeeth' then verily it is from the Prophet Muhammad ﷺ.' Then he said: 'Did Abu Haneefah use this hadeeth?

---

[1]-This wording is for Abu Dawud Book of Hajj, Chapter Tawaf after Asr, #1894, vol. 2/180, and At Tirmidthi in his Jami' 2/22, Book of Hajj, #868 and An Nisaa'ee in his Sunan 1/284, Book of Prayer, Chapter Permissiblity of The Prayer at All hours in Makkah, #2924 and #585 also in the Book of Hajj, Chapter Tawaf at all times, Ibn Majah in his Sunan 1/398, Book of Establishment of Prayer, Chapter that which has been narrated regarding the permissibility of prayer in Makkah at all times, and other then them #1254. The narration is authentic. Please see "al Masjid al Haraam , History and Rulings", By Ash Sheikh al Muhaddith Wasiullah Muhammad Abbaas.

Al 'I'tibaa'a

Then I replied to him: 'As long as it is an established authentic narration from the Prophet Muhammad ﷺ and other scholars of 'fiqh' used it as a proof and they said: 'there is no disliked time for praying in the Masjid al Haraam', then it is permissible for me to pray if Allah wills. He was not pleased with my opposition and he didn't pray after that.

What is clearly evident in this story is: That the bigotry and fanaticism demonstrated by this man is that he didn't even accept nor consider the narration of the Prophet Muhammad ﷺ until his Imam had taken, accepted and used this narration.

This is why some of the people who are followers of the Hanafee school of thought dislike me in Makkah, India and other places and they accuse me of being an enemy of the Imam Abu Hanifah.

I also heard a cassette in which one of them was cursing and slandering me, telling lies about me, may Allah forgive him and guide him-he said: 'that I curse and slander Imam Abu Haneefah,' this is outright blasphemy which he will be held accountable for in front of Allah.

Verily, I am one who follows all of the scholars of 'fiqh', Abu Haneefah, Malik, ash Shafee'ee, Ahmed and others. I benefit from their knowledge and I ask Allah to always send His all encompassing mercy upon them all. This being because I know that they are from Ahlul Hadeeth (the people of hadeeth) and that they all exhorted and urged us in their recommendations and advices to take and adhere to the authentic narrations of the Prophet Muhammad ﷺ and the noble companions.

I say to the people: It is obligatory upon all of us to love the scholars of 'fiqh' and always ask Allah to send His mercy upon them and make supplication for them and benefit from their schools of jurisprudic thought. However it is not obligatory upon us, rather it is not permissible for us to blind follow any of them in particular. This is because Allah and His Messenger ﷺ did not make it obligatory, however the bigoted and fanatical ones are not satisfied with this answer, rather they consider action upon the Sunnah as a crime which is not forgiven.

From amongst the things which I have never forgotten regarding this topic: I was attending a gathering with some of the scholars of India in which some of the 'influential' people of Makkah were present. While sitting in the gathering one of these people of Makkah began advising those Indian scholars with his mellow, lenient and gentle phrases saying: 'O my brothers, don't differ and create dissension with the group over there-meaning the majority group of the Hanafees-and don't be extreme regarding some of the sunan[1]. From amongst the things he said: 'I attended some of the masaajid in India and I found that all of the students place their hands upon their chests when they are standing in the prayer, and they raise their voices saying 'Ameen', and from amongst the Sunnah is leaving off the Sunnah sometimes, as Ibn Taymiyyah mentioned...' This is what he said-may Allah forgive him.

I was not able to remain patient, so I said with the best of manners: 'Didn't Allah and His Messenger ﷺ order with the propagation of and calling to the 'sincere religion' and acting upon it?! Didn't the Prophet ﷺ make supplication for the one who transmits narrations and relates on his behalf? So if everyone who Allah has given knowledge of the Sunnah remains silent, doesn't act upon it and doesn't remind the people about acting upon the Sunnah, we will find that the Prophet's ﷺ traditions and narrations will disappear little by little until people are raised and nurtured and they don't know the religion except that it is equivalent to a mixture of truth with falsehood.

No one payed any attention to what I said, it was as if no one heard me. This 'influential' man continued with his exhortation by advising them to stay with the majority group of Hanafees in India and not to cause problems by acting upon some of the sunan, as he claimed.

My heart was touched with amazement and astonishment, I was startled and surprised, saying to myself: 'how could a man who was raised in the land of Tawheed (monotheism) Saudia Arabia, which revived many of the sunan and destroyed some of the innovations, and revived the rememberence of the rightly guided caliphs; this man speaking with words as though he is free and innocent of the calling to 'tawheed and Sunnah'. How can he be pleased with himself by advising the people to leave off the Sunnah and leave off praying the way the Prophet ﷺ prayed??!!' Then it didn't take long until my astonishment and amazement diminished after knowing that he is one of the major 'du'aat' (callers) to some of the sects in Indian and they are supporters of these groups in Saudia Arabia.

---

[1]-**(TN)**Sayings, actions, approvals, and characteristics of the Prophet Muhammad ﷺ

Al 'I'tibaa'a

I say: The likes of those people do not fear Allah regarding their fellow Muslims nor do they care for, regard nor consider the ties of kinship and covenants if they obtain strength, status, or are placed in positions of authority.

Verily, I have read as many others have read in the authentic history of Islam about occurrences, incidents and scandals which were facilitated by Muslims who showed bigotry and partisanship to their false creed and system of beliefs against the people who call to the Sunnah and the implementation of it into their creed and actions.

The history of Imam Ahmed ibn Hanbal and the harm and torture he suffered at the hands of the rulers of Baghdad at that time who were misguided and deceived by some perverted and misguided people.[1] This is something familiar to all of us and one of the best examples regarding the history of the Islamic creed and legislations.

The great Imam Baqee ibn Makhlad[2] as Imam adh Dha'habee said about him: 'He was a diligent, righteous, truthful, pious Imam, and sincere. He was the chief and leader in knowledge and action, unique without rivals. He used to give religious verdicts with narrations of the Prophet ﷺ and companions and he didn't blind follow or imitate anyone (besides the Prophet and companions).[3] Verily the 'fiqh' scholars of the Maliki school of thought harmed him and put him through the worst type of suffering, until Allah granted him success and aided him.

Ibn al Fardee[4] said: 'Baqee ibn Makhlid brought an enormous amount of narrations into 'Andalus' (Spain)[1], and many of his Spanish companions criticized,

---

[1] -(TN)Ahmed ibn Abee Du'aad and Bishr al-Marrisee were the two important figures behind the Mu'tazilite inquisition, which systematically placed many jurists and traditionists on trial until they were forced to acknowledge that the Quran is created, and their acknowledgement publicised in all major cities. Nearly all the scholars of Baghdad from the jurists and the traditionists were tested, and all of them acknowledged the doctrine of the created Quran, with the exception of the two; Ahmad b. Hanbal and Muhammad b. Nuh.

[2] -(TN) His name was Baqee ibn Makhlad ibn Yazeed, al Imam, Sheikhul Islaam, Abu Abdurahman the Spainard al Qurtubee, al Hafidth, the author of 'al Musnad' and he also has a commentary on the Quran which are unique. He was born around 200 H. and died 276, refer back to 'Seer A'laam an Nubalaa'a 13/285-296

[3] -Seer A'laam an Nubalaa'a 13/286

[4] -(TN)He is al Imam al Hafidth Abul Waleed Abdullah ibn Muhammad ibn Yusuf ibn Nasr, al Qurtubee, the author of 'History of Spain'. It is said that he was a scholar and jurist who was very knowledgeable in all fields of knowledge related to hadeeth and their narrators, he was killed by the Berbers in the year 403 hijri. (Seer A'laam an Nubalaa'a 17/177)

Al 'I'tibaa'a

rebuked and censured him such as Ahmed ibn Khalid, Muhammad ibn al Harith[2], and Abu Zaid for what he brought with him from various types of books and uncommon narrations. His rivals excited, incited and frightened the ruler with the mentioning of these books and their authors. Then Allah granted victory to Baqee over them and protected him from their evil plots and his narrations became well known amongst the people. Then the people became familiar and read Baqee's narrations and from that day on the narrations of the Prophet ﷺ and the companions spread throughout Spain."[3]

Furthermore, Abu Muhammad ibn Hazm ath Thaahiree[4] mentioned: 'Muhammad ibn Abdurahman al Umawee[5] the leader of Spain, was well versed and learned and had a great love for knowledge. Baqee ibn Makhlad entered Spain with 'Musanaf Abee Bakr ibn Abee Shaybah'[6] and it was being read and taught there until a group of people of 'ahl Ray'ee' (personal and subjective opinion) disapproved, renounced and rebuked 'Musanaf Abee Bakr ibn Abee Shaybah' for what they claimed it contained of 'controversial narrations' against their opinions. They considered the book to be repugnant and the people of opinions excited and incited the residents of the city to rebel against Baqee. They eventually prohibited him from teaching and reading the book altogether. Until the leader of Spain, Muhammad al Umawee summoned Baqee and the residents of Spain together to judge between them. Muhammad al Umawee started skimming and browsing through 'Musanaf Abee Bakr ibn Abee Shaybah'

---

[1]-(TN)Prophetic narrations as well as narrations from the companions

[2]-(TN)He is Muhammad ibn Harith ibn Asad al Khushanee al Qeerawaani al Hafidth al Imam. He authored many books: 'al Itifaaq wal Ikhtilaaf' about the Maliki madth'hab, also 'History of Spain', also 'History of the Africaans'. He was known to be from amongst the greatest poets. He died 361 hijri or 371. (Seer A'laam an Nubalaa'a 16/165)

[3]-History of the Scholars of Andulus 1/92-93

[4]-(TN)He is Abū Muḥammad ʿAlī ibn Aḥmad ibn Saʿīd ibn Ḥazm also sometimes known as al-Andalusī ath-Thaāhirī, he died 456 hijri. He was a Spanish scholar of hadeeth, fiqh, litterateur, psychologist, historian, jurist and theologian born in Córdoba, present-day Spain. He has many works from them: Al-Fisal fi al-Milal wa al-Ahwa' wa al-Nihal, Al Kitab al-Muhallā bi'l Athār, Ihkam Al Ahkam fi Usul al Ahkam, usul al fiqh, and many others.

[5]-(TN)He is Muhammad ibn Abdurahman ibnul Hakam, leader of Spain. He used to love knowledge and he was influenced by the People of Hadeeth, while honoring and being generous to them. He is the one who aided Baqee ibn Makhlad when the People of Opinions gathered up against him. He died in the end of Safar 273 hijri. (Seer A'Laam an Nubalaa'a 8/262

[6]-(TN)The author of this book is Abu Bakr Muhammad ibn Abdillah ibn Abee Shaybah who was born in the year 135 hijir and died in the year 235 hijri. This book is considered on of the earliest, biggest and most important sources regarding narrations of the salaf, containing over 35,000 narrations.

Al 'I'tibaa'a

volume by volume until he reached the end of the book. Then he said to the treasurer: 'this book is that which no treasury or library can do without, do whatever you can to get a copy of this book.' Then Muhammad al Umawee said to Baqee: 'spread and propagate your knowledge throughout the land and narrate and teach everything you have. Finally, he prevented the people of the city from challenging and hindering Baqee any further."[1]

Imam adh Dha'habee mentioned in his biography of Asbag ibn Khalil[2] saying: 'He was proficient and an expert in making and deriving jurisprudic and theoretical conditions and stipulations. He had no knowledge of the narrations and he was considered to be weak in transmitting them. It has also been said that he fabricated narrations about not raising the hands in the prayer. Qasim ibn Asbag[3] said about him (Asbag): He prohibited me from listening and learning from Baqee ibn Makhlid and I heard him say: 'It is more loved to me to have a pig in my coffin than to have 'Musanaf ibn Abee Shaybah' in my coffin, then Qasim made supplication against him.'[4]

Furthermore, what occurred in the Masjid al Haraam for eight hundred years of emaciation, the Muslims were split into sects- even while performing their prayers, all of this because of their bigotry and fanaticism shown to their specific 'madthaa'hib'. None of the Imam's would pray behind any of the other Imam's who were followers of another 'madth'hab', while there existed a place of prayer for every Imam and their particular 'madth'hab'. An occurrence which is an embarrassment when observing the history of Islam.[5]

---

[1]-Seer A'Laam an Nubalaa'a 13/288

[2]-(TN)His name is Abul Qaasim al Maliki, he was the jurist of Qurtubaa (city in Spain) and their Mufti. He learned from 'Sahnoon' and many others. He was known for his excessive worship and piety, he lived to be approximately 90 years and he died 273 hijri.

[3]-(TN)He is Ibn Muhammad ibn Yusuf ibn Nasih, also it has been said his name is: 'Wadih ibn Nasih', the great Imam, al Hafidth, al Allaamah, the Muhaddith of Spain. He studied under many great scholars such as Baqee ibn Makhlid, Ibn Abee Dunya, Abee Khaythamah. And he authored many books in his time. He possessed one of the strongest and shortest chains of narration from amongst the scholars in Spain. He was known for his memorization, his strong Arabic Language, and he gave many religious verdicts. He died in Jumada al Uwlaa 340hijri. (Seer A'Laam an Nubalaa'a 15/473-474

[4]-Seer A'Laam an Nubalaa'a 13/202, also see 'al I'tisaam by Ash Shatibee 2/348

[5]-Look for the details of this subject in the authors book "al Masjid al Haraam, History and Rulings' pg. 163-166, also see what Ibn Hajr mentioned in his biography of Ibn Abee Izz from the book 'Inbaa'a al Gamar' 1/258

Al 'I'tibaa'a

Ibn Kathir mentioned in 'al Bidayah wa an Nihayaa': That the leader of Egypt, the king Ibn Salah ad Deen decided in the same year he died 595 (H),with firm intent to exile all of the followers of the Hanbali school of 'fiqh' from Egypt and send letters to all his brothers to do the same in their countries. Ibn Kathir also mentioned: 'During the year 595 there was some strife and tribulations which took place in Damascus because al Hafith Abdul Ganee al Maqdasee[1] was speaking in one of the Hanbali's podiums in Masjid al Umawee. One day he mentioned something from the affairs of creed and then the Judge Ibn Turkey and Dee'yaa'a ad Deen al Khateeb ad Dula'ee[2] gathered together with the prince Sarim ad Deen Bargash. So they arranged a sitting for him regarding the issues related to 'Allah's raising up above the throne, His descending, and the letters and pronunciation of the Quran. So Najm al Hanbali agreed with the majority of the Hanbali scholars and al Hafith al Maqdasee continued and remained firm upon his creed and didn't abandon nor deny anything of the correct creed. Then the remaining 'fiqh' scholars gathered up against him and imposed upon him things which he refused and denied until the Prince Bargash asked him: 'All of those 'fiqh' scholars are upon misguidance and you, alone, are upon the truth? Al Hafith replied: 'Yes.' Then the Prince became extremely angry and ordered that al- Hafith be exiled from his country, in which he asked for a three day delay in which he was granted. Then Prince Bargash sent the captives from the castle to destroy and demolish the podium of the Hanbali scholars. So that day there was no 'Thur' prayer established in the 'mihrab' (prayer area) of the Hanbalis and the treasure chests and valuables were extracted and the problems, confusion and tribulations continued and increased. We seek refuge in Allah from all confusion the apparent and unapparent. Then al Hafith Abdul Ganee traveled to 'Ba'labak[3] and he went on to Egypt where the people and scholars of hadeeth aided and supported him while continuously asking him about what

---

[1]-(TN)He is Abdul Ghanee ibn Abdul Waahid ibn Ja'far al Jammaa'eelee, he was born in the year 541 hijri. He traveled to Baghdaad to seek knowledge of hadeeth, he also visited Egypt, Iran, Damascus. He authored one of the most famous books regarding hadeeth narrators called 'al Kamal fi Asmaa ar Rijaal', and also 'Umdatul Ahkaam'. He died in the year 600 hijri.

[2]-(TN)-He is Sheikh al Imam al Hafidth Dee'yaa'a Deen Abu Abdullah as Sa'dee al Maqdisee al Jammaa'eelee, he was born in the year 569 hijri. He authored many books such as 'Fadaa'il al'Amaal', 'Fadaa'il ash Shaam', 'al Ahaadeeth al Mukhtaarah', and many others. He continued to author books and compilations until he died. He was well known for his memorization and knowledge of hadeeth narrators, and used to be the reference for knowing the authentic ahadeeth from the inauthentic. He died 643 hijri. (Seer A'laam an Nubalaa'a 23/126) This story was also narraated by Abee al Muthafar from 'Miraat az Zamaan' and mentioned in 'Seer A'Laam an Nubalaa'a 21/463.

[3]-(TN) A city which is in modern day Lebanon

happened and treating him with the greatest amount of generousity and kindness.¹

Furthermore, within the story transmitted from ad Dee'yaa'a al Maqdasi :'We were in al- Mowsil² and were listening to the book 'ad Du'afaa'a' by al Uqaylee³, so the people of al- Mowsil took hold of me and placed me in prison and they wanted to assassinate me because Abu Haneefah was mentioned within this book. Then there came upon me a very tall man holding a sword and I said to him: 'You will kill me and I will be at ease'. The narrator mentioned: 'that the man holding the sword didn't do anything.' Ad Dee'yaa'a al Maqdasi then said: 'they released me from prison, and they used to listen to Ibn al Burnee the great exhorter.' The narrator mentioned:' so he tore out the pages with the mention of Abu Haneefah, then they sent the book and examined it closely and diligently without finding anything in it, this was the reason for his liberation and freedom.⁴

The books of history are filled with mention of these stories of trials, tribulations and the outright blatant hatred and malice against those who call to the authentic creed of as-Salifiyyah and call to implementing the Quran and Sunnah. Incidents which disturb and trouble the mind and heart, we are no doubt sad and disappointed about this. We hope that harm, grievances and evil acts against the scholars do not come from their own brothers who may be also scholars, students of knowledge or from amongst the Muslims in general.

---

[1] -Al Bidayah wa Nihayah 13/18-21. This story was also mentioned by Abee al Muthafar from 'Miraat az Zamaan' in 'Seer A'Laam an Nubalaa'a 21/463

[2] -(TN)Mowsil: A northern city in Iraq some 400km of Baghdaad.

[3] -(TN)This book was authored by Abee Ja'far Muhammad ibn Amru ibn Musa ibn Hamaad al Uqaylee who died in the year 322 hijri. This book contains mention of ahadeeth narrators who were known to be weak in their narrating and transmitting of ahadeeth. This book also mentions those narrators who were known to fabricate ahadeeth, narrators who were unknown, also narrators who were innovators and propagated their innovations. It also contains narrators who were imprecise, weak and made many mistakes in their narrating of hadeeth.

[4] -Seer A'Laam an Nubalaa'a 21/459. Sheikh Wasiullah said: I have a copy of 'ad Du'afaa'a' by al Uqaylee which was copied from a handwritten manuscript over 38 years ago. Within it you will find that they erased/blacked out the biography of al Imam Abu Haneefah with a thick black pen.

Certainly, the scholars who lead the masses will be the first ones asked about the sin regarding this type of behavior, Allah the Most High says:

﴿ لِيَحْمِلُوٓا۟ أَوْزَارَهُمْ كَامِلَةً يَوْمَ ٱلْقِيَٰمَةِ ۙ وَمِنْ أَوْزَارِ ٱلَّذِينَ يُضِلُّونَهُم بِغَيْرِ عِلْمٍ ۗ أَلَا سَآءَ مَا يَزِرُونَ ۝ ﴾

"They bear their own burdens (sins) completely on the Day of Resurrection and also the burdens (sins) of those whom they misled without knowledge. Evil indeed is that which they shall bear!" (An Nahl 16:25)

Won't they fear Allah amongst themselves and with regards to Allah servants!

Al 'I'tibaa'a

Chapter One

Definition of al It'ibaa'a'

Al It'ibaa'a in the Arabic Language is a verbal noun, meaning one who follows something. It is said in Arabic 'I followed his path'. It is also said: 'A man who goes ahead and you go behind him or follow him. 'It'ibaa'ul Quran' means: Follow the Quran, in other words: imitate, emulate, follow it's example and act upon what is in it.'[1]

The technical and religious meaning of Al It'ibaa'a is similar to the linguistic meaning: following, walking behind, emulating what the Prophet Muhammad ﷺ came with and imitating it and acting upon it.

Al It'ibaa'a is the opposite of at Taqleed, which means: Acting upon a saying or action from someone whose sayings and actions are not authoritative sources or evidences in the religion.

What we mean by Al It'ibaa'a is: Imitation, adherence, following the Book of Allah and the Sunnah of His Messenger ﷺ and the obligation of following them are upon whoever the Quran and Sunnah reach.

Al'It'ibaa'a' also means: imitating and following the Sunnah of the rightly guided caliphs, based upon the Prophets ﷺ saying:

"عَلَيْكُمْ بِسُنَّتِي وَسُنَّةِ الْخُلَفَاءِ الرَّاشِدِينَ"

'Upon all of you is to adhere to my Sunnah and the Sunnah of the rightly guided caliphs.'[2]

It also means following the consensus of the companions and those who proceeded them from amongst the scholars of Islam if their sayings are

---

[1]-see 'Lisanul Arab' 8/27-28

[2]-(TN)Taken from the long hadeeth in Sunan at Tirmidthi 5/44, Book of Knowledge, Chapter: What came regarding implementing the Sunnah #2676, and at Tirmidthi said 'hasan saheeh'. Sunan Abee Dawud pg.691, Book of the Sunnah, Chapter: Adhering to the Sunnah, #4607. Sunan ibn Majah pg.20, Introduction, Chapter: Following the Sunnah of the Rightly Guided Caliphs #42. Mustadrak al Haakim 1/95, and al Haakim said: 'saheeh and there is no defect in the narration, and adh Dha'habee agreed with him'. And the narration is as they said-authentic.

Al 'I'tibaa'a

authentic. All of this is considered Al'It'ibaa'a because these are legislative evidences which are obligatory to follow.

Also 'it'ibaa'a' of the correct 'qiyas'(analogical reasoning) which is authentic from the Quran and Sunnah is considered 'it'ibaa'a' and not 'taqleed'.

Part One

Creation of mankind and the reason for their creation

Allah the Most Magnificent said:

﴿ وَإِذْ قَالَ رَبُّكَ لِلْمَلَٰٓئِكَةِ إِنِّي جَاعِلٌ فِى ٱلْأَرْضِ خَلِيفَةً ۖ قَالُوٓا۟ أَتَجْعَلُ فِيهَا مَن يُفْسِدُ فِيهَا وَيَسْفِكُ ٱلدِّمَآءَ وَنَحْنُ نُسَبِّحُ بِحَمْدِكَ وَنُقَدِّسُ لَكَ ۖ قَالَ إِنِّىٓ أَعْلَمُ مَا لَا تَعْلَمُونَ ۞ ﴾

"**And remember when your Lord said to the angels: Verily, I am going to place mankind on earth, generations after generations.' They said: Will you place within the earth those who will make mischief therein and shed blood-while we glorify you with praises and thanks and sanctify you." Allah said: "I know that which you do not know."** (al Baqarah 2:30)

'Allah reiterated His favor on the Children of Adam when He stated that He mentioned them in the heavens before He created Adam, He said to the Prophet Muhammad ﷺ: O Muhammad ﷺ remind your people what Allah said to the angels, and tell them that I am going to place people upon the earth reproducing generation after generation, century after century. Allah was not referring to Adam specifically and the angels understood this according to their special knowledge that these people (Khalifah) will cause mischief upon the earth. So the angels asked Allah about the wisdom behind creating them and this was not a form of disputing with Allah nor was it out of envy for the Children of Adam. They understood that the reason behind creating the Children of Adam was: to worship Allah, to praise Him and glorify Him. The angels replied: We praise you and glorify you and sanctify you, and Allah replied to them: I am the most knowledgeable of the wisdom and benefits behind the creation which you all do not know. If there exists amongst these creatures some of the harmful things which you all mentioned (angels) for verily I will create amongst them Prophets, Messengers, truthful people, martyrs, righteous believers, worshippers, ascetics, pious believers, those who get closer to Allah by worshipping Him alone, humble scholars who act upon their knowledge, and those who love Allah and His Messenger ﷺ.'[1]

---

[1]-Tafsir ibn Kathir 1/115

Al 'I'tibaa'a

Part Two

The Sending of the Messengers and the conflict and differing amongst their nations

After the creation of Adam mankind was upon the true and natural inclination 'al-Fitrah' (Islamic Monotheism) which Allah created them upon. The 'fitrah' is the sincere worship of Allah alone without any partners. Allah created all of the followers of the Messengers upon this monotheism until the Shayateen (satans) deceived them and then they started worshipping other than Allah. Allah mentions in the Quran:

﴿ كَانَ ٱلنَّاسُ أُمَّةً وَاحِدَةً فَبَعَثَ ٱللَّهُ ٱلنَّبِيِّنَ مُبَشِّرِينَ وَمُنذِرِينَ وَأَنزَلَ مَعَهُمُ ٱلْكِتَٰبَ بِٱلْحَقِّ لِيَحْكُمَ بَيْنَ ٱلنَّاسِ فِيمَا ٱخْتَلَفُوا۟ فِيهِ ۚ وَمَا ٱخْتَلَفَ فِيهِ إِلَّا ٱلَّذِينَ أُوتُوهُ مِنۢ بَعْدِ مَا جَآءَتْهُمُ ٱلْبَيِّنَٰتُ بَغْيًۢا بَيْنَهُمْ ۖ فَهَدَى ٱللَّهُ ٱلَّذِينَ ءَامَنُوا۟ لِمَا ٱخْتَلَفُوا۟ فِيهِ مِنَ ٱلْحَقِّ بِإِذْنِهِۦ ۗ وَٱللَّهُ يَهْدِى مَن يَشَآءُ إِلَىٰ صِرَٰطٍ مُّسْتَقِيمٍ ۝ ﴾

"Mankind were one community and Allah sent Prophets with glad tidings and warnings. He also sent with them the Scripture in truth to judge between the people in matters wherein they differed. And only those to whom the Scripture was given to, they differed concerning it after clear proofs had come to them through hatred amongst each other. Then Allah by His will guided those who believed to the truth regarding that in which they differed. And Allah guides whom He wills to the straight path." (al Baqarah 2:213)

Al Hakim and others narrated with an authentic chain of narration on the authority of Ibn Abaas he said:

عَنِ ابْنِ عَبَّاسٍ رَضِيَ اللهُ عَنْهُمَا ، قَالَ : " كَانَ بَيْنَ نُوحٍ وَآدَمَ عَشَرَةُ قُرُونٍ كُلُّهُمْ عَلَى شَرِيعَةٍ مِنَ الْحَقِّ ، فَاخْتَلَفُوا (فيه) فَبَعَثَ اللهُ النَّبِيِّينَ مُبَشِّرِينَ وَمُنْذِرِينَ "

Al 'I'tibaa'a

"Between Nuh (Noah) and Adam were ten centuries, all of them were upon the legislation of truth, then they differed regarding it, so Allah sent Prophets as bringers of glad tidings and warners."[1]

Also Ibn Jarir at Tabari narrated this and said: 'and that is the recitation of Abdullah ibn Mas'ud and that was what Ubay' ibn Kab used to recite, this is what Qatadah mentioned while Mujahid said similar to what Ibn Abaas said."[2]

When the people started differing in regards to what Allah created them upon (Islamic Monotheism) Allah sent Prophets to remind them and call the people back to the truth. The believers are the ones who are guided-in the affairs and situations of conflict and differing-to the truth which the Prophets and Messengers came with.

In times of conflict and differing, the true guidance is known by returning back to what the Prophet Muhammad ﷺ came with to his nation from Allah the Most Magnificent, and this is what the Prophet ﷺ used to make supplication for when supplicating.

Imam Muslim narrated on the authority of Aa'isha that the Prophet Muhammad ﷺ when he woke up to pray at night, he would start his prayer with the words:

"اللَّهُمَّ رَبَّ جِبْرِيلَ وَمِيكَائِيلَ وَإِسْرَافِيلَ فَاطِرَ السَّمَوَاتِ وَالأَرْضِ عَالِمَ الْغَيْبِ وَالشَّهَادَةِ أَنْتَ تَحْكُمُ بَيْنَ عِبَادِكَ فِيمَا كَانُوا فِيهِ يَخْتَلِفُونَ لِمَا اخْتُلِفَ فِيهِ مِنَ الْحَقِّ بِإِذْنِكَ إِنَّكَ تَهْدِي مَنْ تَشَاءُ إِلَى صِرَاطٍ مُسْتَقِيمٍ"

'O Allah, Lord of Jibreel, Mikaa'eel, and Isra'feel Originator of the heavens and the earth, knower of the unseen and the seen, you judge between your slaves concerning that wherein they differ. Guide me concerning that wherein they

---

[1] -This wording is for al Haakim in al Mustadrak 2/546-547 #4009, and at Tabari narrated it in his tafsir 2/194 see 'Silsilah al Ahadeeh as Saheehah by Sheikh Muhammad Naasirud Deen al Albaani 7/854. **(TN)** Sheikh al Albaani said: This narration contains an important benefit it is that the first generation of people were one unified nation upon pure 'tawheed' monotheism then the emergence of 'shirk' polytheism became apparent. This narration is a refutation to the philosophers and atheists who say that in the beginning there was polytheism then monotheism emerged after it...

[2] -Tafsir Ibn Jarir at Tabari 2/194, under the mentioned verse.

differ of truth by your leave, for verily You guide whomsoever you will to a straight path."[1]

Then Allah sent His Messengers and Prophets one after the other to various nations while some Prophets were sent specifically to their own nations. Verily it occurred in the past that there were many Prophets who were sent to their nations all at one time. Allah the Most Gracious mentions:

﴿ وَلَقَدْ أَرْسَلْنَا نُوحًا إِلَىٰ قَوْمِهِ إِنِّي لَكُمْ نَذِيرٌ مُبِينٌ ۝ ﴾

"And verily we sent Nuh (Noah) to his people saying: 'I have come to you as a plain warner." (Hud 11:25) And Allah says:

﴿ وَإِلَىٰ عَادٍ أَخَاهُمْ هُودًا ۚ قَالَ يَـٰقَوْمِ ٱعْبُدُوا۟ ٱللَّهَ مَا لَكُم مِّنْ إِلَـٰهٍ غَيْرُهُۥٓ ۖ إِنْ أَنتُمْ إِلَّا مُفْتَرُونَ ۝ ﴾

"And to Ad's people We sent their brother Hud saying: 'O my people! Worship Allah! You have no other god except Him. Certainly, you do nothing but invent lies." (Hud 11:50) And Allah says:

﴿ ۞ وَإِلَىٰ ثَمُودَ أَخَاهُمْ صَـٰلِحًا ۚ قَالَ يَـٰقَوْمِ ٱعْبُدُوا۟ ٱللَّهَ مَا لَكُم مِّنْ إِلَـٰهٍ غَيْرُهُۥ ۖ هُوَ أَنشَأَكُم مِّنَ ٱلْأَرْضِ وَٱسْتَعْمَرَكُمْ فِيهَا فَٱسْتَغْفِرُوهُ ثُمَّ تُوبُوٓا۟ إِلَيْهِ ۚ إِنَّ رَبِّي قَرِيبٌ مُّجِيبٌ ۝ ﴾

"And to Thamud's people We sent their brother Salih saying: O my people! Worship Allah, you have no other god except him..." (Hud 11:61) And Allah says:

﴿ وَإِلَىٰ مَدْيَنَ أَخَاهُمْ شُعَيْبًا ۚ قَالَ يَـٰقَوْمِ ٱعْبُدُوا۟ ٱللَّهَ مَا لَكُم مِّنْ إِلَـٰهٍ غَيْرُهُۥ ۖ وَلَا تَنقُصُوا۟ ٱلْمِكْيَالَ وَٱلْمِيزَانَ ۚ إِنِّيٓ أَرَىٰكُم بِخَيْرٍ وَإِنِّيٓ أَخَافُ عَلَيْكُمْ عَذَابَ يَوْمٍ مُّحِيطٍ ۝ ﴾

"And to Madyan's people we sent their brother Shu'aib saying: O my people! Worship Allah, you have no other god except him..." (Hud 11:84)

---

[1]-Saheeh Muslim 1/534, Book of the Travelers prayer, chapter: Supplication in the night prayer, #770

This is how Allah sent the Messengers as bringers of glad tidings and warners of Allah's punishment in order that mankind should have no plea against Allah after the coming of the Messengers. Allah says:

﴿ ثُمَّ أَرْسَلْنَا رُسُلَنَا تَتْرَا ۖ كُلَّ مَا جَاءَ أُمَّةً رَّسُولُهَا كَذَّبُوهُ ۚ فَأَتْبَعْنَا بَعْضَهُم بَعْضًا وَجَعَلْنَاهُمْ أَحَادِيثَ ۚ فَبُعْدًا لِّقَوْمٍ لَّا يُؤْمِنُونَ ﴾

"Then we sent Our Messengers in succession. Every time a Messenger came to a nation, the people denied him. So we made them follow one another to destruction and we made them as stories and tales for mankind to learn a lesson from. So away with the people who do not believe!" (al Mu'minun 23:44)
Allah also says:

﴿ إِنَّا أَوْحَيْنَا إِلَيْكَ كَمَا أَوْحَيْنَا إِلَىٰ نُوحٍ وَالنَّبِيِّينَ مِن بَعْدِهِ ۚ وَأَوْحَيْنَا إِلَىٰ إِبْرَاهِيمَ وَإِسْمَاعِيلَ وَإِسْحَاقَ وَيَعْقُوبَ وَالْأَسْبَاطِ وَعِيسَىٰ وَأَيُّوبَ وَيُونُسَ وَهَارُونَ وَسُلَيْمَانَ ۚ وَآتَيْنَا دَاوُودَ زَبُورًا ۞ وَرُسُلًا قَدْ قَصَصْنَاهُمْ عَلَيْكَ مِن قَبْلُ وَرُسُلًا لَّمْ نَقْصُصْهُمْ عَلَيْكَ ۚ وَكَلَّمَ اللَّهُ مُوسَىٰ تَكْلِيمًا ۞ ﴾

"Verily, We have sent the revelation to you O Muhammad as We have sent the revelation to Nuh and the Prophets after him, We also sent the revelation to Ibrahim (Abraham), Isma'eel (Ishmael), Ishaq (Isaac), Ya'cub (Jacob), and the twelve offspring from the sons of Ya'cub, Isa (Jesus), Ayyub (Job), Yunus (Jonah), Harun (Aaron), and Sulaiman (Soloman), and We gave the Zabur (Psalms) to Dawud (David).-And Messengers which We have mentioned to you previously and Messengers which we have not mentioned to you-and Allah spoke to Musa (Moses) directly." (an Nisa 4:163-164)

The Messengers which Allah mentioned in the Quran are: Adam, Idrees, Nuh, Hud, Salih, Ibrahim, Lut, Isma'eel, Ishaaq, Ya'qub, Yusuf, Ayyub, Shu'aib, Musa, Harun, Yunus, Dawud, Sulaiman, Ilyaas, al Yas'a, Zakariyyah, Yahya, Isa, and also Dhul Kifl amongst many of the commentators of the Quran and the leader of them, Muhammad ibn Abdullah ﷺ.

Al 'I'tibaa'a

A narration came on the authority of Abu Umaamah he said:

عَنْ أَبِي أُمَامَةَ رَضِيَ اللَّهُ عَنْهُ ، أَنَّ رَجُلًا قَالَ : يَا رَسُولَ اللَّهِ ، أَنَبِيًّا كَانَ آدَمُ ؟ قَالَ : " نَعَمْ ، مُعَلَّمٌ مُكَلَّمٌ " قَالَ : كَمْ بَيْنَهُ وَبَيْنَ نُوحٍ ؟ قَالَ : " عَشْرَةُ قُرُونٍ " قَالُوا : يَا رَسُولَ اللَّهِ ، كَمْ كَانَتِ الرُّسُلُ ؟ قَالَ : " ثَلَاثُمِائَةٍ وَخَمْسَةَ عَشَرَ "

A man said: 'O Messenger of Allah ﷺ, was Adam a Prophet? The Prophet ﷺ replied: Yes, one who Allah spoke to'. Then the man said: 'How much time was between Adam and Nuh? The Prophet ﷺ replied: 'Ten centuries'. Then the man said: 'O Messenger of Allah, how many Messengers were there? The Prophet ﷺ said: 'three hundred and fifteen." [1]

Also Ibn Hibban[2] narrated in his 'Saheeh' in the long narration on the authority of Abu Dharr, which contains:

...قُلْتُ : يَا رَسُولَ اللَّهِ كَمِ الْأَنْبِيَاءُ؟ قَالَ : مِائَةُ أَلْفٍ وَعِشْرُونَ أَلْفًا. قُلْتُ يَا رَسُولَ اللَّهِ كَمِ الرُّسُلُ مِنْ ذَلِكَ؟ قَالَ : ثَلَاثُمِائَةٍ وَثَلَاثَةَ عَشَرَ جَمًّا غَفِيرًا ، قُلْتُ يَا رَسُولَ اللَّهِ مَنْ كَانَ أَوَّلُهُمْ؟ قَالَ : آدَمُ. قُلْتُ : يَا رَسُولَ اللَّهِ أَنَبِيٌّ مُرْسَلٌ؟ قَالَ : نَعَمْ خَلَقَهُ اللَّهُ بِيَدِهِ...

'I said O Messenger of Allah, how many Prophets were there? The Prophet replied ﷺ: 'one hundred and twenty thousand'. Then I said, how many messengers from amongst them? He ﷺ replied: 'three hundred and thirteen a vast multitude', then I said: who was the first of them? He replied ﷺ: 'Adam'. Then I said: O Messenger of Allah: was he a prophet and messenger?

---

[1] -Ibn Hibbaan transmitted this narration in his Saheeh (#2085-mawaarid) and Ibn Mundah in at Tawheed (104/2) and al Haakim 2/262 and al Haakim said: this narration is authentic in accordance to the conditions of Imam Muslim and adh Dhahabee agreed with him. At Tabaraani in al Awsat 1/24/2/398 and in Mu'jam al Kabeer 8/139-140. Sheikh al Albaani also said it is authentic. see 'Silsilah al ahadeeh as Saheehah #668

[2] -(TN)He is the Imam al Hafidth Muhammad ibn Hibbaan ibn Ahmed ibn Hibbaan Abu Haatim al Bustee as Sijistaani. He was born in modern day Afghanistaan between the years 280-290 and died in 354 hijri. He authored the great book called 'al Musnad as Saheeh alaa at Taqaaseem wal Anwaa'a min ghairi wujood qat'i fi sanadihaa wa laa thuboot jarh fi naqileehaa', which is considered one of the authentic ahadeeth collections after Ibn Khuzaimah, Saheeh Bukhari and Saheeh Muslim.

Al 'I'tibaa'a

The Prophet ﷺ replied: **Yes, Allah created him with His own hand."**[1] This narration is evidence that Adam was the first messenger sent to earth. Imam Bukhari narrated in the hadeeth of 'Intercession' on the authority of Abu Hurairah and it contains:

...فَيَأْتُونَ نُوحًا، فَيَقُولُونَ: يَا نُوحُ، أَنْتَ أَوَّلُ الرُّسُلِ إِلَى أَهْلِ الأَرْضِ...

'So they come to Nuh and they say: 'O Nuh you are the first messenger sent to the people of the earth.'[2]

This narration proves that the first messenger was Nuh and not Adam. This narration is interpreted-Allah knows best: that Nuh was the first messenger of the progeny of Adam, so with this explanation there is no confliction in the narrations seeing that Adam was the first messenger without exception.

As Sindi[3] said: **'Nuh was the first messenger**, it is said that: 'the intent here is that Nuh was the first messenger who was sent to call the disbelievers to believe and have faith, and before him was Adam, Sheet/Sheeth, and Idrees who were not sent for this duty. However, they were sent to teach the believers the religious rulings and legislations, because at that time there were no disbelievers upon the earth.'[4]

---

[1]-Al Ihsaan Saheeh ibn Hibbaan bi tarteeb ibn Bulbaan 2/77 #361. The chain of narration used by Ibn Hibbaan is very weak due to the condition of Ibrahim ibn Hishaam al Ghasaani, however the hadeeth has many other supporting narrations which are authentic especially regarding the mention of the number of Prophets and Mesengers. So with these supporting evidences the part of the hadeeth mentioning the Prophets and Messenger is 'Hasan li gharihi' and 'Saheeh li dthatihi', this is clear by the narration which Abu Ja'far ar Razaaz mentioned with an authentic chain of narration on the authority of Abu Umaamah: that a man said: O Messenger of Allah, was Adam a Prophet? He replied: yes, one who was spoken to. Then the man asked: 'How much time was between Adam and Nuh? He replied: ten generations. Then the man said: 'O Messenger of Allah How many Messengers were there? He replied: three hundred and fifteen.' Please refer to see 'Silsilah Saheehah' al Albaani 6/1/358-369 #2668

[2]-Saheeh Bukhari 8/504, Book: The hadeeth of the prophets, Chapter: (إنا أرسلنا نوحا إلى قومه....) #3340

[3]-(TN)He is Sheikh al Imam Abul Hasan Nur Deen Muhammad ibn Abdul Haadi at Tatwee al Madani. He died in the year 1138 hijri in al Madinah an Nabiwiyyah, Saudia Arabia. He was known to be a scholar of hadeeth as well as many other fields of knowledge.

[4]-Explanation of Ibn Majah, by as Sindi 4/525

Al 'I'tibaa'a

Al Mubaarakfuri[1] said: 'this issue of Adam being the first Prophet and Messenger is somewhat problematic as well as Sheeth and Idrees and other than them. I will respond to this by saying: 'that the precedence which is mentioned here is restricted in the saying: **'to the people of the earth'**. This is problematic while keeping in mind the narration of Jabir ibn Abdullah in Saheeh Bukhari regarding 'tayamum' which contains in it: **'That a Prophet would be sent specifically to his nation only'**. This may be answered by saying that: the generality mentioned did not exist initially when Nuh was sent and verily it is in agreement considering the fact of restricting and limiting the creation to those who existed after the destruction and drowning of the people. The most apparent answer to this is to say: The three of them were Messengers sent to the believers and disbelievers, as for Nuh, then verily he was sent to the people of the earth and all of them were disbelievers.'[2]

---

[1]-**(TN)** He is Imam al Hafidth Muhammad ibn Abdur Rahmaan ibn Abdur Raheem al Mubararakfuri, the author of 'Tuhfatul Ah'wadthee', which is an explanation of Sunnan at Tirmidthi. He was born in 1283 and died in 1353 hijri.
[2]-Tuhfatul Ah'wadthee 2/297

Part Three

What is obligatory upon the nations with regards to the Messengers

It was obligatory upon every nation to obey and follow their Prophets in everything they brought their people from the divine revelation which Allah sent to them. Regardless of whether it was in book form or not in book form. Allah says:

﴿ وَمَآ أَرْسَلْنَا مِن رَّسُولٍ إِلَّا لِيُطَاعَ بِإِذْنِ ٱللَّهِ ﴾

"We sent no Messenger except that he be obeyed, by Allah's will" (An Nisa 4:64) Allah also says:

﴿ يَٰبَنِىٓ ءَادَمَ إِمَّا يَأْتِيَنَّكُمْ رُسُلٌ مِّنكُمْ يَقُصُّونَ عَلَيْكُمْ ءَايَٰتِى فَمَنِ ٱتَّقَىٰ وَأَصْلَحَ فَلَا خَوْفٌ عَلَيْهِمْ وَلَا هُمْ يَحْزَنُونَ ۝ وَٱلَّذِينَ كَذَّبُوا۟ بِـَٔايَٰتِنَا وَٱسْتَكْبَرُوا۟ عَنْهَآ أُو۟لَٰٓئِكَ أَصْحَٰبُ ٱلنَّارِ هُمْ فِيهَا خَٰلِدُونَ ۝ ﴾

"O Children of Adam! If there comes to you Messengers from amongst yourselves, reciting to you My verses, then whomsoever becomes pious and righteous then they shall have no fear nor shall they grieve.-But those who rejected our verses, proofs, evidences, revelations and treat these things with arrogance, then they are the dwellers of the Hellfire and will abide therein forever." (al A'raaf 7:35-36) Allah also mentions:

﴿ وَمَآ أَرْسَلْنَا مِن رَّسُولٍ إِلَّا بِلِسَانِ قَوْمِهِۦ لِيُبَيِّنَ لَهُمْ ۖ فَيُضِلُّ ٱللَّهُ مَن يَشَآءُ وَيَهْدِى مَن يَشَآءُ ۚ وَهُوَ ٱلْعَزِيزُ ٱلْحَكِيمُ ﴾

"And We didn't send any Messenger except with the language of his people, so that he might explain and make the message clear for them. Then Allah misleads whom He wills and guides whom He wills, and He is the All Mighty the All Wise." (Ibrahim 14:4)

Allah also says:

﴿ إِنَّا أَوْحَيْنَا إِلَيْكَ كَمَا أَوْحَيْنَا إِلَىٰ نُوحٍ وَالنَّبِيِّينَ مِنْ بَعْدِهِ ۚ وَأَوْحَيْنَا إِلَىٰ إِبْرَاهِيمَ ﴾

"Verily, We have sent the revelation to you O Muhammad just as We sent the revelation to Nuh and the Prophets after him. We also sent the revelation Ibrahim..." (an Nisa 4:163)

It is well known that many of the Prophets did not have a book of divine revelation nor was the revelation revealed to them in book form. Furthermore, it was still obligatory upon their nations and followers to obey their Messengers in everything they came with- without differentiating between the type of divine revelation which was sent to them. They made no distinction whether the revelation was recited in book form or not in book form. The Sunnah of the Prophet Muhammad ﷺ is considered as the second type (non-book form) which contains his sayings, actions and approvals.

The understanding of this is made clear by observing the story of Musa when he encountered and disputed with Firoun (Pharoah) and his people, which is a prime example of the type of revelation which was not recited nor was it in book form. In addition, the destruction of Firoun and his nation happened before Musa received the Torah, as Allah says:

﴿ وَلَقَدْ ءَاتَيْنَا مُوسَى ٱلْكِتَٰبَ مِنۢ بَعْدِ مَآ أَهْلَكْنَا ٱلْقُرُونَ ٱلْأُولَىٰ بَصَآئِرَ لِلنَّاسِ وَهُدًى وَرَحْمَةً لَّعَلَّهُمْ يَتَذَكَّرُونَ ﴾

" And indeed We gave Musa-after We destroyed the old generations-the Scripture (Torah) as an enlightenment for mankind and a guidance and a mercy that they might remember and receive admonition." (Al Qasas 28:43)

The domination and reign of humiliation and shame upon the nations was the result of them differing and disobeying what their Messengers came with from the divine revelation.

Al 'I'tibaa'a

Allah said about the Children of Israel:

﴿ وَضُرِبَتْ عَلَيْهِمُ ٱلذِّلَّةُ وَٱلْمَسْكَنَةُ وَبَآءُو بِغَضَبٍ مِّنَ ٱللَّهِ ۗ ذَٰلِكَ بِأَنَّهُمْ كَانُوا۟ يَكْفُرُونَ بِـَٔايَٰتِ ٱللَّهِ وَيَقْتُلُونَ ٱلنَّبِيِّـۧنَ بِغَيْرِ ٱلْحَقِّ ۗ ذَٰلِكَ بِمَا عَصَوا۟ وَّكَانُوا۟ يَعْتَدُونَ ﴾

"And they were overwhelmed and covered with humiliation and misery and they earned for themselves the wrath and anger of Allah. That was because they used to disbelieve in the proofs, evidences, verses, revelation from Allah and they also killed the Prophets wrongfully. That was because they disobeyed and used to transgress the limits by disobeying Allah and committing sins." (al Baqarah 2:61) Allah also says:

﴿ وَتِلْكَ عَادٌ ۖ جَحَدُوا۟ بِـَٔايَٰتِ رَبِّهِمْ وَعَصَوْا۟ رُسُلَهُۥ وَٱتَّبَعُوٓا۟ أَمْرَ كُلِّ جَبَّارٍ عَنِيدٍ ۝ وَأُتْبِعُوا۟ فِى هَٰذِهِ ٱلدُّنْيَا لَعْنَةً وَيَوْمَ ٱلْقِيَٰمَةِ ۗ أَلَآ إِنَّ عَادًا كَفَرُوا۟ رَبَّهُمْ ۗ أَلَا بُعْدًا لِّعَادٍ قَوْمِ هُودٍ ۝ ﴾

"Such were Ad's people who rejected the verses, proofs, revelation of their Lord and disobeyed His Messengers and followed the command of every proud, obstinate oppressor of truth from their leaders.-And a curse was made to pursue and follow them in this world and also on the Day of Resurrection. No doubt! That verily, Ad' disbelieved in their Lord, so away with Ad', the people of Hud." (Hud 11:59-60)

The destruction of some of the nations was due to the lack of obedience to their Messengers in what they brought of divine revelation from Allah. Allah says:

﴿ وَتِلْكَ ٱلْقُرَىٰٓ أَهْلَكْنَٰهُمْ لَمَّا ظَلَمُوا۟ وَجَعَلْنَا لِمَهْلِكِهِم مَّوْعِدًا ۝ ﴾

"And those towns of Ad and Thamud, We destroyed them with they did wrong. And we appointed a fixed time for their destruction." (al Kahf 18:59)

Amongst the most common things which the nations and people disobeyed their Lord and their Messengers in- was their division, separation, disunity and differing in Allah's religion. Verily Allah condemned, reviled and censured the Children of Israel and the People of the Book (Jews and Christians) in general because of their disputing and differing regarding Allah's religion.

Al 'I'tibaa'a

Allah says:

﴿ رَسُولٌ مِّنَ ٱللَّهِ يَتْلُوا۟ صُحُفًا مُّطَهَّرَةً ۝ فِيهَا كُتُبٌ قَيِّمَةٌ ۝ وَمَا تَفَرَّقَ ٱلَّذِينَ أُوتُوا۟ ٱلْكِتَٰبَ إِلَّا مِنۢ بَعْدِ مَا جَآءَتْهُمُ ٱلْبَيِّنَةُ ۝ ﴾

"A Messenger-Muhammad- sent from Allah reciting the purified pages (Quran)-Wherein are correct and straight laws from Allah-And the people of the Scripture (Jews and Christians) did not differ until after there came to them clear evidence from the Prophet Muhammad." (al Bayyinah 98:2-4)

Allah The Most Gracious warned the Muslims from dissension, splitting and differing as He said:

﴿ وَلَا تَكُونُوا۟ كَٱلَّذِينَ تَفَرَّقُوا۟ وَٱخْتَلَفُوا۟ مِنۢ بَعْدِ مَا جَآءَهُمُ ٱلْبَيِّنَٰتُ ۚ وَأُو۟لَٰٓئِكَ لَهُمْ عَذَابٌ عَظِيمٌ ﴾

"And do not be like those who split up and differed amongst themselves after the clear proofs had come to them. It is them who will receive an awful torment." (Al Imran 3:105)

Then Allah sent the last of the prophets and messengers-Muhammad ﷺ after a pause in the sending of the messengers.

Part Four

The time period between the Prophet Muhammad ﷺ and the Prophet who preceded him

We should know that Isa (Jesus) was the last Messenger before the Prophet Muhammad ﷺ as it has been established in Saheeh Bukhari on the authority of Abu Hurairah that the Prophet Muhammad ﷺ said:

عَنْ أَبِي هُرَيْرَةَ، قَالَ: قَالَ رَسُولُ اللَّهِ صَلَّى اللهُ عَلَيْهِ وَسَلَّمَ: «إِنَّ أَوْلَى النَّاسِ بِابْنِ مَرْيَمَ لَأَنَا،لِيس بيني و بينه وَالْأَنْبِيَاءُ إِخْوَةٌ لِعَلَّاتٍ، أُمَّهَاتُهُمْ شَتَّى وَدِينُهُمْ وَاحِدٌ"

"The most deserving people of Isa the son of (Mary) is me, there is no Prophet which came between me and him, and the Prophets are brothers with the same fathers and their mothers are different and their religion is one."[1]

Within this narration is a reply to those who claim that there was a Prophet sent after Isa, such as Khalid ibn Sinaan[2]; as al Qadaa'ee[3] and others mentioned.[4] Allah mentioned:

﴿ يَٰٓأَهْلَ ٱلْكِتَٰبِ قَدْ جَآءَكُمْ رَسُولُنَا يُبَيِّنُ لَكُمْ عَلَىٰ فَتْرَةٍ مِّنَ ٱلرُّسُلِ أَن تَقُولُوا۟ مَا جَآءَنَا مِنۢ بَشِيرٍ وَلَا نَذِيرٍ ۖ فَقَدْ جَآءَكُم بَشِيرٌ وَنَذِيرٌ ۗ وَٱللَّهُ عَلَىٰ كُلِّ شَىْءٍ قَدِيرٌ ﴾

"O People of the Scripture (Jews and Christians). Verily Our Messenger (Muhammad) has come to you making things clear to you after a pause in the sending of the Messengers, or do you say: 'No one came to us as a bringer of glad tidings nor as a warner.' However, now there is a Messenger who has come to you as a bringer of glad tidings and a warner, and Allah is Able to do all things." (al Ma'idah 5:19)

Allah the Most Magnificent says addressing the People of the Book from the Jews and Christians that verily He has sent to them His final Messenger

---

[1]-Saheeh Bukhari, Fatul Baari 6/591 Book Hadeeth of the Prophets #3442,3443
[2]-(TN)A man who claimed to be a Prophet after the time of Isa (Jesus).
[3]-(TN)He is Abu Abdullah Muhammad ibn Salaamah ibn Ja'far ibn Ali al Qadaa'ee, one of the judges of Egypt. He died in the year 454 hijri.
[4]-Tafsir ibn Kathir 2/52

Al 'I'tibaa'a

Muhammad ﷺ whom there is no Prophet or Messenger after him. Muhammad ﷺ has pursued and followed all of them- this is why Allah said: *"after a pause in the sending of the Messengers"* i.e. after a long period of time between his (Muhamad's) sending and the sending of Isa ibn Maryam.

There is difference of opinion regarding the period of time between Isa and Muhammad ﷺ.

Abu Uthmaan an Nah'dee[1] and Qatadah[2] said in a narration: there was six hundred years between them. Also Bukhari narrated on the authority of Salman al Farasee and Qatadah: five hundred and sixty years.

Ma'mar[3] mentioned on the authority of some of his companions: five hundred and forty years. Also ad Dah'haak[4] said: Four hundred and thirty some odd years.

Ibn Asaakir mentioned in his biography of Isa on the authority of ash Sha'bee[5] that he said: 'From the time that Isa ascended to the heavens until the migration of the Prophet Muhammad ﷺ to al Madinah is nine hundred and thirty three years, and the widely known report is the first statement of six hundred years."[6]

---

[1] -Abu Uthmaan an Nah'dee is Abdurahman ibn Mul, a 'mukhadram' (one who lived during the time of the prophet but didn't get to meet him), trustworthy worshipper, he died 95 hijri. He lived to be 130 years old and it is said longer than that. (taqreeb ut Tah'theeb pg. 601)

[2] -Qatadah ibn Du'aamah as Sadusee, Abu al Khattab al Basree, trustworthy, it is said that he was born blind. He died sometime after 100 hijri. (taqreeb ut Tah'theeb pg. 798)

[3] -Ma'mar ibn Rashid al Azdee , Abu Urwah al Basree, traveled and resided in Yemen, virtuous and trustworthy narrator. He died 154 hijri. (taqreeb ut Tah'theeb pg. 961)

[4] -ad Dah'haak ibn Muzahim al Hilaali, Abul Qasim or Abu Muhammad al Khurasaani, died after the year 100.

[5] -(TN)He is Aamir ibn Sharaaheel ash Sha'bee, Abu Amru, he was one of the best and most knowledgeable jurists of his time. There are various statements regarding his birthdate, in 'Mu'jam al Buldaan', 'Tarikh at Tabari and Ibn Atheer it is said the year 16 hijri. Others said he was born in the caliphate of Umar ibn al Khattab and many other statements. He died between 103-106 hijri. (Seer A'laam an Nubalaa'a 4/294)

[6] -Tafsir ibn Kathir 2/52

Part Five

The condition of the world when the Prophet Muhammad ﷺ was sent to mankind

The entire world at the time of the sending of the Prophet Muhammad ﷺ was detached and isolated from Allah's divine religion except for a few who were still upon what they found from the remnants of the previous religions.

A period of six hundred years in which the era of prophethood became ancient and the majority of the prophetic knowledge was forgotten and people became oblivious of it. The nation that was closest to the Messengers and Divine Books were the The People of Israel(followers of Musa). Verily, Allah mentioned them numerous times in the Quran and clarified their misguidance, arrogance, stubbornness, filth, and their abandonment of Allah's religion and their alteration of Allah's holy books.

Similar to them are the Christians who went astray from the correct way, who altered and changed Allah's divine revelation that was revealed to them. They changed and altered Allah's religion based upon their own desires and left off the religion of Ibrahim and associated partners with Allah. Allah says:

﴿ وَقَالُوا۟ كُونُوا۟ هُودًا أَوْ نَصَـٰرَىٰ تَهْتَدُوا۟ۗ قُلْ بَلْ مِلَّةَ إِبْرَٰهِـۧمَ حَنِيفًاۖ وَمَا كَانَ مِنَ ٱلْمُشْرِكِينَ ﴾

"And they say: 'Be Jews or Christians then you will be guided.' Rather say to them O Muhammad: 'Nay we follow the religion of Ibrahim (Islamic Monotheism) and he was not of the polytheists."* (al Baqarah 2:135)

Then the Jews and the Christians were constantly hostile and inimical to each other and they used to say that the other is misguided and astray as Allah mentions:

﴿ وَقَالَتِ ٱلْيَهُودُ لَيْسَتِ ٱلنَّصَـٰرَىٰ عَلَىٰ شَىْءٍ وَقَالَتِ ٱلنَّصَـٰرَىٰ لَيْسَتِ ٱلْيَهُودُ عَلَىٰ شَىْءٍ وَهُمْ يَتْلُونَ ٱلْكِتَـٰبَ كَذَٰلِكَ قَالَ ٱلَّذِينَ لَا يَعْلَمُونَ مِثْلَ قَوْلِهِمْ فَٱللَّهُ يَحْكُمُ بَيْنَهُمْ يَوْمَ ٱلْقِيَـٰمَةِ فِيمَا كَانُوا۟ فِيهِ يَخْتَلِفُونَ ﴾

"The Jews said that the Christians are not upon the right religion and the Christians say that the Jews are not upon the right religion. They both recite the Scripture and similar to what they say, is that which the pagans and ignorant people say. Allah will judge between them on the Day of Resurrection about that which they have been differing." (al Baqarah 2:113)

The Jews throughout their history have always been the most deceptive of Allah's creation, as well as the most tyrannical enemies against the Prophets, while being the filthiest of those who set foot upon the face of the earth, all of this while disregarding and abandoning the teachings of Musa. As a result of this, Allah split them up into many sects leaving them to wander blindly throughout the earth. They never had a country, city, or land to go to nor a group or sect to gather them together. Allah mentioned in the Quran:

﴿ وَقُلْنَا مِنْ بَعْدِهِۦ لِبَنِىٓ إِسْرَٰٓءِيلَ ٱسْكُنُوا۟ ٱلْأَرْضَ فَإِذَا جَآءَ وَعْدُ ٱلْـَٔاخِرَةِ جِئْنَا بِكُمْ لَفِيفًا ﴾

"And We said to the Children of Israel after Musa: 'Dwell in the land, then when the final and last promise comes near We shall bring you altogether as a mixed crowd gathered out of various nations." (al Isra 17:104)

The Jews and Christians were continuously showing enmity towards each other based upon their strict adherence and devotion to their altered religions, while fighting and killing each other constantly.

When these two sects abandoned their creed which they used to be devoted to and practiced as their religion, it became easy for them to be at harmony with each other and agree in their political affairs as we see today.

Al 'I'tibaa'a

The Jews are the ones who imposed their ideas and filthy manners upon the Christians with their deception and cunning.

In these days the Jews have taken advantage and exploited their religion for their political agendas so that they can gather and congregate the masses to establish an Israeli state, after the fact that they have been overwhelmed with humiliation and misery by their evil past. The reality of this is that the Jews have no religion.

As for the Arab and the illiterate people than verily Allah has mentioned them in the Quran clarifying their status as well as Allah's blessings and favors upon them and upon all of creation, as Allah says:

﴿ هُوَ ٱلَّذِى بَعَثَ فِى ٱلۡأُمِّيِّـۧنَ رَسُولًا مِّنۡهُمۡ يَتۡلُوا۟ عَلَيۡهِمۡ ءَايَـٰتِهِۦ وَيُزَكِّيهِمۡ وَيُعَلِّمُهُمُ ٱلۡكِتَـٰبَ وَٱلۡحِكۡمَةَ وَإِن كَانُوا۟ مِن قَبۡلُ لَفِى ضَلَـٰلٍ مُّبِينٍ ۝ ﴾

"He (Allah) it is who sent among the illiterate people a Messenger (Muhammad) from amongst themselves, reciting to them Allah's verses, purifying them from falsehood (polytheism and disbelief) and teaching them the Quran and Sunnah. And verily in the past they had been in manifest error." (al Jumu'ah 62:2) Allah also says:

﴿ لَقَدۡ مَنَّ ٱللَّهُ عَلَى ٱلۡمُؤۡمِنِينَ إِذۡ بَعَثَ فِيهِمۡ رَسُولًا مِّنۡ أَنفُسِهِمۡ يَتۡلُوا۟ عَلَيۡهِمۡ ءَايَـٰتِهِۦ وَيُزَكِّيهِمۡ وَيُعَلِّمُهُمُ ٱلۡكِتَـٰبَ وَٱلۡحِكۡمَةَ وَإِن كَانُوا۟ مِن قَبۡلُ لَفِى ضَلَـٰلٍ مُّبِينٍ ۝ ﴾

"Indeed Allah bestowed a great favor upon the believers when He sent amongst them a Messenger from amongst themselves, reciting to them His verses and purifying them from their sins by their following of him and instructing them with the Quran and the Sunnah. While previously they had been in manifest error." (Ali Imran 3:164)

Allah sent Muhammad ﷺ after a pause in the sending of Messengers, after the corruption of the paths, and after the changing of the religions, after the widespread worship of idols, fire and crosses. The blessing of the sending of the Prophet Muhammad ﷺ was the most complete and the need for him was the most universal and beneficial at that time. Verily, corruption was prevalent throughout all the land. Tyranny, oppression and ignorance were most apparent

Al 'I'tibaa'a

amongst the worshippers except for a few who were adhering to the remnants of the earlier Prophet's religions which was found amongst some of the Jewish rabbis and the Christian worshippers and the Saa'bi'een'[1]

Verily this condition of misguidance throughout the world was mentioned by one of the scholars of history he said: 'We must remember that the era in which the Prophet Muhammad ﷺ was sent with his 'da'wa', was a time in which the entire world was corrupted and drowned in the darkness of ignorance. Savageness and barbarity was prevalent throughout the entire world. Perhaps there may have been witness of some talk of humanity, civilization and manners contained in some pages of books, except for the fact that these words had no affect upon the hearts of the people.'

A) The People of Israel before the Messiah (Jesus) deserved to be called 'serpents and sons of serpents', and with the curse of the Messiah upon them there remained no trace of humanity for them.

B) Europe was witnessing the times of ignorance and savageness, and in Britian the worship of idols became widespread. Furthermore, some places within France and the surrounding countries- superstitions, fables and myths were most common, and many of the priests were calling the people to do obscene, vulgar and despicable acts.

C) The al Mazdkiyyah[2] had taken control over Iran and called the people to communism and the sharing of women, money and land.

D) In India there were idols and sculptures of naked women and men placed inside the temples for the people to worship. The doors and walls of these temples were covered and adorned with pictures of abominable and atrocious acts.

E) As for the people of China, they deemed their country to be under the ownership of a divine son who descended from the heavens, and turned away from Allah and made idols and sculptures for every affair.

---

[1]-(TN)The Saa'bi'eens were a past nation who used to live in Mowsil (Iraq) who used to believe that there was no deity worthy of worship except Allah, and they used to read the az Zabur (Psalms) and they were neither Jews nor Christians. Tafsir ibn Kathir 2/52

[2]-(TN)An atheist group who were followers of Mazdak ibn Namidan who alleged that he was a prophet and eventually called the people to the legalization of all things. They believe that the origin of the creation are two main sources: light and darkness. (see 'al Milal wa an Nihal' by ash Shirastaani)

F) In Egypt the Christians had taken power and day after day there would arise new and invented beliefs and articles of faith. This is how the many different sects emerged, while each sect used to call the opposing sects apostates and infidels. To the point where they didn't refrain from nor did they show any regard in killing and burning of their opponents.

This is a summary of the situations and conditions of the countries which were subjugated to their great governments and submissive to their laws and legislations. Every one of these nations used to boast and brag to the other nations about their level of knowledge and civilization.

This situation in the Land of Arabia was similar to these previously mentioned countries. With one exception: the Land of Arabia was not subjugated nor influenced by any type of law, king or ruler. Similarly, there never came anyone to guide them to the right path in addition to some of the uncivilized bestial customs which existed. For verily ignorance, seclusion and being isolated and remote from the civilized nations had indeed intensified the conditions and situations which led to declination, degeneration and regression of the people. This extreme vile and wicked situation is that which made the Arabic people the most deserving of mercy, so Allah willed and destined that the Land of Arabia be made as the starting point and base for the propagation of that which would reform, rectify and guide the entire world and all of the creation."[1]

So when Allah honored our Prophet Muhammad ﷺ with the Prophetic mission and revealed to him Allah's statement:

﴿ اقْرَأْ بِاسْمِ رَبِّكَ الَّذِي خَلَقَ ۝ خَلَقَ الْإِنسَانَ مِنْ عَلَقٍ ۝ ﴾

"**Read! In the name of your Lord who created all that exists. He has created man from a clot.**" (al Alaq 96:1-2) Also Allah said:

﴿ وَأَنذِرْ عَشِيرَتَكَ الْأَقْرَبِينَ ۝ ﴾

"**And warn your tribe and your kin O Muhammad**" (ash Shu'ara 26:214)

The land of the Arabs was thirsty for the religion of truth which the majority of its features, marks and milestones were extinct, forgotten and non-existent.

---

[1]-see 'Rahmatu lilAlaameen pgs.45-46

Abdullah ibn Mas'ud said:

عَنْ عَبْدِ اللهِ بْنِ مَسْعُودٍ، قَالَ: " إِنَّ اللهَ نَظَرَ فِي قُلُوبِ الْعِبَادِ، فَوَجَدَ قَلْبَ مُحَمَّدٍ صَلَّى اللهُ عَلَيْهِ وَسَلَّمَ خَيْرَ قُلُوبِ الْعِبَادِ، فَاصْطَفَاهُ لِنَفْسِهِ، فَابْتَعَثَهُ بِرِسَالَتِهِ، ثُمَّ نَظَرَ فِي قُلُوبِ الْعِبَادِ بَعْدَ قَلْبِ مُحَمَّدٍ، فَوَجَدَ قُلُوبَ أَصْحَابِهِ خَيْرَ قُلُوبِ الْعِبَادِ، فَجَعَلَهُمْ وُزَرَاءَ نَبِيِّهِ، يُقَاتِلُونَ عَلَى دِينِهِ، فَمَا رَأَى الْمُسْلِمُونَ حَسَنًا، فَهُوَ عِنْدَ اللهِ حَسَنٌ، وَمَا رَأَوْا سَيِّئًا فَهُوَ عِنْدَ اللهِ سَيِّئٌ "

"Verily Allah looked into the hearts of His servants, He found that Muhammad's heart was the best of all His servants, so Allah selected Him, and sent him with His Prophetic mission. Then Allah looked into the hearts of the servants again and found that the Prophet's companions had the best of hearts, so He made them ministers and helpers of the Prophet, they fight and exert their efforts in defense of their religion. So whatever the Muslims see as good (consensus of the companions) than Allah views it as being good, and whatever the Muslims see as bad than Allah views it as being bad."[1]

So the Prophet ﷺ started calling his tribe and relatives to Islam, as Bukhari narrated

عَنِ ابْنِ عَبَّاسٍ رَضِيَ اللهُ عَنْهُمَا قَالَ: لمَّا نَزَلَتْ: ﴿وَأَنْذِرْ عَشِيرَتَكَ الْأَقْرَبِينَ﴾ [الشعراء: 214]، صَعِدَ النَّبِيُّ صَلَّى اللهُ عَلَيْهِ وَسَلَّمَ عَلَى الصَّفَا، فَجَعَلَ يُنَادِي: «يَا بَنِي فِهْرٍ، يَا بَنِي عَدِيٍّ» - لِبُطُونِ قُرَيْشٍ - حَتَّى اجْتَمَعُوا فَجَعَلَ الرَّجُلُ إِذَا لَمْ يَسْتَطِعْ أَنْ يَخْرُجَ أَرْسَلَ رَسُولًا لِيَنْظُرَ مَا هُوَ، فَجَاءَ أَبُو لَهَبٍ وَقُرَيْشٌ، فَقَالَ: «أَرَأَيْتَكُمْ لَوْ أَخْبَرْتُكُمْ أَنَّ خَيْلًا بِالوَادِي تُرِيدُ أَنْ تُغِيرَ عَلَيْكُمْ، أَكُنْتُمْ مُصَدِّقِيَّ؟» قَالُوا: نَعَمْ، مَا جَرَّبْنَا عَلَيْكَ إِلَّا صِدْقًا، قَالَ: «فَإِنِّي نَذِيرٌ لَكُمْ بَيْنَ يَدَيْ عَذَابٍ شَدِيدٍ» فَقَالَ أَبُو لَهَبٍ: تَبًّا لَكَ سَائِرَ الْيَوْمِ، أَلِهَذَا جَمَعْتَنَا؟ فَنَزَلَتْ: ﴿تَبَّتْ يَدَا أَبِي لَهَبٍ وَتَبَّ مَا أَغْنَى عَنْهُ مَالُهُ وَمَا كَسَبَ﴾ [المسد: 2]

On the authority of Abdullah ibn Abaas who said: 'when Allah's statement: 'Warn your tribe and your kin O Muhammad'(ash'Shu'araa:214) was revealed, the Prophet ﷺ ascended upon the Mountain of Safa as began to shout: 'O Children of 'Fihr', O Children of 'Adee'-who were two tribes from Quraish-until they

---

[1]-Imam Ahmed narrated it in his 'Musnad' 1/379, #3600 he said: Abu Bakr said to us, from Aasim, from Zir ibn Hubaysh, from Abdullah ibn Mas'ud, and the chain is 'Hasan' (Good). Also at Tayalaasee narrated it in his Musnad pg. 23, see the introduction of 'al Muwafaqaat' by ash Shaatibee 3/4.

gathered around him. If some of the men were not able to attend they sent someone to go and see what was happening. So Abu Lahab and Quraish came and the Prophet ﷺ said to them: "What would you think if I told you that there were some horsemen in the valley planning to raid you, would you all believe me? They replied: Yes, we only know you to be truthful. The Prophet than said: 'Verily I am a warner sent to you, warning you of a severe torment." Then Abu Lahab replied: 'May you perish eternally! For this reason you have summoned us?! Then the Quranic verses were immediately revealed to the Prophet ﷺ: "Perish the two hands of Abu Lahab-His wealth and children will not benefit him anything!" (al Mas'ad 111:1-2)[1]

Bukhari also narrated on the authority of Abu Hurairah who said:

قَالَ: قَامَ رَسُولُ اللَّهِ صَلَّى اللهُ عَلَيْهِ وَسَلَّمَ حِينَ أَنْزَلَ اللَّهُ: ﴿وَأَنذِرْ عَشِيرَتَكَ ٱلْأَقْرَبِينَ﴾ [الشعراء: 214] قَالَ: «يَا مَعْشَرَ قُرَيْشٍ - أَوْ كَلِمَةً نَحْوَهَا - اشْتَرُوا أَنْفُسَكُمْ لاَ أُغْنِي عَنْكُمْ مِنَ اللَّهِ شَيْئًا، يَا بَنِي عَبْدِ مَنَافٍ لاَ أُغْنِي عَنْكُمْ مِنَ اللَّهِ شَيْئًا، يَا عَبَّاسُ بْنَ عَبْدِ المُطَّلِبِ لاَ أُغْنِي عَنْكَ مِنَ اللَّهِ شَيْئًا، وَيَا صَفِيَّةُ عَمَّةَ رَسُولِ اللَّهِ لاَ أُغْنِي عَنْكِ مِنَ اللَّهِ شَيْئًا، وَيَا فَاطِمَةُ بِنْتَ مُحَمَّدٍ سَلِينِي مَا شِئْتِ مِنْ مَالِي لاَ أُغْنِي عَنْكِ مِنَ اللَّهِ شَيْئًا»

'The Prophet ﷺ went out to call the people after the revealing of Allah's statement: 'And warn your tribe and your kin O Muhammad' and he shouted: "O people of Quraish" or something similar to this, and said: ' Save yourselves, I cannot save you from Allah, O People of Abdu Manaf I cannot save you from Allah, O Abaas ibn Abdul Muttalib I cannot save you from Allah, O Safiyyah the aunt of the Prophet Muhammad ﷺ, I cannot save you from Allah, O Fatimah the daughter of Muhammad ﷺ, ask me for anything you desire from my wealth, for verily I cannot save you from Allah."[2]

Then Allah ordered him to proclaim the revelation publicly, and call all of the people to Islam as Allah says:

﴿ فَٱصْدَعْ بِمَا تُؤْمَرُ وَأَعْرِضْ عَنِ ٱلْمُشْرِكِينَ ﴾

"Therefore proclaim openly everything which you are commanded and shun/abandon the polytheists" (al Hijr 15:94)

---

[1]-Saheeh Bukhari 8/642, The book of Tafsir, #4770
[2]-Saheeh Bukhari 8/643, The book of Tafsir, #4771

Al 'I'tibaa'a

Also as Allah says:

﴿ قُلْ يَٰٓأَيُّهَا ٱلنَّاسُ إِنِّى رَسُولُ ٱللَّهِ إِلَيْكُمْ جَمِيعًا ٱلَّذِى لَهُۥ مُلْكُ ٱلسَّمَٰوَٰتِ وَٱلْأَرْضِ ۖ لَآ إِلَٰهَ إِلَّا هُوَ يُحْىِۦ وَيُمِيتُ ۖ فَـَٔامِنُوا۟ بِٱللَّهِ وَرَسُولِهِ ٱلنَّبِىِّ ٱلْأُمِّىِّ ٱلَّذِى يُؤْمِنُ بِٱللَّهِ وَكَلِمَٰتِهِۦ وَٱتَّبِعُوهُ لَعَلَّكُمْ تَهْتَدُونَ ۝ ﴾

"Say O Muhammad : 'O mankind, verily I have been sent to all of you as a Messenger from Allah-to whom belongs the dominion of the heavens and the earth. None has the right to be worshipped except Him. It is He who gives life and causes death. So believe in Allah and His Messenger Muhammad, the Prophet who can neither read nor write, and who believes in Allah and all His words (Quran), the Torah and Gospels and also Allah's word: 'Be'! and he was, (Isa/Jesus) the son of Maryam (Mary) and follow him so that you may be guided." (al A'raaf 7:158)

Ibn Kathir said: 'Allah The Most High said to His Prophet and Messenger Muhammad ﷺ: **'Say O Muhammad "O Mankind"** this message is for the red (white)people, the black people, the Arabs and non- Arabs. **"Verily I have been sent as a Messenger to all of you"** i.e. to all of you, this is from the nobility, honor and greatness of the Prophet Muhammad ﷺ , and that he is the last of the Prophets, and he has been sent to all the people, Allah says:

﴿ قُلِ ٱللَّهُ شَهِيدٌۢ بَيْنِى وَبَيْنَكُمْ ۚ وَأُوحِىَ إِلَىَّ هَٰذَا ٱلْقُرْءَانُ لِأُنذِرَكُم بِهِۦ وَمَنۢ بَلَغَ ﴾

"Say Allah is the Witness between me and you all, and verily this Quran has been revealed to me that I may warn you all and whomsoever it reaches." (al An'am 6:19) And Allah says:

﴿ وَمَن يَكْفُرْ بِهِۦ مِنَ ٱلْأَحْزَابِ فَٱلنَّارُ مَوْعِدُهُۥ ﴾

"But those of the sects from the Jews, Christians and Non Muslims that reject the Quran, the Fire is their appointed and promised meeting-place..." (Hud 11:17)

And Allah says:

$$\left\{ \text{وَقُل لِّلَّذِينَ أُوتُوا۟ ٱلْكِتَٰبَ وَٱلْأُمِّيِّۦنَ ءَأَسْلَمْتُمْ ۚ فَإِنْ أَسْلَمُوا۟ فَقَدِ ٱهْتَدَوا۟ ۖ وَّإِن تَوَلَّوْا۟ فَإِنَّمَا عَلَيْكَ ٱلْبَلَٰغُ ۗ وَٱللَّهُ بَصِيرٌۢ بِٱلْعِبَادِ} \right\}$$

"Say to those who were given the Scripture from the Jews and Christians and to those illiterate Arab pagans: 'Do you all submit yourselves to Allah in Islam?" If they do so, then verily they are rightly guided, but if they turn away than know that your duty is only to convey the divine message..." (al Imran 3:20)

The Quranic verses and prophetic narrations containing this meaning are many, and this is something that is necessary to have knowledge about within the religion of Islam-that is to know that the Prophet Muhammad ﷺ is Allah's messenger <u>sent to all of mankind</u>.

Allah the Most Gracious made him the last of the Prophets which there are no Prophets after him, as Allah mentions:

$$\left\{ \text{مَّا كَانَ مُحَمَّدٌ أَبَآ أَحَدٍ مِّن رِّجَالِكُمْ وَلَٰكِن رَّسُولَ ٱللَّهِ وَخَاتَمَ ٱلنَّبِيِّۦنَ ۗ وَكَانَ ٱللَّهُ بِكُلِّ شَىْءٍ عَلِيمًا} \right\}$$

"Muhammad is not the father of any of your people, but he is the Messenger of Allah and the last of the Prophets, and Allah is Ever All-Aware of everything." (al Ahzab 33:40)

Then Ibn Kathir said: 'This verse is evidence that there is no prophet after Muhammad ﷺ. So if there is no prophet after him then this is all the more reason for there not being a messenger after him. This is because the status of messengerhood is more specific than prophethood. For verily every Messenger is a Prophet but not every Prophet is a Messenger. This is what came in all of the various narrations of the Prophet ﷺ on the authority of numerous companions.'[1]

The Prophet ﷺ set out on his mission calling people to Allah's religion with wisdom and fine preaching, he debated with the people using the best of

---

[1]-Tafsir Ibn Kathir 3/665

Al 'I'tibaa'a

manners. He continued propagating this message day and night, publicly and privately. Nothing could dissuade him from his mission, nor ward him off. However, the affair of being a messenger -and he was not the first messenger- is that few people believe in them and the majority of them disbelieve in them and what they call to. The Prophet Muhammad would present himself and go out to see the different tribes during the seasonal festivals and holidays. The Prophet himself as well as whoever was with him would be hurt, offended and harassed in the worst types of ways. Allah says in the Quran:

﴿ سُنَّةَ ٱللَّهِ فِى ٱلَّذِينَ خَلَوْا۟ مِن قَبْلُ ﴾

"And that was Allah's way with those who passed away of old" (al Ahzab 33:62)

Until it came to the point where the Prophet's companions were forced to leave their homeland, so the Prophet Muhammad suggested that whoever had the ability that they should migrate to Ethiopia. Some of them who had the ability made the migration while others stayed in Makkah. The Prophet Muhammad was eventually compelled to migrate to al Madinah where some of al Madinah's residents believed in him and others did not. The residents of al Madinah were honored with the Prophet's invitation and gladly accepted it.

Certainly, leaving your homeland where you used to rest your head, and traversed the many streets is definitely not something easy to do. No doubt that this is something painful, saddening and depressing which definitely wrings the heart with pain. The statement of the Prophet Muhammad can describe to us the pain and distress which he experienced, when he said on the authority of Abdullah ibn Adee' ibnil Hamraa'a when he said:

عَنْ عَبْدِ اللهِ بْنِ عَدِيِّ بْنِ حَمْرَاءَ، قَالَ: رَأَيْتُ رَسُولَ اللهِ صَلَّى اللهُ عَلَيْهِ وَسَلَّمَ وَاقِفًا عَلَى الحَزْوَرَةِ فَقَالَ: وَاللهِ إِنَّكِ لَخَيْرُ أَرْضِ اللهِ، وَأَحَبُّ أَرْضِ اللهِ إِلَى اللهِ، وَلَوْلاَ أَنِّي أُخْرِجْتُ مِنْكِ مَا خَرَجْتُ"

'I saw the Messenger of Allah standing upon 'al-Hazwarah'[1] and he said: "I swear by Allah, that verily you (Makkah) are the best of Allah's lands, and the

---

[1] -a market in Makkah, and it is now part of the Masjid al Haram after the expansions.

Al 'I'tibaa'a

most beloved land to Allah, if I wasn't forced and compelled to leave you (Makkah) I would never have left."[1]

In another narration which at Tirmidthi, Ibn Hibban, at Tabaraani and al Hakim mentioned on the authority of Ibn Abaas he said: the Messenger of Allah ﷺ said:

عَنْ ابْنِ عَبَّاسٍ، قَالَ: قَالَ رَسُولُ اللهِ صَلَّى اللهُ عَلَيْهِ وَسَلَّمَ لِمَكَّةَ: «مَا أَطْيَبَكِ مِنْ بَلَدٍ، وَأَحَبَّكِ إِلَيَّ (إلى الله)، وَلَوْلَا أَنَّ قَوْمِي أَخْرَجُونِي مِنْكِ مَا سَكَنْتُ غَيْرَكِ»

"There is no better city than you (Makkah), and most beloved to me (to Allah), If it wasn't for the fact that my people forced me to leave, I wouldn't have resided in any other place besides you (Makkah)."[2]

At Tirmidthi said about this narration: it is a 'hasan ghareeb' narration from this route. Al Hakim[3] said: the chain of narration is authentic, and adh Dhahabee agreed with him in this.

Ibn Hajar al Asqalaani said: 'this is an authentic narration, the scholars of hadeeth have mentioned it in their books, and at Tirmidthi, Ibn Khuzaimah, Ibn Hibaan and others said it is authentic.[4]

The Prophet Muhammad ﷺ and those of his companions who had the ability migrated to al Madinah. However, disbelief and the people of disbelief did not approve nor agree with this nor would they be satisfied with the prevalence and spreading of Islam amongst Allah's servants. So the Prophet ﷺ was compelled to

---

[1]-This wording is for Tirmidthi 5/723, Book of Manaaqib, Chapter: Virtues of Makkah #3925 and Abdur Razaaq as San'aani narrated it in his 'Musanaf' 5/270, , and Ahmed in his Musnad with three chains of narration 4/305, and Abdu ibn Humaid relating from the book 'Shifaa'a al Garam' 1/74 . The chain of narration is authentic

[2]-Jami at Tirmidthi, The Book of Manaqib, Chapter: The Virtues of Makkah #3926, 5/723, and 'Mawaarid ath Tham'aan pg. 253. In one narration it mentions: 'most loved to Me' and another narration mentions ' most loved to Allah'

[3]-(TN)He is Abu Abd-Allah Muhammad ibn Abd-Allah al-Hakim al-Nisaburi was a scholar of hadeeth and one of the most knowledgeable people of his time. He was frequently referred to as the "Imam of the Muhaddithin" or the "Muhaddith of Khorasan. He died 403 hijri. He authored his book called 'al Mustadrak' in which he claimed all the ahadeeth in it were authentic according to the conditions of either Sahih Bukhari or Sahih Muslim or both of them. Imam Adh-Dha'habi made an abridged version of the collection named Talkhis al-Mustadrak where he commented on its authenticity.

[4]-Fathul Baari 3/67

go out on war campaigns and battles in which Allah aided his combatants and defeated the disbelieving parties all by Himself. Then the day came for the Conquest of Makkah- the same city that the Prophet ﷺ was driven out of (Makkah)-the Prophet ﷺ and his Companions entered and conquered, all due to the aid and victory that Allah bestowed upon them. This is in agreement to Allah's statement:

﴿ إِنَّ ٱلَّذِى فَرَضَ عَلَيْكَ ٱلْقُرْءَانَ لَرَآدُّكَ إِلَىٰ مَعَادٍ ﴾

"Verily, He (Allah) who has given you the Quran will surely bring you back to 'Ma'aad' (Place of return, Makkah) (al Qasas 28:85)

After that the people started entering Allah's religion in enormous crowds, as Allah mentions:

﴿ إِذَا جَآءَ نَصْرُ ٱللَّهِ وَٱلْفَتْحُ ۝ وَرَأَيْتَ ٱلنَّاسَ يَدْخُلُونَ فِى دِينِ ٱللَّهِ أَفْوَاجًا ۝ فَسَبِّحْ بِحَمْدِ رَبِّكَ وَٱسْتَغْفِرْهُ إِنَّهُ كَانَ تَوَّابًا ۝ ﴾

"When there comes the Help of Allah and the conquest of Makkah-And you see that the people enter Allah's religion in crowds. So glorify with the praises of you Lord and ask for His forgiveness. Verily He is the One who accepts the repentance and forgives." (an Nasr 110:1-3)

The Land of Arabia submitted to that which they were at first hesitant to do and the people of Makkah entered into Islam. Then Allah's religion spread amongst the people and Allah was highly pleased and satisfied with the Prophet's companions after being abhorred, detested and hated people in the time prior to Islam. Iyaad ibn Himaar al Mujaasha'ee said that the Prophet Muhammad ﷺ said:

...إِنَّ اللهَ نَظَرَ إِلَى أَهْلِ الْأَرْضِ، فَمَقَتَهُمْ عَرَبَهُمْ وَعَجَمَهُمْ، إِلَّا بَقَايَا مِنْ أَهْلِ الْكِتَابِ، وَقَالَ: إِنَّمَا بَعَثْتُكَ لِأَبْتَلِيَكَ وَأَبْتَلِيَ بِكَ، وَأَنْزَلْتُ عَلَيْكَ كِتَابًا لَا يَغْسِلُهُ الْمَاءُ، تَقْرَؤُهُ نَائِمًا وَيَقْظَانَ....

"Allah looked at the people of the earth and hated them, Arabs and non-Arabs alike, except a remnant of the People of the Book. He said: I have only sent you to test you and test others through you. I have also revealed to you a book that

cannot be washed away with water, which you recite while sleeping and when you're awake."¹ Then Allah announced and proclaimed His pleasure and satisfaction of the companions of Allah's Messenger ﷺ by saying:

$$\langle\!\langle\text{ وَٱلسَّٰبِقُونَ ٱلۡأَوَّلُونَ مِنَ ٱلۡمُهَٰجِرِينَ وَٱلۡأَنصَارِ وَٱلَّذِينَ ٱتَّبَعُوهُم بِإِحۡسَٰنٍ رَّضِيَ ٱللَّهُ عَنۡهُمۡ وَرَضُواْ عَنۡهُ وَأَعَدَّ لَهُمۡ جَنَّٰتٍ تَجۡرِي تَحۡتَهَا ٱلۡأَنۡهَٰرُ خَٰلِدِينَ فِيهَآ أَبَدٗاۚ ذَٰلِكَ ٱلۡفَوۡزُ ٱلۡعَظِيمُ }\rangle\!\rangle$$

"Those who took precedence in embracing Islam of those who migrated from Makkah to al Madinah and the citizens of al Madinah who helped and gave aid to the migrating people and those who imitate them in their beliefs. Allah is well pleased with them as they are pleased with Him. He has prepared for them Gardens under which rivers flow (paradise) to dwell therein forever. That is the great success." (at Tawbah 9:100) Allah also says:

$$\langle\!\langle\text{ لَّقَدۡ رَضِيَ ٱللَّهُ عَنِ ٱلۡمُؤۡمِنِينَ إِذۡ يُبَايِعُونَكَ تَحۡتَ ٱلشَّجَرَةِ فَعَلِمَ مَا فِي قُلُوبِهِمۡ فَأَنزَلَ ٱلسَّكِينَةَ عَلَيۡهِمۡ وَأَثَٰبَهُمۡ فَتۡحٗا قَرِيبٗا }\rangle\!\rangle$$

"Indeed Allah was pleased with the believers when they gave the pledge to you O Muhammad under the tree, Allah knew what was in their hearts, and He sent down calmness and tranquility upon them and He rewarded them with a near victory." (al Fath 48:18)

The conflict, confusion and differences between the people were eventually eliminated and became non-existent. This led to the unification of these people (companions) until they became as one heart upon the best of guidance (Quran and Sunnah). Becomng leaders and guiding others, after they used to be misguided and enemies constantly fighting and killing each other. Allah the Most Gracious granted them victory and opened up the treasures of the earth for them after being from those who suffered from starvation and hunger; where the strong devoured the weak, by looting, plundering, and robbery. They were

---

¹-Saheeh Muslim 4/2197, Book of Paradise and the description of its delights, chapter: characteristics which the people of world are known to be from the people of paradise or hellfire, #2865

given all of these things solely because of their adherence to the 'sincere religion' of Islam, and implementing it into their beliefs and actions.

Furthermore, Allah warned the companions about splitting up and differing, and He ordered everyone to hold fast and adhere to all the means and reasons for unification, and to remember Allah's favor upon them. Allah said:

﴿ وَٱعْتَصِمُوا بِحَبْلِ ٱللَّهِ جَمِيعًا وَلَا تَفَرَّقُوا ۚ وَٱذْكُرُوا نِعْمَتَ ٱللَّهِ عَلَيْكُمْ إِذْ كُنتُمْ أَعْدَآءً فَأَلَّفَ بَيْنَ قُلُوبِكُمْ فَأَصْبَحْتُم بِنِعْمَتِهِۦٓ إِخْوَٰنًا وَكُنتُمْ عَلَىٰ شَفَا حُفْرَةٍ مِّنَ ٱلنَّارِ فَأَنقَذَكُم مِّنْهَا ۗ كَذَٰلِكَ يُبَيِّنُ ٱللَّهُ لَكُمْ ءَايَٰتِهِۦ لَعَلَّكُمْ تَهْتَدُونَ ۝ ﴾

"And hold fast, all of you together, to the Rope of Allah (Quran, Sunnah) and do not be divided amongst yourselves and remember Allah's favor upon you. For you were once enemies against each other but Allah joined your hearts together, so by His Grace you became brothers in Islamic Faith. And you were on the brink of a pit of Fire and Allah saved you from it. Thus Allah makes His verses, proofs, revelation clear to you, that you may be guided." (Ali Imran 3:103)

Preservation, safety and security of the creed became widespread as well as everlasting security for the countries and cities which governed with the pure, immaculate Islamic Creed and Islamic Legislations. And finally the time which the Prophet ﷺ gave his promise and gave glad tidings about had become a reality. Imam Bukhari narrated on the authority of Adee ibn Hatim who said:

عَنْ عَدِيِّ بْنِ حَاتِمٍ، قَالَ: بَيْنَا أَنَا عِنْدَ النَّبِيِّ صَلَّى اللهُ عَلَيْهِ وَسَلَّمَ إِذْ أَتَاهُ رَجُلٌ فَشَكَا إِلَيْهِ الفَاقَةَ، ثُمَّ أَتَاهُ آخَرُ فَشَكَا إِلَيْهِ قَطْعَ السَّبِيلِ، فَقَالَ: «يَا عَدِيُّ، هَلْ رَأَيْتَ الحِيرَةَ؟» قُلْتُ: لَمْ أَرَهَا، وَقَدْ أُنْبِئْتُ عَنْهَا، قَالَ «فَإِنْ طَالَتْ بِكَ حَيَاةٌ، لَتَرَيَنَّ الظَّعِينَةَ تَرْتَحِلُ مِنَ الحِيرَةِ، حَتَّى تَطُوفَ بِالكَعْبَةِ لَا تَخَافُ أَحَدًا إِلَّا اللَّهَ، - قُلْتُ فِيمَا بَيْنِي وَبَيْنَ نَفْسِي فَأَيْنَ دُعَّارُ طَيِّئٍ الَّذِينَ قَدْ سَعَّرُوا البِلاَدَ -، وَلَئِنْ طَالَتْ بِكَ حَيَاةٌ لَتُفْتَحَنَّ كُنُوزُ كِسْرَى»، قُلْتُ: كِسْرَى بْنِ هُرْمُزَ؟ قَالَ: " كِسْرَى بْنِ هُرْمُزَ، وَلَئِنْ طَالَتْ بِكَ حَيَاةٌ، لَتَرَيَنَّ الرَّجُلَ يُخْرِجُ مِلْءَ كَفِّهِ مِنْ ذَهَبٍ أَوْ فِضَّةٍ، يَطْلُبُ مَنْ يَقْبَلُهُ مِنْهُ فَلاَ يَجِدُ أَحَدًا يَقْبَلُهُ مِنْهُ، وَلَيَلْقَيَنَّ اللَّهَ أَحَدُكُمْ يَوْمَ يَلْقَاهُ، وَلَيْسَ بَيْنَهُ وَبَيْنَهُ تُرْجُمَانٌ يُتَرْجِمُ لَهُ، فَلَيَقُولَنَّ لَهُ: أَلَمْ أَبْعَثْ إِلَيْكَ رَسُولًا فَيُبَلِّغَكَ؟ فَيَقُولُ: بَلَى، فَيَقُولُ: أَلَمْ أُعْطِكَ مَالًا وَأُفْضِلْ عَلَيْكَ؟ فَيَقُولُ: بَلَى، فَيَنْظُرُ عَنْ يَمِينِهِ فَلاَ يَرَى إِلَّا جَهَنَّمَ، وَيَنْظُرُ عَنْ يَسَارِهِ فَلاَ يَرَى إِلَّا جَهَنَّمَ " قَالَ عَدِيٌّ: سَمِعْتُ النَّبِيَّ صَلَّى اللهُ عَلَيْهِ وَسَلَّمَ، يَقُولُ: «اتَّقُوا النَّارَ وَلَوْ بِشِقَّةِ

Al 'I'tibaa'a

تَمْرَةٍ فَمَنْ لَمْ يَجِدْ شِقَّةَ تَمْرَةٍ فَبِكَلِمَةٍ طَيِّبَةٍ» قَالَ عَدِيٌّ: فَرَأَيْتُ الظَّعِينَةَ تَرْتَحِلُ مِنَ الحِيرَةِ حَتَّى تَطُوفَ بِالكَعْبَةِ لاَ تَخَافُ إِلَّا اللهَ، وَكُنْتُ فِيمَنِ افْتَتَحَ كُنُوزَ كِسْرَى بنِ هُرْمُزَ وَلَئِنْ طَالَتْ بِكُمْ حَيَاةٌ، لَتَرَوُنَّ مَا قَالَ النَّبِيُّ أَبُو القَاسِمِ: صَلَّى اللهُ عَلَيْهِ وَسَلَّمَ يُخْرِجُ مِلْءَ كَفِّهِ."

'While I was with the Prophet Muhammad ﷺ a man came to him complaining about poverty, then another man came to him complaining about highway robbery, so the Prophet ﷺ said: "O Adee have you seen al Heerah?[1] Adee replied: "I have not seen it, but I have heard of it.' Then the Prophet ﷺ said: "If you are alive for verily you will see a woman in a covered saddle on a camel traveling from al Heerah until she goes around the Ka'bah and does not fear anyone except Allah alone."Then I (Adee) said to myself: where is the lewd/immoral tribe of Ta'y who have caused confusion throughout the land?- Then the Prophet ﷺ said: "If you are still alive than verily you will conquer and open the treasures of Kisra", I replied: "Kisra ibn Hurmuz?" The Prophet ﷺ than said: "Kisra ibn Hurmuz, if it so happens that you are still alive you will verily see that a man's hand will be filled with gold and silver and ask people to accept it from him, and he won't find anyone who will accept it from him. And verily you will meet Allah the day in which there is no intercessor between himself and Allah, no one to speak for him. Then Allah will say: "Didn't I send to you all a Messenger who conveyed My message to you?, He will reply: 'Of course'. Then Allah will say to him: "Didn't I give you wealth and bestow my favors, graces and kindness upon you". He will reply: 'Of course', and he will look to his right and not see anything except the hellfire, and then he will look to his left and not see anything except the hellfire." Then Adee said: "I heard the Prophet Muhammad ﷺ say: "Fear the hellfire even if it is with half of a date, and whoever does not find a half of a date than with a good word." Then Adee said: 'Verily I saw the woman on a camel with a covered saddle traveling from al Heerah until going around the Ka'bah and she didn't fear anyone except Allah, and I was from amongst the ones who aided in the conquest of Kisra ibn Hurmuz, perhaps if you are all alive you will all come to see what the Prophet (Abul Qaasim) said: "Take out his hands filled with gold and silver..."[2]

---

[1]-**(TN)**An Arabic Kingdom which was under the rule of the Farisee people.
[2]-Saheeh Bukhari, with Fatul Baari 6/757-758, Book of Virtues, Chapter: Signs of Prophethood #3595

Part Six

How the Companions learned and acquired the religion from the Prophet Muhammad ﷺ

The people (prior to the Prophet Muhammad ﷺ) were upon misguidance in their creed as well as in their acts of worship except for those who believed in the Prophet ﷺ and the delight of true faith entered and mixed with their hearts. So when Allah sent the final Messenger Muhammad ﷺ, the companions used to learn Islam directly from the Prophet Muhammad ﷺ without any intermediaries or agents.

The Prophet ﷺ used to teach them the Book (Quran) and the Hikmah (Sunnah) and the companions would imitate and follow the 'illiterate' Prophet ﷺ in all of his sayings, actions, verily they truly believed in Allah's saying:

﴿ وَمَا كَانَ لِمُؤْمِنٍ وَلَا مُؤْمِنَةٍ إِذَا قَضَى ٱللَّهُ وَرَسُولُهُۥ أَمْرًا أَن يَكُونَ لَهُمُ ٱلْخِيَرَةُ مِنْ أَمْرِهِمْ وَمَن يَعْصِ ٱللَّهَ وَرَسُولَهُۥ فَقَدْ ضَلَّ ضَلَٰلًا مُّبِينًا ﴾

"It is not for a believing man or woman when Allah and His Messenger have decreed a matter that they should have any choice or option in their decision. And whoever disobeys Allah and His Messenger, he has indeed strayed away into clear misguidance." (al Ahzab 33:36)

The companions also believed that Allah ordered them to take every single affair which the Prophet Muhammad ﷺ conveyed to them from Allah the Most High, except for those things which authentic evidences specificied for the Prophet Muhammad ﷺ as Allah says:

﴿ لَّقَدْ كَانَ لَكُمْ فِى رَسُولِ ٱللَّهِ أُسْوَةٌ حَسَنَةٌ لِّمَن كَانَ يَرْجُوا۟ ٱللَّهَ وَٱلْيَوْمَ ٱلْءَاخِرَ وَذَكَرَ ٱللَّهَ كَثِيرًا ﴾

"Indeed in the Messenger of Allah you have a excellent role model/example to follow for he who hopes to meet Allah and the Last Day and verily Allah remembers much." (al Ahzab 33:21)

The companions also believed that the Prophet ﷺ was the most compassionate and merciful with them, even more than their own fathers were.

Al 'I'tibaa'a

The Prophet's status was that of a father to them, as Abu Hurairah mentioned that the Prophet Muhammad ﷺ said:

عَنْ أَبِي هُرَيْرَةَ قَالَ قَالَ رَسُولُ اللَّهِ -صلى الله عليه وسلم- « إِنَّمَا أَنَا لَكُمْ بِمَنْزِلَةِ الْوَالِدِ أُعَلِّمُكُمْ فَإِذَا أَتَى أَحَدُكُمُ الْغَائِطَ فَلاَ يَسْتَقْبِلِ الْقِبْلَةَ وَلاَ يَسْتَدْبِرْهَا وَلاَ يَسْتَطِبْ بِيَمِينِهِ »

"Verily my status (to you all) is that of a father, I teach you. If one of you goes to answer the call of nature then he should neither face nor turn his back towards the Qiblah (Ka'bah/Makkah), and do not clean yourself with your right hand."[1]

The companions never approved of nor allowed the abandonment, deviation or desertion of anything that the Prophet Muhammad ﷺ came with. In addition to that, even when the companions saw the Prophet Muhammad ﷺ take his sandals off during the prayer they removed their sandals, without the Prophet Muhammad ﷺ gesturing to them and without commanding them to do so. Abu Dawud as Sijistaani narrated with an authentic chain of narration on the authority of Abu Saeed al Khudri that he said:

عَنْ أَبِي سَعِيدٍ الْخُدْرِيِّ قَالَ بَيْنَمَا رَسُولُ اللَّهِ -صلى الله عليه وسلم- يُصَلِّي بِأَصْحَابِهِ إِذْ خَلَعَ نَعْلَيْهِ فَوَضَعَهُمَا عَنْ يَسَارِهِ فَلَمَّا رَأَى ذَلِكَ الْقَوْمُ أَلْقَوْا نِعَالَهُمْ فَلَمَّا قَضَى رَسُولُ اللَّهِ -صلى الله عليه وسلم- صَلاَتَهُ قَالَ « مَا حَمَلَكُمْ عَلَى إِلْقَائِكُمْ نِعَالَكُمْ ». قَالُوا رَأَيْنَاكَ أَلْقَيْتَ نَعْلَيْكَ فَأَلْقَيْنَا نِعَالَنَا. فَقَالَ رَسُولُ اللَّهِ -صلى الله عليه وسلم- « إِنَّ جِبْرِيلَ -صلى الله عليه وسلم- أَتَانِي فَأَخْبَرَنِي أَنَّ فِيهِمَا قَذَرًا ». وَقَالَ « إِذَا جَاءَ أَحَدُكُمْ إِلَى الْمَسْجِدِ فَلْيَنْظُرْ فَإِنْ رَأَى فِي نَعْلَيْهِ قَذَرًا أَوْ أَذًى فَلْيَمْسَحْهُ وَلْيُصَلِّ فِيهِمَا »

While the Messenger of Allah ﷺ was praying with his companions he took off his sandals and placed them on his left side. So when the companions saw him do this they also took off their sandals. Then when the Prophet ﷺ finished his prayer he said: "What caused you to take your sandals off?" They replied: 'We saw you take your sandals off so we took our sandals off.' Then the Prophet

---

[1]-This wording is from Abu Dawud in his Sunan, Book of Purification pg.6, #8 with a 'Hasan'- good- chain of narration. Imam Ahmed narrated it in his Musnad 2/250, Sunan ibn Majah pg. 73, Book of Purification, Chapter of Cleansing with water, also Chapter of Cleansing with rocks and the prohibition of using dung and bones, #313. Ibn Hibbaan also narrated it in his Saheeh 4/279, Book of Purification, in which is mention of the rebuking of cleansing oneself with dung or bones, also Ibn Hibbaan 4/288, Chapter the mention of the command to cleanse oneself with three rocks.... See Silsilah Saheehah by al Albaani #1301

Muhammad ﷺ said: "Verily the angel Jibreel came to me and informed me that there was some filth on them-or he said impurity." Then the Prophet said ﷺ: "When one of you comes to the mosque than he must look (at his sandals), and if he sees any filth or impurities upon his sandals then let him wipe them off and let him perform the prayer while wearing them."[1] The Prophet ﷺ ordered the companions to pray the same way that the Prophet ﷺ prayed, so they used to pray the way they learned directly from the Prophet ﷺ.

Imam Bukhari narrated on the authority of Malik ibn ul Huwayrith who said:

حَدَّثَنَا مَالِكٌ، أَتَيْنَا إِلَى النَّبِيِّ صَلَّى اللهُ عَلَيْهِ وَسَلَّمَ وَنَحْنُ شَبَبَةٌ مُتَقَارِبُونَ، فَأَقَمْنَا عِنْدَهُ عِشْرِينَ يَوْمًا وَلَيْلَةً، وَكَانَ رَسُولُ اللهَ صَلَّى اللهُ عَلَيْهِ وَسَلَّمَ رَحِيمًا رَفِيقًا، فَلَمَّا ظَنَّ أَنَّا قَدِ اشْتَهَيْنَا أَهْلَنَا - أَوْ قَدِ اشْتَقْنَا - سَأَلَنَا عَمَّنْ تَرَكْنَا بَعْدَنَا، فَأَخْبَرْنَاهُ، قَالَ: «ارْجِعُوا إِلَى أَهْلِيكُمْ، فَأَقِيمُوا فِيهِمْ وَعَلِّمُوهُمْ وَمُرُوهُمْ - وَذَكَرَ أَشْيَاءَ أَحْفَظُهَا أَوْ لاَ أَحْفَظُهَا - وَصَلُّوا كَمَا رَأَيْتُمُونِي أُصَلِّي، فَإِذَا حَضَرَتِ الصَّلاَةُ فَلْيُؤَذِّنْ لَكُمْ أَحَدُكُمْ، وَلْيَؤُمَّكُمْ أَكْبَرُكُمْ»

"We visited the Prophet ﷺ and we were young men who were almost the same age, we remained with the Prophet ﷺ twenty days and nights. The Prophet ﷺ was so compassionate, kind and merciful with us, so when he realized that we were longing to be with our families, he asked us about who we have left behind us so we told him, then he replied to us: "Go back to your families and remain with them, and teach them the religion, and order them..." and the Prophet ﷺ mentioned some things which I recall and other things which I don't recall-The Prophet ﷺ also said: "Pray as you have seen me praying, and if the time for prayer comes, then one of you should pronounce the 'Adhaan' (call for prayer), and let the oldest one amongst you lead the prayer."[2]

Also Imam Muslim narrated on the authority of Jabir ibn Abdullah he said:

أَخْبَرَنِي أَبُو الزُّبَيْرِ، أَنَّهُ سَمِعَ جَابِرًا، يَقُولُ: " رَأَيْتُ النَّبِيَّ صَلَّى اللهُ عَلَيْهِ وَسَلَّمَ يَرْمِي عَلَى رَاحِلَتِهِ يَوْمَ النَّحْرِ، وَيَقُولُ: «لِتَأْخُذُوا (عني) مَنَاسِكَكُمْ، فَإِنِّي لَا أَدْرِي لَعَلِّي لَا أَحُجُّ بَعْدَ حَجَّتِي هَذِهِ»

---

[1]-Sunan Abee Dawud pg. 106, Book of Prayer, the Chapters of the Leaders in the Prayer, #650, and Al Bayhaqi 2/43 and Al Haakim in 'al Mustadrak' 1/260 and Al Haakim said: the narration is authentic upon the conditions of Imam Muslim and adh Dha'habee agreed with him. See 'Illal ibn Abee Haatim' 1/121 . It is an authentic narration.
[2]-Saheeh Bukhari 2/142,Book of Adthaan, Chapter The Call for prayer for the travelers if they are a congregation...#631

Al 'I'tibaa'a

'I saw the Prophet Muhammad ﷺ throw the stones (at the Jamarat) the day of 'an Nahr'1 while sitting on his camel and he said: "Take and learn your rituals from me, for verily I do not know, perhaps I will not perform another Hajj after this one."2 Also an- Nisaa'ee narrated and the wording is:

حَدَّثَنِي أَبُو الزُّبَيْرِ، أَنَّهُ سَمِعَ جَابِرًا هُوَ ابْنُ عَبْدِ الله، يَقُولُ: رَأَيْتُ رَسُولَ اللهِ صَلَّى اللهُ عَلَيْهِ وَسَلَّمَ يَرْمِي الجُمْرَةَ، وَهُوَ عَلَى بَعِيرِهِ، وَهُوَ يَقُولُ: «يَا أَيُّهَا النَّاسُ خُذُوا مَنَاسِكَكُمْ، فَإِنِّي لَا أَدْرِي لِعَلِّي لَا أَحُجُّ بَعْدَ عَامِي

"O Mankind, take from your rituals from me, for verily I don't know, perhaps I will not make Hajj after this year."3 Other authors also mentioned these narrations.

Ibnul Qayyim mentioned: 'When the techniques of learning and acquiring the religion from the Prophet Muhammad ﷺ were of two types: indirectly and directly. The companions were fortunate because they learned and acquired their religion from the Prophet ﷺ directly and they were the forerunners and achieved the best, and the companions seized and captured the time and opportunity, so there is no chance or aspiration for anyone from the Muslims after them to catch up with them or exceed them. However, the distinguished and illustrious one is he who follows the straight path, and the one who imitates and follows the companion's correct methodology and ways. And he who opposes, contradicts and differs is the one who deviates from the companion's way and methodology, straying to the right and to the left. Verily he is the one who has been cut off and he is wandering in the wilderness of destruction and misguidance."4

1-(TN)The 10th day of Dhul Hijjah, after the day of Arafat. This is the day which the ones performing Hajj stone the Jamarat (stone pillars) in Mina, and this is also the day of Eid (festival) in which sacrificial animals are slaughtered.

2-Saheeh Muslim, 2/943, the Book of Hajj, Chapter Recommended to stone jamarat on a riding animal, #310

3-Sunan an Nisaa'ee, Book of Rituals pg. 472, #4054. **(TN)** There are many examples of how the companions used to emulate and imitate the Prophet in all of his actions not just actions of worship. Another example of this is what Ibn Umar and Anas ibn Malik narrated from the Prophet Muhammad when he started wearing a silver ring (gold ring in another narration), so the companions all wore silver rings, then the Prophet Muhammad threw away his silver ring and then all the companions threw away their silver rings... This can be found in Saheeh Bukhari #'s 5867, 5868, 6651, 7298 and others mentioned these narrations also.

4-'I'laam al Muwa'qa'eeen' 1/6

Al 'I'tibaa'a

Part Seven

Allah and His Messenger ordered with the imitation and following of the Prophet Muhammad

Allah the Most Wise ordered all of His believing servants with the complete imitation and following of what the Prophet Muhammad ﷺ came with from the Quran and the Sunnah, without taking anyone other than Allah, His Messenger, or the true believers as intimate friends, while giving complete and sincere advice for Allah and His Messenger's sake only. Allah says:

﴿ إِن كُنتُمْ تُحِبُّونَ ٱللَّهَ فَٱتَّبِعُونِى يُحْبِبْكُمُ ٱللَّهُ وَيَغْفِرْ لَكُمْ ذُنُوبَكُمْ ۗ وَٱللَّهُ غَفُورٌ رَّحِيمٌ ﴾

"If you really love Allah than follow me (Muhammad), Allah will love you and forgive you your sins. And Allah is the oft forgiving, Most Merciful." (Ali Imran 3:31)

This verse is the judge and test for everyone who claims that one loves Allah and is not following the path of the Prophet Muhammad ﷺ. Verily this person's claim is false until one follows the methodology and legislations of the Prophet Muhammad ﷺ. This person should follow the Prophetic religion completely- the Prophet's ﷺ sayings, actions and situations as has been established in Saheeh Bukhari and Saheeh Muslim as the Prophet ﷺ said:

أَنَّ رَسُولَ اللهِ صَلَّى اللهُ عَلَيْهِ وَسَلَّمَ قَالَ: "مَنْ عَمِلَ عَمَلًا لَيْسَ عَلَيْهِ أَمْرُنَا فَهُوَ رَدٌّ"

"Whoever does an action which is not from our affairs (Islam) than it is rejected,"[1] for this reason Allah said: *"If you really love Allah than follow me, and Allah will love you"*, i.e.-you will receive more than what you desire which is Allah's love of you. Allah said:

﴿ قُلْ أَطِيعُوا۟ ٱللَّهَ وَٱلرَّسُولَ ۖ فَإِن تَوَلَّوْا۟ فَإِنَّ ٱللَّهَ لَا يُحِبُّ ٱلْكَٰفِرِينَ ﴾

"Say O Muhammad: 'Obey Allah and the Messenger, but if they turn away then Allah does not like the disbelievers." (Ali Imran 3:32)

---

[1] -Saheeh Bukhari 5/377, Book of reconciliation, #2697, Saheeh Muslim, Chapter: Nullification of the false rulings #1718, the wording is for Muslim.

Al 'I'tibaa'a

In this verse Allah commanded the people with the obedience of Himself and His Messenger ﷺ, if they turn away, abandon or contradict Allah's and His Messenger's ﷺ orders, individually or collectively than it is considered disbelief. This verse is evidence proving that violating and disobeying the orders of the Prophet Muhammad ﷺ in his methodology and Sunnah is considered disbelief. Allah says:

$$\left\{ \text{وَأَطِيعُوا۟ ٱللَّهَ وَٱلرَّسُولَ لَعَلَّكُمْ تُرْحَمُونَ} \right\}$$

"And obey Allah and the Messenger that you may obtain mercy." (Ali Imran 3:132)

This verse is evidence proving that Allah's mercy is obtained by those who obey Allah and His Messenger ﷺ, and whoever does not obey them has verily gone astray and will be destroyed.

Allah the Most High says:

$$\left\{ \text{يَٰٓأَيُّهَا ٱلَّذِينَ ءَامَنُوٓا۟ أَطِيعُوا۟ ٱللَّهَ وَأَطِيعُوا۟ ٱلرَّسُولَ وَأُو۟لِى ٱلْأَمْرِ مِنكُمْ ۖ فَإِن تَنَٰزَعْتُمْ فِى شَىْءٍ فَرُدُّوهُ إِلَى ٱللَّهِ وَٱلرَّسُولِ إِن كُنتُمْ تُؤْمِنُونَ بِٱللَّهِ وَٱلْيَوْمِ ٱلْءَاخِرِ ۚ ذَٰلِكَ خَيْرٌ وَأَحْسَنُ تَأْوِيلًا} \right\}$$

"O you who believe! Obey Allah and obey the Messenger and those of you (Muslims) who are in authority. And if you differ in anything amongst yourselves, than refer it back to Allah and His Messenger, if you truly believe in Allah and in the Last Day. That is better and more suitable for final determination." (An Nisa 4:59)

In this verse are several commands to be obedient to the scholars and the leaders, for this reason Allah said: **"Obey Allah"** i.e. follow His book, and He said **"Obey the Messenger"** i.e. take his Sunnah, and He said: **"And those of you in authority"** i.e. regarding everything you are ordered with from obedience of Allah and not disobedience of Allah, for verily there is no obedience to the creation in affairs in which there is disobedience of Allah.

And Allah's statement:

$$\text{﴿ فَإِن تَنَازَعْتُمْ فِي شَيْءٍ فَرُدُّوهُ إِلَى ٱللَّهِ وَٱلرَّسُولِ ﴾}$$

"And if you differ in anything amongst yourselves, than refer it back to Allah and His Messenger", i.e. This meaning that many of the 'salaf' (righteous predecessors): i.e.-referred their differences back to the book of Allah and the Sunnah of Allah's Messenger ﷺ. This is a command from Allah The Most High, that everything which people differ about from the fundamentals of the religion as well as the subdivisions, refer it back to the Quran and the Sunnah when differing, as Allah said:

$$\text{﴿ وَمَا ٱخْتَلَفْتُمْ فِيهِ مِن شَيْءٍ فَحُكْمُهُ إِلَى ٱللَّهِ ﴾}$$

"And in whatsoever you differ in, the decision thereof is with Allah…" (Ash Shura 42:10)

So whatever the Quran and Sunnah have decided, judged and confirmed as being authentic, then it is the truth, and that which is subsequent to the truth is nothing but falsehood. So refer all arguments, disputes, and ignorance back to the Book of Allah and the Sunnah of Allah's Messenger ﷺ. Litigate and judge between yourselves with these two sources in everything which you differ in. Then Allah says:

$$\text{﴿ إِن كُنتُمْ تُؤْمِنُونَ بِٱللَّهِ وَٱلْيَوْمِ ٱلْآخِرِ ﴾}$$

"If you truly believe in Allah and the Last Day", this is evidence proving that whoever does not litigate or judge with the Quran and Sunnah in times of conflict and differing and doesn't refer back to them than he is not a believer in Allah nor in the Last Day."[1]

---

[1]-Tafsir ibn Kathir 1/713

Allah the Most Magnificent also says:

﴿ يَسْأَلُونَكَ عَنِ ٱلْأَنفَالِ قُلِ ٱلْأَنفَالُ لِلَّهِ وَٱلرَّسُولِ فَٱتَّقُوا۟ ٱللَّهَ وَأَصْلِحُوا۟ ذَاتَ بَيْنِكُمْ وَأَطِيعُوا۟ ٱللَّهَ وَرَسُولَهُۥٓ إِن كُنتُم مُّؤْمِنِينَ ۝ ﴾

"They ask you O Muhammad about the spoils of war. Say: the spoils of war are for Allah and His Messenger. So fear Allah and reconcile all matters of differences amongst you, and obey Allah and His Messenger, if you are believers." (al Anfal 8:1)

In this verse Allah also commanded us to be obedient to Him and His Messenger ﷺ, and made it a condition for having faith. So whoever does not obey Allah and His Messenger ﷺ than one is not a believer. Allah also says:

﴿ يَٰٓأَيُّهَا ٱلَّذِينَ ءَامَنُوٓا۟ أَطِيعُوا۟ ٱللَّهَ وَرَسُولَهُۥ وَلَا تَوَلَّوْا۟ عَنْهُ وَأَنتُمْ تَسْمَعُونَ ۝ ﴾

"O you who believe! Obey Allah and His Messenger, and do not turn away from him (Muhammad) while listening to him." (al Anfal 8:20) And Allah says:

﴿ وَأَطِيعُوا۟ ٱللَّهَ وَرَسُولَهُۥ وَلَا تَنَٰزَعُوا۟ فَتَفْشَلُوا۟ وَتَذْهَبَ رِيحُكُمْ ﴾

"And obey Allah and His Messenger, and do not dispute with one another, lest you lose courage and your strength/power is removed...." (al Anfal 8:46)

This verse proves that obedience to Allah and His Messenger ﷺ is a cause and means of harmony and unification and these are the two means which lead to strength and power. Furthermore, differing, conflicting, disputing and abandoning obedience to Allah and His Messenger ﷺ is from the means and causes of failure, weakness and the removal of power and strength. What a great statement that ibn Kathir made in his commentary of this verse: 'Verily the companions-in their courage, obedience and submission to Allah and His Messenger's ﷺ guidance- reached a level and possessed that which no other nation or generation before them possessed, nor any nation proceeding them will ever possess. For verily through the blessings and virtues of the Messenger of Allah ﷺ and their obedience to what he ordered them with, the companions were able to open the hearts of the people, in all parts of the world from East to West, in a very short period of time. This occurred even though they were few in number compared to the armies of the various nations of that time such as the Romans, Persians, Turks, Slavs, Berbers, Ethiopians, Sudanese tribes, the Copts and the rest of the mankind. The companions defeated all of these nations, until Allah's Word (La ilaha ill Allah) became the highest and His religion became the most predominant over all the other religions. The Islamic state spread from the far East to West of the world in less than thirty years. May Allah grant all the Companions His pleasure and may He be pleased with them, and gather us with them in the paradise, for verily Allah is the Most Generous and Most Giving."[1]

Certainly, Allah's words came to reality within the first generation of Muslims. Allah aided the companions because of their obedience to Allah and His Messenger. Similarly, Allah's words became a reality amongst the later generations of Muslims, who differed, split up and disputed amongst each other- as we see in our modern day. They have become some of the most humiliated of nations and people throughout the world, even with their large numbers and numerous amounts of blessings, bounties, and resources which Allah bestowed upon them. Allah says:

﴿ وَلَا تَنَٰزَعُوا۟ فَتَفْشَلُوا۟ وَتَذْهَبَ رِيحُكُمْ ﴾

"Do not dispute with one another, lest you lose courage and your strength and power is removed". Power and strength have been removed and the other nations throughout the world have rushed madly upon the Muslims, afflicting them with a horrible torment because of what they do. And to Allah are the complaints. Allah says:

﴿ قُلْ أَطِيعُوا۟ ٱللَّهَ وَأَطِيعُوا۟ ٱلرَّسُولَ ۖ فَإِن تَوَلَّوْا۟ فَإِنَّمَا عَلَيْهِ مَا حُمِّلَ وَعَلَيْكُم مَّا حُمِّلْتُمْ ۖ وَإِن تُطِيعُوهُ تَهْتَدُوا۟ ۚ وَمَا عَلَى ٱلرَّسُولِ إِلَّا ٱلْبَلَٰغُ ٱلْمُبِينُ ﴾

"Say: Obey Allah and obey the Messenger, but if you turn away, Muhammad is only responsible for the duty placed upon him which is conveying the message, and you are responsible for that placed upon you. If you obey Muhammad, you shall be upon right guidance. The Messenger's duty is only to convey the message in a clear way." (an Nur 24:54)

---

[1]-Tafsir ibn Kathir 2/433

Al 'I'tibaa'a

This verse is a clear-cut text proving that obedience to the Messenger of Allah ﷺ is clear guidance and contrary to it is misguidance. Allah says:

$$ \text{﴿ وَأَقِيمُوا۟ ٱلصَّلَوٰةَ وَءَاتُوا۟ ٱلزَّكَوٰةَ وَأَطِيعُوا۟ ٱلرَّسُولَ لَعَلَّكُمْ تُرْحَمُونَ ﴾} $$

"And perform the prayers and give the obligatory charity and obey the Messenger of Allah that you may receive mercy from Allah." (an Nur 24:56)

And Allah says:

$$ \text{﴿ يَٰٓأَيُّهَا ٱلَّذِينَ ءَامَنُوٓا۟ أَطِيعُوا۟ ٱللَّهَ وَأَطِيعُوا۟ ٱلرَّسُولَ وَلَا تُبْطِلُوٓا۟ أَعْمَٰلَكُمْ ﴾} $$

"O you who believe! Obey Allah and obey the Messenger and do not nullify your deeds." (Muhammad 47:33)

This verse proves that all actions are false, vain, and invalid if they are not done in obedience to Allah and His Messenger ﷺ. Allah says:

$$ \text{﴿ ءَأَشْفَقْتُمْ أَن تُقَدِّمُوا۟ بَيْنَ يَدَىْ نَجْوَىٰكُمْ صَدَقَٰتٍ ۚ فَإِذْ لَمْ تَفْعَلُوا۟ وَتَابَ ٱللَّهُ عَلَيْكُمْ فَأَقِيمُوا۟ ٱلصَّلَوٰةَ وَءَاتُوا۟ ٱلزَّكَوٰةَ وَأَطِيعُوا۟ ٱللَّهَ وَرَسُولَهُۥ ۚ وَٱللَّهُ خَبِيرٌۢ بِمَا تَعْمَلُونَ ﴾} $$

"Is it difficult for you to spend your wealth in charity before taking private consultation with Muhammad? And if you do not do it, and Allah has forgiven you, than at least perform the prayer and give the obligatory charity and obey Allah and His Messenger. And Allah is All Aware of what you do." (al Mujadilah 58:13) Allah also says:

$$ \text{﴿ وَأَطِيعُوا۟ ٱللَّهَ وَأَطِيعُوا۟ ٱلرَّسُولَ ۚ فَإِن تَوَلَّيْتُمْ فَإِنَّمَا عَلَىٰ رَسُولِنَا ٱلْبَلَٰغُ ٱلْمُبِينُ ﴾} $$

"Obey Allah and obey the Messenger Muhammad, but if you turn away then verily the duty of the Messenger is only to convey the message clearly." (at Taghabun 64:12)

Indeed, that which the Prophet ﷺ propagates and calls to contains life, and the opposite of what the Prophet ﷺ calls to contains destruction and death.

Al 'I'tibaa'a

Allah says in the Quran:

$$\text{﴿ يَٰٓأَيُّهَا ٱلَّذِينَ ءَامَنُوا۟ ٱسْتَجِيبُوا۟ لِلَّهِ وَلِلرَّسُولِ إِذَا دَعَاكُمْ لِمَا يُحْيِيكُمْ ۖ وَٱعْلَمُوٓا۟ أَنَّ ٱللَّهَ يَحُولُ بَيْنَ ٱلْمَرْءِ وَقَلْبِهِۦ وَأَنَّهُۥٓ إِلَيْهِ تُحْشَرُونَ ﴾}$$

"O you who believe! Answer Allah and His Messenger by obeying them, when Muhammad calls you to that which gives you life, and know that Allah intervenes between a person and the conditions of his heart. And verily to Him you shall all be gathered." (al Anfal 8:24)

Allah the Most Knowledgeable promised that whoever obeys Him and His Messenger ﷺ that they will have paradises under which rivers flow. Allah also specified the obedient ones with the bestowing of His mercy upon them, and He has prepared for them things which they can never imagine.

Allah also warned of the result of contradicting, abandoning and disobeying Allah and His Messenger ﷺ as Allah says:

$$\text{﴿ تِلْكَ حُدُودُ ٱللَّهِ ۚ وَمَن يُطِعِ ٱللَّهَ وَرَسُولَهُۥ يُدْخِلْهُ جَنَّٰتٍ تَجْرِى مِن تَحْتِهَا ٱلْأَنْهَٰرُ خَٰلِدِينَ فِيهَا ۚ وَذَٰلِكَ ٱلْفَوْزُ ٱلْعَظِيمُ ﴾}$$

"These are Allah's limits and ordainments and whomsoever obeys Allah and His Messenger will be admitted to Gardens under with rivers flow, to eternally abide therein, and that will be the great success." (an Nisa 4:13) And Allah says:

$$\text{﴿ وَمَن يُطِعِ ٱللَّهَ وَٱلرَّسُولَ فَأُو۟لَٰٓئِكَ مَعَ ٱلَّذِينَ أَنْعَمَ ٱللَّهُ عَلَيْهِم مِّنَ ٱلنَّبِيِّۦنَ وَٱلصِّدِّيقِينَ وَٱلشُّهَدَآءِ وَٱلصَّٰلِحِينَ ۚ وَحَسُنَ أُو۟لَٰٓئِكَ رَفِيقًا ﴾}$$

"And whosoever obeys Allah and the Messenger then they will be in the company of those upon whom Allah has bestowed His Grace, from the Prophets, the Truthful ones who followed the Prophets, the martyrs, and the righteous. And how excellent these companions are!" (an Nisa 4:69)

Al 'I'tibaa'a

Allah also says:

﴿ وَٱلْمُؤْمِنُونَ وَٱلْمُؤْمِنَٰتُ بَعْضُهُمْ أَوْلِيَآءُ بَعْضٍ يَأْمُرُونَ بِٱلْمَعْرُوفِ وَيَنْهَوْنَ عَنِ ٱلْمُنكَرِ وَيُقِيمُونَ ٱلصَّلَوٰةَ وَيُؤْتُونَ ٱلزَّكَوٰةَ وَيُطِيعُونَ ٱللَّهَ وَرَسُولَهُۥٓ أُو۟لَٰٓئِكَ سَيَرْحَمُهُمُ ٱللَّهُ إِنَّ ٱللَّهَ عَزِيزٌ حَكِيمٌ ﴾

"The male and female believers are helpers, supporters, protectors of one another; they enjoin all that is good and forbid and prohibit all that is evil, they perform the prayers and give the obligatory charity ad they obey Allah and His Messenger. Allah will surely send His Mercy upon them. Surely Allah is the Most Mighty the Most Wise." (at Tawbah 9:71) Allah also says:

﴿ وَمَن يُطِعِ ٱللَّهَ وَرَسُولَهُۥ وَيَخْشَ ٱللَّهَ وَيَتَّقْهِ فَأُو۟لَٰٓئِكَ هُمُ ٱلْفَآئِزُونَ ﴾

"And whomsoever obeys Allah and His Messenger and fears Allah and keeps his duty to Him, such are the successful." (an Nur 24:52) And Allah says:

﴿ وَمَن يُطِعِ ٱللَّهَ وَرَسُولَهُۥ فَقَدْ فَازَ فَوْزًا عَظِيمًا ﴾

"...And whomsoever obeys Allah and His Messenger than he has indeed achieved a great achievement (entrance into the Paradise and protection from the hellfire)" (al Ahzab 33:71)

And Allah says:

﴿ وَمَن يُطِعِ ٱللَّهَ وَرَسُولَهُۥ يُدْخِلْهُ جَنَّٰتٍ تَجْرِى مِن تَحْتِهَا ٱلْأَنْهَٰرُ وَمَن يَتَوَلَّ يُعَذِّبْهُ عَذَابًا أَلِيمًا ﴾

"And whomsoever obeys Allah and His Messenger, Allah will admit him to gardens in which rivers flow underneath them, and whomever turns away/back, Allah will punish him with a painful torment." (al Fath 48:17)

Al 'I'tibaa'a

And Allah says:

﴿ وَإِن تُطِيعُوا۟ ٱللَّهَ وَرَسُولَهُۥ لَا يَلِتْكُم مِّنْ أَعْمَـٰلِكُمْ شَيْـًٔا ۚ إِنَّ ٱللَّهَ غَفُورٌ رَّحِيمٌ ﴾

"And if you obey Allah and His Messenger, Allah will not decrease anything in reward for your deeds, Allah is the All Forgiving and Most Merciful." (al Hujurat 49:14)

Furthermore, Allah has warned the Muslims of contradicting and disobeying the Prophet Muhammad's ﷺ commands particularly in a specific verse, as Allah says:

﴿ فَلْيَحْذَرِ ٱلَّذِينَ يُخَالِفُونَ عَنْ أَمْرِهِۦٓ أَن تُصِيبَهُمْ فِتْنَةٌ أَوْ يُصِيبَهُمْ عَذَابٌ أَلِيمٌ ﴾

"Let those who oppose the Messenger's commandments beware, lest some afflictions, disbelief, trials, should befall them or a painful torment be inflicted upon them." (an Nur 24:63)

Ibn Kathir said about this verse: " *oppose the Messenger's commandments*", i.e.-against the commandments of the Prophet ﷺ, which is his way, his methodology, his Sunnah, his legislations. All words and deeds should be compared to the Prophet's ﷺ words and deeds, those that are in accordance with the Prophet's ﷺ words and deeds will be accepted, and those which are not in accordance with the Prophet's ﷺ words and deeds will be rejected, no matter who the person is.

It has been narrated in Saheehul Bukhari, Muslim and other that the Messenger of Allah ﷺ said:

أَنَّ رَسُولَ اللهِ صَلَّى اللهُ عَلَيْهِ وَسَلَّم قَالَ: "مَنْ عَمِلَ عَمَلًا لَيْسَ عَلَيْهِ أَمْرُنَا فَهُوَ رَدٌّ"

"Whoever does an action which is not from our affairs (Islam) than it is rejected," [1] meaning: let those who go against the legislations -in private or public-of the Prophet Muhammad ﷺ beware *"lest some affliction should befall them"* i.e.-lest some disbelief, hypocrisy, or innovation enter their hearts *"or a painful torment be inflicted upon them"* i.e.-means in this world by afflicting

---

[1]-Saheeh Bukhari 5/377, Book of reconciliation, #2697, Saheeh Muslim, Chapter: Nullification of the false rulings# 1718, the wording is for Muslim.

Al 'I'tibaa'a

them with capital punishment (death), prescribed punishment, or imprisonment and so on."[1]

Allah the Most Wise did not give the believers a choice to give or take if Allah and His Messenger ﷺ ruled, judged or ordained in the affair. Meaning that it is obligatory upon them to accept what Allah and His Messenger ﷺ legislated and act upon it as soon as it reaches them.

As Allah mentions:

﴿ وَمَا كَانَ لِمُؤْمِنٍ وَلَا مُؤْمِنَةٍ إِذَا قَضَى ٱللَّهُ وَرَسُولُهُۥٓ أَمْرًا أَن يَكُونَ لَهُمُ ٱلْخِيَرَةُ مِنْ أَمْرِهِمْۗ وَمَن يَعْصِ ٱللَّهَ وَرَسُولَهُۥ فَقَدْ ضَلَّ ضَلَٰلًا مُّبِينًا ﴾

"It is not for a believing man or woman; when Allah and His Messenger have decreed a matter, that they should have any choice in their decision. And whoever disobeys Allah and His Messenger has indeed strayed away into clear error." (Al Ahzab 33:36)

Similarly the Prophet ﷺ ordered his companions and the Muslims in general with the absolute following and imitation of him, which is found in numerous prophetic narrations. Al Bukhari narrated on the authority of Abu Hurairah that he said: the Messenger of Allah ﷺ said:

عَنْ أَبِي هُرَيْرَةَ أَنَّ رَسُولَ اللَّهِ صَلَّى اللهُ عَلَيْهِ وَسَلَّمَ، قَالَ: «كُلُّ أُمَّتِي يَدْخُلُونَ الجَنَّةَ إِلَّا مَنْ أَبَى»، قَالُوا: يَا رَسُولَ اللَّهِ، وَمَنْ يَأْبَى؟ قَالَ: «مَنْ أَطَاعَنِي دَخَلَ الجَنَّةَ، وَمَنْ عَصَانِي فَقَدْ أَبَى»

"All of my nation will enter the paradise except for those who refuse", it was said: who will refuse?, The Prophet ﷺ replied: "Whoever obeys me will enter paradise, and whoever disobeys me has refused."[2]

---

[1]-Tafsir ibn Kathir 2/422
[2]-Saheeh Bukhari 13/310 Book of Holding Firmly onto the Quran and Sunnah, Chapter: following the Prophets Sunnah #7280

Al 'I'tibaa'a

Imam Bukhari and Muslim narrated on the authority of Aa'isha who said:

قَالَ رَسُولُ اللَّهِ صَلَّى اللهُ عَلَيْهِ وَسَلَّمَ: «مَنْ أَحْدَثَ فِي أَمْرِنَا هَذَا مَا لَيْسَ فِيهِ، فَهُوَ رَدٌّ»

'The Messenger of Allah said ﷺ: "Whoever innovates in our affair (Islam) something which is not from our affair (Islam) than it is rejected."[1] Imam Muslim narrated on the authority of Jabir who said 'The Messenger of Allah ﷺ said:

"فَإِنَّ خَيْرَ الْحَدِيثِ كِتَابُ الله، وَخَيْرُ الْهُدَى هُدَى مُحَمَّدٍ، وَشَرُّ الْأُمُورِ مُحْدَثَاتُهَا، وَكُلُّ بِدْعَةٍ ضَلَالَةٌ» ثُمَّ يَقُولُ: «أَنَا أَوْلَى بِكُلِّ مُؤْمِنٍ مِنْ نَفْسِهِ..."

"Verily the best of speech is the speech of Allah and the best of guidance is the guidance of Muhammad, and the most evil affairs are the innovated affairs, and every innovation is misguidance," then he said: "I am more entitled to the believers than their own selves."[2]

Furthermore, the authentic Sunnah is revelation from Allah so it is obligatory for the Muslim to follow and imitate it, just as it is obligatory to follow and imitate what is in the Quran.

This can be proved by what the scholars of hadeeth narrated on the authority of al Miqdaam ibn Ma'deeka'rib from the Prophet Muhammad ﷺ that he said:

«أَلاَ إِنِّي أُوتِيتُ الْكِتَابَ وَمِثْلَهُ مَعَهُ أَلاَ يُوشِكُ رَجُلٌ شَبْعَانُ عَلَى أَرِيكَتِهِ يَقُولُ عَلَيْكُمْ بِهَذَا الْقُرْآنِ فَمَا وَجَدْتُمْ فِيهِ مِنْ حَلاَلٍ فَأَحِلُّوهُ وَمَا وَجَدْتُمْ فِيهِ مِنْ حَرَامٍ فَحَرِّمُوهُ أَلاَ لاَ يَحِلُّ لَكُمْ لَحْمُ الْحِمَارِ الْأَهْلِيِّ وَلاَ كُلُّ ذِي نَابٍ مِنَ السَّبُعِ وَلاَ لُقَطَةُ مُعَاهِدٍ إِلاَّ أَنْ يَسْتَغْنِيَ عَنْهَا صَاحِبُهَا وَمَنْ نَزَلَ بِقَوْمٍ فَعَلَيْهِمْ أَنْ يَقْرُوهُ فَإِنْ لَمْ يَقْرُوهُ فَلَهُ أَنْ يُعْقِبَهُمْ بِمِثْلِ قِرَاهُ»

"Don't you know that verily I have been given the Quran and that which is similar to it[3], verily the time is near that a man who has eaten to his full, reclining on a couch will say: 'Upon you is to follow this Quran, whatever you find the Quran as being legislated than consider it permissible, and whatever you find the Quran prohibiting than deem it as being prohibited. Indeed it is

---

[1] -Saheeh Bukhari 5/377, Book of Reconciliation, #2697, Saheeh Muslim 3/1343, Book of Judicial Decisions, Chapter: Rejection of incorrect rulings #1718
[2] -Saheeh Muslim, Book of Jumu'ah, Chapter: Imam shortening the Prayer and Sermon #867
[3] -(TN)The Sunnah is similar to the Quran in its legislations and its status regarding rulings and judgments.

not permissible for you to eat the meat of domesticated donkeys, and also it is not permissible to eat predatory animals with canine teeth, and also it is not permissible to take lost property of someone who is under a peace treaty with you except if the owner can do without it, and whoever takes lodging with a people then it is upon them to treat him generously and if they don't then he can from their wealth that which is equivalent for his entertainment and lodging(accomodations)."[1]

So it is obligatory upon the Muslims to unify upon the belief and understanding that whatever the Prophet ﷺ passed judgement in then it is not permissible to use personal opinion, 'qiyas'[2], nor trickery in rejecting these rulings. It is also obligatory upon the Muslims that they do not differ nor conflict amongst each other in taking these articles (Sunnah) as legitimate proofs and evidences for their religion. However, as Allah has predestined-as a test-that differences and conflicts have occurred as have occurred with the previous nations. Imam Bukhari narrated on the authority of Abu Sa'eed al Khudri that the Prophet Muhammad ﷺ said:

عَنْ أَبِي سَعِيدٍ رَضِيَ اللهُ عَنْهُ، أَنَّ النَّبِيَّ صَلَّى اللهُ عَلَيْهِ وَسَلَّمَ، قَالَ: «لَتَتَّبِعُنَّ سَنَنَ مَنْ قَبْلَكُمْ شِبْرًا بِشِبْرٍ، وَذِرَاعًا بِذِرَاعٍ، حَتَّى لَوْ سَلَكُوا جُحْرَ ضَبٍّ لَسَلَكْتُمُوهُ»، قُلْنَا يَا رَسُولَ اللهِ!! اليَهُودَ، وَالنَّصَارَى؟ قَالَ: «فَمَنْ»

"Indeed you will verily follow the ways of the nations before you, handspan by handspan, and armslength by armslength (cubit), until they enter a lizard's hole, then verily you will follow them in. The companions asked: O Messenger of Allah! The Jews and the Christians? Then the Prophet replied: Who else!"[3]

However the Prophet ﷺ warned from differing and instructed and guided us how to stay away and escape these problems of discord and dissension.

---

[1]-Sunan Abee Dawud pg. 690, Book of the Sunnah, Chapter: Adhering to the Sunnah #4604, Sunan Ibn Majah pg.14, Chapter: Glorifying the narrations of the Messenger of Allah being harsh with those who contradict them #12

[2]-**(TN)** Analogical reasoning

3-Saheeh Bukhari 6/613, Book of Prophets, Chapter: what has been mentioned about the Children of Israel #3456, as Book of Holding firmly onto the Quran and Sunnah, Chapter: Saying of the Prophet: 'You will verily follow the ways of those who came before you #7319

Al 'I'tibaa'a

Abu Dawud and others narrated on the authority of Abdur Rahman ibn Amru as Sulami and Hujr ibn Hujr who both said:

قَالَ: حَدَّثَنِي عَبْدُ الرَّحْمَنِ بْنُ عَمْرٍو السُّلَمِيُّ، وَحُجْرُ بْنُ حُجْرٍ، قَالَا: أَتَيْنَا الْعِرْبَاضَ بْنَ سَارِيَةَ، وَهُوَ مِمَّنْ نَزَلَ فِيهِ ﴿وَلَا عَلَى الَّذِينَ إِذَا مَا أَتَوْكَ لِتَحْمِلَهُمْ قُلْتَ لَا أَجِدُ مَا أَحْمِلُكُمْ عَلَيْهِ﴾ [التوبة: 92] فَسَلَّمْنَا، وَقُلْنَا: أَتَيْنَاكَ زَائِرِينَ وَعَائِدِينَ وَمُقْتَبِسِينَ، فَقَالَ الْعِرْبَاضُ: صَلَّى بِنَا رَسُولُ اللَّهِ صَلَّى اللَّهُ عَلَيْهِ وَسَلَّمَ ذَاتَ يَوْمٍ، ثُمَّ أَقْبَلَ عَلَيْنَا فَوَعَظَنَا مَوْعِظَةً بَلِيغَةً ذَرَفَتْ مِنْهَا الْعُيُونُ وَوَجِلَتْ مِنْهَا الْقُلُوبُ، فَقَالَ قَائِلٌ: يَا رَسُولَ اللَّهِ كَأَنَّ هَذِهِ مَوْعِظَةُ مُوَدِّعٍ، فَمَاذَا تَعْهَدُ إِلَيْنَا؟ فَقَالَ «أُوصِيكُمْ بِتَقْوَى اللَّهِ وَالسَّمْعِ وَالطَّاعَةِ، وَإِنْ عَبْدًا حَبَشِيًّا، فَإِنَّهُ مَنْ يَعِشْ مِنْكُمْ بَعْدِي فَسَيَرَى اخْتِلَافًا كَثِيرًا، فَعَلَيْكُمْ بِسُنَّتِي وَسُنَّةِ الْخُلَفَاءِ الْمَهْدِيِّينَ الرَّاشِدِينَ، تَمَسَّكُوا بِهَا وَعَضُّوا عَلَيْهَا بِالنَّوَاجِذِ، وَإِيَّاكُمْ وَمُحْدَثَاتِ الْأُمُورِ، فَإِنَّ كُلَّ مُحْدَثَةٍ بِدْعَةٌ، وَكُلَّ بِدْعَةٍ ضَلَالَةٌ»

'We came across al Irbaad ibn Sariyah and he was the one intended in the revealing of the Quranic verse: "Nor is there blame on those who came to you requesting to be provided with riding mounts, when you said: I cannot find any riding mounts for you…" (at Tawbah 9:92), so we greeted him and we said: We have come to you as visitors, and al Irbaad replied: 'The Prophet prayed with us one day, then he turned around and faced us, and exhorted us with an eloquent exhortation which filled our eyes with tears and filled our hearts with fear, then someone said: O Messenger of Allah ! This sounds like a farewell exhortation, what do you advise us with? So the Prophet said: "I advise you to fear Allah and advise you to listen and obey (the rulers), even if it is an Ethiopian slave. For verily those of you who live after me will definitely see much differing and conflict, so it is obligatory upon you to follow my Sunnah and the Sunnah of the rightly guided caliphs, hold firmly onto it, and bite onto it firmly with your molar teeth. And beware of the newly invented affairs, indeed every innovation is a misguidance."[1]

In this narration the Prophet Muhammad informed us about the occurrence of much differing and conflict amongst the Muslims, and this if from the most evident proofs of his prophethood. Furthermore, this is a command from the

---

[1]-This is the wording in Sunan Abee Dawud pg.691, Book of the Sunnah, Chapter: Adhering to the Sunnah, #4607.Sunan at Tirmidthi 5/44, Book of Knowledge, Chapter: What came regarding implementing the Sunnah #2676, and at Tirmidthi said 'hasan saheeh'. Sunan ibn Majah pg.20, Introduction, Chapter: Following the Sunnah of the Rightly Guided Caliphs #42. Mustadrak al Haakim 1/95, and al Haakim said: 'saheeh and there is no defect in the narration, and adh Dha'habee agreed with him'. And the narration is as they said.

Al 'I'tibaa'a

Prophet Muhammad ﷺ to return back to his Sunnah and the Sunnah of the rightly guided caliphs and hold firmly onto it in times of differing and conflict. As he also warned from innovations and newly invented affairs which have entered Allah's religion and will continue to occur until the Day of Resurrection. So whatever was not considered religion (Islam) in the era of the Prophet Muhammad ﷺ and the rightly guided caliphs, will never be considered religion (Islam) after that era.

Here we will mention a summary as to what Allah has made obligatory upon the Muslims. This is the preparation of answers to three questions which every human being will be asked, Muslim as well as non-Muslim, in his or her grave after the sending of the Prophet Muhammad ﷺ.

These questions are: **Who is your lord?, What is your religion?, Who is your Prophet?**[1]

Most importantly, one should not worship any Lord other than Allah, as Allah mentions in the Quran:

﴿ وَمَا خَلَقْتُ ٱلْجِنَّ وَٱلْإِنسَ إِلَّا لِيَعْبُدُونِ ﴾

"And I did not create the jinn and mankind except to worship Me alone." (adh Dhariyat 51:56) meaning: do not worship other than him, nor worship Him with partners. Nor should one follow any other religion besides Islam, which the Prophet Muhammad ﷺ came with, as Allah says:

﴿ إِنَّ ٱلدِّينَ عِندَ ٱللَّهِ ٱلْإِسْلَٰمُ ﴾

"Truly the religion with Allah is Islam" (ali Imran 3:19)

---

[1]-See the hadeeth of al Baraa'a ibn Aazib about the questions of the two angels after the deceased person is buried. Abu Dawud narrated it in the Book of Funeral Prayers, Chapter: Sitting near the graves #3212, #4753. An Nisaa'ee Book of Funeral Prayers, Chapter: What the believer experiences from generosity, #1833, also #2057 from the narration of Abu Hurairah. Also Ibn Majah, Ahmed as well as others narrated this hadeeth. Al Albaani gathered together all the different wordings of this narration in his book 'Funeral Prayers' pgs. 198-202, please refer back to that book.

Al 'I'tibaa'a

And Allah said:

﴿ وَمَن يَبْتَغِ غَيْرَ ٱلْإِسْلَٰمِ دِينًا فَلَن يُقْبَلَ مِنْهُ وَهُوَ فِى ٱلْأَخِرَةِ مِنَ ٱلْخَٰسِرِينَ ۝ ﴾

"*And whoever seeks a religion other than Islam, it will never be accepted of him...*" (ali Imran 3:85)

Just as Allah created mankind and the jinn for the sole purpose of worshipping Him, similarly He created them to follow the Prophet Muhammad ﷺ and not to disobey him. There does not exist, nor will there exist any human being to be followed or imitated unconditionally except the Prophet Muhammad ﷺ. So therefore it is not permissible to leave off or abandon what the Prophet Muhammad ﷺ came with from his Lord. It is also obligatory that we believe that Allah's religion has been completed and perfected in the form of the Quran and the Sunnah, as Allah gave us the glad tidings about this:

﴿ ٱلْيَوْمَ أَكْمَلْتُ لَكُمْ دِينَكُمْ وَأَتْمَمْتُ عَلَيْكُمْ نِعْمَتِى وَرَضِيتُ لَكُمُ ٱلْإِسْلَٰمَ دِينًا ﴾

"*This day, I have perfected your religion for you and completed My favor upon you and have chosen for you Islam as your religion.*" (al Ma'idah 5:3)

In addition, it is not permissible for anyone to say anything in the religion: 'this is from Allah's religion' except with a legislative proof and evidence.

As Allah says:

﴿ وَلَا تَقُولُوا۟ لِمَا تَصِفُ أَلْسِنَتُكُمُ ٱلْكَذِبَ هَٰذَا حَلَٰلٌ وَهَٰذَا حَرَامٌ لِّتَفْتَرُوا۟ عَلَى ٱللَّهِ ٱلْكَذِبَ ۚ إِنَّ ٱلَّذِينَ يَفْتَرُونَ عَلَى ٱللَّهِ ٱلْكَذِبَ لَا يُفْلِحُونَ ۝ ﴾

"*And do not say that which you tongues put forth falsely or assert as being truth: "This is lawful and that is forbidden", so as to invent lies and falsehood about/against Allah. Verily those who invent lies and falsehood about Allah will never prosper.*" (an Nahl 16:116)

This is because the religious laws are completely and solely from Allah alone, and it is not permissible for anyone to come along and legislate anything while not possessing a proof or evidence from Allah and His Messenger.

Al 'I'tibaa'a

As Allah says:

$$\text{﴿ أَمْ لَهُمْ شُرَكَٰٓؤُا۟ شَرَعُوا۟ لَهُم مِّنَ ٱلدِّينِ مَا لَمْ يَأْذَنۢ بِهِ ٱللَّهُ ۚ وَلَوْلَا كَلِمَةُ ٱلْفَصْلِ لَقُضِىَ بَيْنَهُمْ ۗ وَإِنَّ ٱلظَّٰلِمِينَ لَهُمْ عَذَابٌ أَلِيمٌ ﴾}$$

"Or do they have partners with Allah who have instituted/invented for them a religion which Allah has not ordained? And had it not been for a decisive Word, the matter would have been judged between them. And verily, for the polytheists and wrong doers is a painful torment." (ash Shura 42:21)

Shah Waliuallah adh Dhalawee[1] said: "Know that there doesn't exist any way for us to know the rulings, regulations, and legislations except by knowing what the Prophet Muhammad informed us about. Contrary to beneficial affairs, indeed the benefits may be realized or recognized by experiment or trial and error, they may also be realized by perception, insight, intuition or any other of the various ways to perceive them. Furthermore, there is absolutely no way for us to know what the Prophet informed us about except by learning and taking the narrations which have connected chains of narration and the chains which contain 'al an'ana'[2] ending at the Prophet Muhammad. Just as the Prophet Muhammad said:

$$\text{قَالَ رَسُولُ اللَّهِ صَلَّى اللَّهُ عَلَيْهِ وَسَلَّمَ: «مَنْ أَحْدَثَ فِي أَمْرِنَا هَذَا مَا لَيْسَ فِيهِ، فَهُوَ رَدٌّ»}$$

"Whoever innovates in our affair (Islam) that which is not from our affair (Islam) than this act is rejected."[3]

It is obligatory upon all of mankind to make the religion sincere for Allah alone. Especially if they find that their religion has been afflicted by defects, faults and deficiencies, and has been afflicted with things which are not from the sincere religion.

---

[1]-(TN)He is Ahmed ibn Abdur Raheem ibn Wajeehu Deen al Umaree ad Dhalawee, he was born 1114 hijri in Dehli (India) and died in the year 1176 hijri.

[2]-(TN)This is when the narrator says: "on the authority of" عن أو أن. The chains of narration which contain this wording need to be studied because it is possible that the narrator didn't hear the narration from his teacher.

[3]-(TN) Saheeh Bukhari 5/377, Book of Reconciliation, #2697, Saheeh Muslim 3/1343, Book of Judicial Decisions, Chapter: Rejection of incorrect rulings #1718

As Allah says:

$$\text{﴿ أَلَا لِلَّهِ الدِّينُ الْخَالِصُ ۚ وَالَّذِينَ اتَّخَذُوا مِن دُونِهِ أَوْلِيَاءَ مَا نَعْبُدُهُمْ إِلَّا لِيُقَرِّبُونَا إِلَى اللَّهِ زُلْفَىٰ إِنَّ اللَّهَ يَحْكُمُ بَيْنَهُمْ فِي مَا هُمْ فِيهِ يَخْتَلِفُونَ ۗ إِنَّ اللَّهَ لَا يَهْدِي مَنْ هُوَ كَاذِبٌ كَفَّارٌ ﴾}$$

"Surely the sincere religion is for Allah alone. And those who take protectors, lords, helpers and gods besides Allah say: 'We only worship them so that they may bring us closer to Allah" Verily Allah will judge between them concerning that wherein they differ. Truly Allah does not guide he who is a liar and a disbeliever." (az Zumar 39:3) And Allah says:

$$\text{﴿ وَمَا أُمِرُوا إِلَّا لِيَعْبُدُوا اللَّهَ مُخْلِصِينَ لَهُ الدِّينَ حُنَفَاءَ وَيُقِيمُوا الصَّلَاةَ وَيُؤْتُوا الزَّكَاةَ ۚ وَذَٰلِكَ دِينُ الْقَيِّمَةِ ﴾}$$

"And they were not commanded except that they should worship Allah alone and make the religion sincere for Him, and perform the prayers and pay the obligatory charity and that is the true religion." (Al Bayyinah 98:5)

The sincere religion is that which was completed in the time of the Messenger of Allah ﷺ. Islam was never blemished with any defects, faults, or deficiencies in it's creed nor in its legislations. Nothing from the religion was ever ascribed to other than Allah and His Messenger ﷺ. Nothing was obligatory except that which Allah and His Messenger ﷺ made obligatory, and nothing was permissible or prohibited except that which Allah and His Messenger ﷺ made permissible or prohibited.

These affairs are obvious and self-evident within the texts of the Quran and the Sunnah, and this is the methodology that the companions of Allah's Messenger ﷺ were raised and nurtured upon. They were under the care and hands of the best of Messengers ﷺ, the best of human beings, our Prophet Muhammad ibn Abdullah ﷺ.

Al 'I'tibaa'a

The companions never gave precedence to themselves over Allah and His Messenger ﷺ, as Allah had raised, refined and taught them the best of etiquettes and manners as He said:

﴿ يَٰٓأَيُّهَا ٱلَّذِينَ ءَامَنُواْ لَا تُقَدِّمُواْ بَيْنَ يَدَىِ ٱللَّهِ وَرَسُولِهِۦ ۖ وَٱتَّقُواْ ٱللَّهَ ۚ إِنَّ ٱللَّهَ سَمِيعٌ عَلِيمٌ ﴾

"*O you who believe do not give precedence to yourselves (decisions, sayings, actions) over Allah and His Messenger. And fear Allah. Verily, Allah is All Hearing and All Knowing.*" (al Hujurat 49:1)

This was implemented by the companions even to the extent that one of them may have known something or the answer to a question which the Prophet Muhammad ﷺ may have asked them, they would reply: Allah and His Messenger ﷺ know best.

On the authority of Abee Bakrah who said:

عَنْ أَبِي بَكْرَةَ رَضِيَ اللهُ عَنْهُ، قَالَ: خَطَبَنَا النَّبِيُّ صَلَّى اللهُ عَلَيْهِ وَسَلَّمَ يَوْمَ النَّحْرِ، قَالَ: «أَتَدْرُونَ أَيُّ يَوْمٍ هَذَا؟»، قُلْنَا: اللهُ وَرَسُولُهُ أَعْلَمُ، فَسَكَتَ حَتَّى ظَنَنَّا أَنَّهُ سَيُسَمِّيهِ بِغَيْرِ اسْمِهِ، قَالَ: «أَلَيْسَ يَوْمَ النَّحْرِ؟» قُلْنَا: بَلَى، قَالَ: «أَيُّ شَهْرٍ هَذَا؟»، قُلْنَا: اللهُ وَرَسُولُهُ أَعْلَمُ، فَسَكَتَ حَتَّى ظَنَنَّا أَنَّهُ سَيُسَمِّيهِ بِغَيْرِ اسْمِهِ، فَقَالَ «أَلَيْسَ ذُو الحَجَّةِ؟»، قُلْنَا: بَلَى، قَالَ «أَيُّ بَلَدٍ هَذَا؟» قُلْنَا: اللهُ وَرَسُولُهُ أَعْلَمُ، فَسَكَتَ حَتَّى ظَنَنَّا أَنَّهُ سَيُسَمِّيهِ بِغَيْرِ اسْمِهِ، قَالَ «أَلَيْسَتْ بِالْبَلْدَةِ الحَرَامِ؟» قُلْنَا بَلَى، قَالَ: «فَإِنَّ دِمَاءَكُمْ وَأَمْوَالَكُمْ عَلَيْكُمْ حَرَامٌ، كَحُرْمَةِ يَوْمِكُمْ هَذَا، فِي شَهْرِكُمْ هَذَا، فِي بَلَدِكُمْ هَذَا...

'The Prophet ﷺ addressed us on the Day of an Nahr[1] (sacrifice) and he said: "Do you all know what day this is?" we replied: Allah and His Messenger know best, and we remained silent until we thought the Prophet ﷺ was going to name the day with another name, then the Prophet ﷺ said: "isn't it the day of sacrifice?", we replied: Of course. Then he asked: "what month is this?", we replied: Allah and His Messenger know best and we remained silent until we thought he was going to name the month with another name, then he said: "Isn't this the month of Dhul Hijjah?" and we replied: Of course. Then the Prophet ﷺ asked: "which city is this?", we replied: Allah and His Messenger know best and we remained silent until we thought he was going to name it with another name, then he said: "Isn't this the city of the Haram?", we replied: of course. Then he

---

[1]-(TN)Day of Eid, the 10th of Dhul Hijjah

Al 'I'tibaa'a

said: *"Verily you blood and money amongst each other is sacred, as the sacredness of this day of yours, in the sacred month, in this sacred city."*[1]

If any mishap, misfortune, or calamity took place and the companions were in the company of the Prophet Muhammad ﷺ, they would immediately return and refer back to him and find the answer, cure and solution for their lack of knowledge, inability and helplessness in the issue. The Prophet Muhammad ﷺ would teach them all what Allah had taught him. Certainly, this issue does not need evidence to support it as it is self evident and clearly understood.

As we know that the Prophet Muhammad ﷺ would not speak nor answer their questions except with revelation from Allah, as Allah says:

﴿ وَمَا يَنطِقُ عَنِ ٱلۡهَوَىٰٓ ۝ إِنۡ هُوَ إِلَّا وَحۡيٞ يُوحَىٰ ۝ ﴾

"Nor does Muhammad speak of his own desires-It is only from Revelation which is revealed to him." (an Najm 53:3-4)

Al Bukhari narrated on the authority of Safwan ibn Ya'la ibn Umayah from his father who said:

حَدَّثَنِي صَفْوَانُ بْنُ يَعْلَى بْنِ أُمَيَّةَ - يَعْنِي -، عَنْ أَبِيهِ، أَنَّ رَجُلًا أَتَى النَّبِيَّ صَلَّى اللهُ عَلَيْهِ وَسَلَّمَ وَهُوَ بِالجِعْرَانَةِ، وَعَلَيْهِ جُبَّةٌ وَعَلَيْهِ أَثَرُ الخَلُوقِ - أَوْ قَالَ: صُفْرَةٌ -، فَقَالَ: كَيْفَ تَأْمُرُنِي أَنْ أَصْنَعَ فِي عُمْرَتِي؟ فَأَنْزَلَ اللهُ عَلَى النَّبِيِّ صَلَّى اللهُ عَلَيْهِ وَسَلَّمَ فَسُتِرَ بِثَوْبٍ، وَوَدِدْتُ أَنِّي قَدْ رَأَيْتُ النَّبِيَّ صَلَّى اللهُ عَلَيْهِ وَسَلَّمَ وَقَدْ أُنْزِلَ عَلَيْهِ الوَحْيُ، فَقَالَ عُمَرُ: تَعَالَ أَيَسُرُّكَ أَنْ تَنْظُرَ إِلَى النَّبِيِّ صَلَّى اللهُ عَلَيْهِ وَسَلَّمَ، وَقَدْ أَنْزَلَ اللهُ عَلَيْهِ الوَحْيَ؟ قُلْتُ: نَعَمْ، فَرَفَعَ طَرَفَ الثَّوْبِ، فَنَظَرْتُ إِلَيْهِ لَهُ غَطِيطٌ، - وَأَحْسِبُهُ قَالَ: كَغَطِيطِ البَكْرِ قَالَ - فَلَمَّا سُرِّيَ عَنْهُ قَالَ: «أَيْنَ السَّائِلُ عَنِ العُمْرَةِ اخْلَعْ عَنْكَ الجُبَّةَ، وَاغْسِلْ أَثَرَ الخَلُوقِ عَنْكَ، وَأَنْقِ الصُّفْرَةَ، وَاصْنَعْ فِي عُمْرَتِكَ كَمَا تَصْنَعُ فِي حَجِّكَ»

"A man came to the Prophet ﷺ while he was in 'al-Ji'raanah[2] *and he was wearing a cloak which had traces of Khalooq or Sufra (perfume). The man asked the Prophet ﷺ: 'What do you command me to do regarding my Umrah? So Allah inspired the Prophet ﷺ with divine revelation while he was screened with a piece of clothing. I was hoping to see the Prophet ﷺ while being inspired with divine revelation, so Umar said to me: 'Come, wouldn't It please you to*

---

[1] -Saheeh Bukhari 3/732, Book of Hajj, Chapter: The sermon in Mina #1741
[2] -**(TN)** A place which is on the outskirts of Makkah in the direction of Taif

Al 'I'tibaa'a

see the Prophet ﷺ while being inspired by revelation? I replied: yes of course! Umar then lifted the corner of the piece of clothing which was screening the Prophet ﷺ and I looked at the Prophet ﷺ who was snoring. (the sub-narrator thought he said : the snoring was like that of a camel). When the time of inspiration was over, the Prophet ﷺ asked the man: "Where is the questioner about Umrah? Take your cloak off and wash away the traces of Khalooq from your body and clean the Sufra (yellow color) and do in your Umrah what you do in your Hajj."[1]

If the companions were not in the presence of the Prophet Muhammad ﷺ then they pondered, reflected and considered carefully the issue at hand with their 'ijtihaad'[2] or personal judgments. They never considered, deemed or made their opinions or judgments to be the final decision or ruling in the issue. Rather they understood whether their opinions or judgements were correct or incorrect after asking the Prophet Muhammad ﷺ. If the companions differed in their 'ijtihaad' or rulings they would never be harsh, cruel or violent with their brothers, nor would they force their opinions upon others or coerce others into accepting them. Abu Dawud narrated with an authentic chain of narration, on the authority of Abu Sa'eed al Khudri who said:

عَنْ أَبِى سَعِيدٍ الْخُدْرِىِّ قَالَ خَرَجَ رَجُلاَنِ فِى سَفَرٍ فَحَضَرَتِ الصَّلاَةُ وَلَيْسَ مَعَهُمَا مَاءٌ فَتَيَمَّمَا صَعِيدًا طَيِّبًا ثُمَّ وَجَدَا الْمَاءَ فِى الْوَقْتِ فَأَعَادَ أَحَدُهُمَا الصَّلاَةَ وَالْوُضُوءَ وَلَمْ يُعِدِ الآخَرُ ثُمَّ أَتَيَا رَسُولَ اللَّهِ -صلى الله عليه وسلم- فَذَكَرَا ذَلِكَ لَهُ فَقَالَ لِلَّذِى لَمْ يُعِدْ « أَصَبْتَ السُّنَّةَ وَأَجْزَأَتْكَ صَلاَتُكَ ». وَقَالَ لِلَّذِى تَوَضَّأَ وَأَعَادَ « لَكَ الأَجْرُ مَرَّتَيْنِ »

'Two men went out on a journey and the time for prayer was established, and neither of them had water (to make ablution), so they both made 'tayammum'[3] and they both prayed . Then they came across some water while the prayer time still being valid, so one of them repeated the prayer and made ablution with the water and the other man did not. Then they went to see the Prophet Muhammad ﷺ and mentioned to him what occurred, and the Prophet ﷺ said to

---

[1] -Saheeh Bukhari 3/783, Book of Umrah, Chapter: Perform in Umrah what one performs in Hajj #1789

[2] -(TN) The meaning of 'al ijtihaad' is: The scholar or jurist exerting all of his efforts and doing everything in his ability to know a religious ruling which contains no text, by the way of deductive and inferential reasoning.

[3] -(TN)Tayammum:to strike the earth with the hands and then blow the dust off and pass the palm of each hand over the other and then to pass them over the face. This is perfomed in the absence of water or when water is not available.

Al 'I'tibaa'a

the one who didn't repeat the prayer: "you have performed the Sunnah, and your prayer is accepted. And he said to the one who made ablution and repeated the prayer: "You have a double reward."[1]

Al Bukhari narrated on the authority of Sa'eed ibn Abdur Rahman ibn Abzaa from his father who said:

عَنْ سَعِيدِ بْنِ عَبْدِ الرَّحْمَنِ بْنِ أَبْزَى، عَنْ أَبِيهِ، قَالَ: جَاءَ رَجُلٌ إِلَى عُمَرَ بْنِ الخَطَّابِ، فَقَالَ: إِنِّي أَجْنَبْتُ فَلَمْ أُصِبِ المَاءَ، فَقَالَ عَمَّارُ بْنُ يَاسِرٍ لِعُمَرَ بْنِ الخَطَّابِ: أَمَا تَذْكُرُ أَنَّا كُنَّا فِي سَفَرٍ أَنَا وَأَنْتَ، فَأَمَّا أَنْتَ فَلَمْ تُصَلِّ، وَأَمَّا أَنَا فَتَمَعَّكْتُ فَصَلَّيْتُ، فَذَكَرْتُ لِلنَّبِيِّ صلّى الله عليه وسلم، فَقَالَ النَّبِيُّ صَلَّى اللهُ عَلَيْهِ وَسَلَّمَ: «إِنَّمَا كَانَ يَكْفِيكَ هَكَذَا» فَضَرَبَ النَّبِيُّ صَلَّى اللهُ عَلَيْهِ وَسَلَّمَ بِكَفَّيْهِ الأَرْضَ، وَنَفَخَ فِيهِمَا، ثُمَّ مَسَحَ بِهِمَا وَجْهَهُ وَكَفَّيْهِ"

'A man came to Umar ibn al Khattab and he said: I became sexually impure and didn't find any water, so Amaar ibn Yasir said to Umar ibn al Khattab: 'Don't you remember when we were both on a journey, and you didn't pray, as for me than I rolled around in the dirt and then I prayed. Then we informed the Prophet ﷺ what occurred and he said: "It would have been sufficient for you to do like this", then the Prophet ﷺ stroke the earth lightly with his hands then blew the dust off and passed his hands over his hands and face."[2]

Furthermore, the companions never used to make distinctions nor discriminate between the actions of the Prophet Muhammad ﷺ, saying this is 'a pillar and that is 'basic element' (rukn) or this is an obligation and that is Sunnah, rather they were the most persistent in adherence and imitating the Prophet Muhammad ﷺ in all of his actions except those which were specific for himself.

Shah Wailullah adh Dhalawee said: 'Know that the 'fiqh' in the time of the Prophet Muhammad ﷺ was not recorded or written down. The search for the 'fiqh' rulings in his time was not like how it was amongst those 'fuqahaa'[3] in which they tried to clarify-to the utmost extreme and strenuous exertion-the conditions, pillars, basic elements, rules and etiquettes of everything. Each part separate and distinguished from the other parts with the proofs and evidences. They assumed, supposed, and invented hypothetical situations then they would talk about these situations. Sometimes they would limit, define and restrict that

---

[1]-Sunan Abee Dawud,pg.60, Book of Purification, Chapter: Tayammum if he doesn't find water after praying in the legislated time, #338, with an authentic chain.
[2]-Saheeh Bukhari, pg. 1/583, Book of Tayammum, Chapter: Does a person blow the dust off his hands after making tayammum #338
[3]-(TN) later generation 'fiqh' scholars

which can be restricted, defined or limited and the many other ways and techniques which are popular amongst the 'fuqahaa'.

As for the Messenger of Allah ﷺ, then he used to make ablution, then the companions would observe carefully and watch how the Prophet ﷺ would make his ablution. They would take this from the Prophet ﷺ without the Prophet ﷺ clarifying: this is 'a basic element, and that is a condition and these are the etiquettes'. Also the Prophet ﷺ would pray, and the companions would observe his prayer, then they would pray exactly as they observed the Prophet ﷺ praying. The Prophet ﷺ made Hajj and the companions closely observed how the Prophet ﷺ made Hajj, so they did exactly as he did. The majority of the affairs of the Prophet ﷺ were like this, he never mentioned that the 'necessities or obligations for ablution are four or six, nor did he assume hypothetical situations where perhaps a person may make ablution without continuation until one decides or makes a judgment that this ablution is correct or corrupt, except for what Allah willed, and very seldom did the companions use to ask about these affairs."[1]

Ibnul Qayyim said: "When the techniques of learning and acquiring the religion from the Prophet Muhammad ﷺ were of two types: indirectly and directly. The companions were fortunate because they learned and acquired their religion from the Prophet ﷺ directly and they were the forerunners and achieved the best, and the companions seized and utilized the time and opportunity, so there is no chance or aspiration for anyone from amongst the Muslims who come after them to exceed them. However the distinguished and illustrious one is he who follows the straight path, and the one who imitates and follows the companions correct methodology and ways. He who opposes, contradicts and differs is the one who deviates from the companions way and methodology, straying to the right and to the left. Verily he is the one who has been cut off and he is wandering in the wilderness of destruction and misguidance. The companions main source and chain of narration was from the Prophet ﷺ who heard from the angel Jibreel who heard from the Lord of all of creation, an authentic lofty chain of narration with few narrators. The companions said to their students: This is the covenant of our Prophet ﷺ for us, and verily we have entrusted you with it, and this is the legacy of our Lord, and His obligation upon us, and it is his recommendation and obligation for you all. "[2]

---

[1]-Hujjatullahi al Baligah 1/140-141
[2]-'I'laam al Muwa'qa'eeen' 1/6

Part Eight

Methodology of the Companions when differing, after the time of the Prophet Muhammad

The companions of Allah's Messenger- may Allah be pleased with them- were the first believers to believe in what Allah ordered the creation to believe in. They never differed in anything in the affairs of creed nor actions, except that they hastened and acted quickly to find out what is Allah and His Messenger's decision in the affair. Allah has ordered all of the people in general:

﴿ وَمَا ٱخْتَلَفْتُمْ فِيهِ مِن شَىْءٍ فَحُكْمُهُۥٓ إِلَى ٱللَّهِ ذَٰلِكُمُ ٱللَّهُ رَبِّى عَلَيْهِ تَوَكَّلْتُ وَإِلَيْهِ أُنِيبُ ﴾

"And whatsoever you differ in, the decision thereof is with Allah. And say O Muhammad: 'This is Allah, my Lord, whom I put my trust...'" (ash Shura 42:10)

Allah's statement: *'whatever you differ in from affairs'*, this is general regarding all affairs and situations, the decision is up to Allah, meaning: He is the judge in the affair, with His Book (Quran) and the Sunnah of His Messenger ﷺ, as Allah mentioned:

﴿ فَإِن تَنَازَعْتُمْ فِى شَىْءٍ فَرُدُّوهُ إِلَى ٱللَّهِ وَٱلرَّسُولِ ﴾

"If you differ in anything amongst yourselves, refer it to Allah and His Messenger..." (an Nisa 4:59), then Allah says: *"This is Allah, my Lord"* i.e.-The judge in everything." [1]

Verily, Allah the Most Wise has dispraised differing and dissension in many places within the Noble Quran, and Allah has prohibited from it, as He says:

﴿ وَٱعْتَصِمُوا۟ بِحَبْلِ ٱللَّهِ جَمِيعًا وَلَا تَفَرَّقُوا۟ وَٱذْكُرُوا۟ نِعْمَتَ ٱللَّهِ عَلَيْكُمْ إِذْ كُنتُمْ أَعْدَآءً فَأَلَّفَ بَيْنَ قُلُوبِكُمْ فَأَصْبَحْتُم بِنِعْمَتِهِۦٓ إِخْوَٰنًا وَكُنتُمْ عَلَىٰ شَفَا حُفْرَةٍ مِّنَ ٱلنَّارِ فَأَنقَذَكُم مِّنْهَا كَذَٰلِكَ يُبَيِّنُ ٱللَّهُ لَكُمْ ءَايَٰتِهِۦ لَعَلَّكُمْ تَهْتَدُونَ ۝ ﴾

---

[1] -Tafsir ibn Kathir 4/139

Al 'I'tibaa'a

"And hold fast, all of you together to the Rope of Allah (Quran and Sunnah) and do not be divided amongst yourselves, and remember Allah's favor upon you, when you were once enemies to one another, but Allah joined your hearts together, so that by His grace you became brothers in Islamic Faith and you were on the brink of a pit of fire and Allah saved you from it..." (al Imran 3:103)

Allah also says:

﴿ وَأَنَّ هَٰذَا صِرَٰطِى مُسْتَقِيمًا فَٱتَّبِعُوهُ ۖ وَلَا تَتَّبِعُوا۟ ٱلسُّبُلَ فَتَفَرَّقَ بِكُمْ عَن سَبِيلِهِۦ ۚ ذَٰلِكُمْ وَصَّىٰكُم بِهِۦ لَعَلَّكُمْ تَتَّقُونَ ۝ ﴾

"And verily this is my straight path, so follow it and do not follow the other paths, for they will deter you and lead you astray from His path..." (al An' am 6:153) Allah says:

﴿ وَمَا ٱخْتَلَفَ فِيهِ إِلَّا ٱلَّذِينَ أُوتُوهُ مِنۢ بَعْدِ مَا جَآءَتْهُمُ ٱلْبَيِّنَٰتُ بَغْيًۢا بَيْنَهُمْ ۖ فَهَدَى ٱللَّهُ ٱلَّذِينَ ءَامَنُوا۟ لِمَا ٱخْتَلَفُوا۟ فِيهِ مِنَ ٱلْحَقِّ بِإِذْنِهِۦ ۗ وَٱللَّهُ يَهْدِى مَن يَشَآءُ إِلَىٰ صِرَٰطٍ مُّسْتَقِيمٍ ﴾

"And only those to whom the Scripture was given differed concerning it by after clear proofs had come to them through hatred, oppression and mutual jealously between them..." (al Baqarah 2:213) Allah says:

﴿ وَمَا ٱخْتَلَفَ ٱلَّذِينَ أُوتُوا۟ ٱلْكِتَٰبَ إِلَّا مِنۢ بَعْدِ مَا جَآءَهُمُ ٱلْعِلْمُ ﴾

"Those who were given the Scripture (Jews and Christians) did not differ except out of mutual jealousy, hatred and oppression; after knowledge had come to them." (Ali Imran 3:19) Allah says:

﴿ وَإِنَّ ٱلَّذِينَ ٱخْتَلَفُوا۟ فِى ٱلْكِتَٰبِ لَفِى شِقَاقٍۭ بَعِيدٍ ۝ ﴾

"And verily those who disputed regarding the Book are far away in opposition." (al Baqarah 2:176)

Al 'I'tibaa'a

Allah says:

$$﴿ وَلَا تَكُونُوا۟ كَٱلَّذِينَ تَفَرَّقُوا۟ وَٱخْتَلَفُوا۟ مِنۢ بَعْدِ مَا جَآءَهُمُ ٱلْبَيِّنَٰتُ ۚ وَأُو۟لَٰٓئِكَ لَهُمْ عَذَابٌ عَظِيمٌ ﴾$$

"And do not be as those who divided and differed amongst themselves after the clear proofs had come to them. It is them whom there is an awful torment." (Ali Imran 3:105) Allah says:

$$﴿ وَأَطِيعُوا۟ ٱللَّهَ وَرَسُولَهُۥ وَلَا تَنَٰزَعُوا۟ فَتَفْشَلُوا۟ وَتَذْهَبَ رِيحُكُمْ ۖ وَٱصْبِرُوٓا۟ ۚ إِنَّ ٱللَّهَ مَعَ ٱلصَّٰبِرِينَ ﴾$$

"And obey Allah and His Messenger and do not dispute with each other lest you lose courage and your strength departs and be patient. Verily Allah is with those who are patient." (al Anfal 8:46)

And Allah exempted and freed His Prophet ﷺ from differing, splitting, and dissension in the religion, as He says:

$$﴿ إِنَّ ٱلَّذِينَ فَرَّقُوا۟ دِينَهُمْ وَكَانُوا۟ شِيَعًا لَّسْتَ مِنْهُمْ فِى شَىْءٍ ﴾$$

"Verily those who divide their religion and break up into sects, You (Muhammad) are not from them nor do you have any concern with them in the least..." (al An'am 6:159) Allah says:

$$﴿ ۞ شَرَعَ لَكُم مِّنَ ٱلدِّينِ مَا وَصَّىٰ بِهِۦ نُوحًا وَٱلَّذِىٓ أَوْحَيْنَآ إِلَيْكَ وَمَا وَصَّيْنَا بِهِۦٓ إِبْرَٰهِيمَ وَمُوسَىٰ وَعِيسَىٰٓ ۖ أَنْ أَقِيمُوا۟ ٱلدِّينَ وَلَا تَتَفَرَّقُوا۟ فِيهِ ﴾$$

"Allah has ordained for you the same religion (Islamic Monotheism) which He ordained for Nuh and that which We have revealed to you (Muhammad) and that which We ordained for Ibrahim, Musa, Isa saying that you should establish the religion and do not differ in the religion..." (ash Shura 42:13)

Ibn Kathir said:' Allah's statement: "To establish the religion and do not differ in the religion", i.e.-Allah The Most High advised all of the Prophets with unification and harmony and prohibited them from splitting up into groups and differing.'[1]

Sheikh al Alaamah Abdur Rahman ibn Naasir as Sa'dee[2] mentioned about this verse: **"To establish the religion"**, i.e.-Allah ordered you all to establish and practice all of the religious legislations, the fundamentals and the sub-divisions. Establish them amongst yourselves first, then work hard in establishing them amongst others. Work together upon righteousness and piety, and do not cooperate upon sin, enmity and evil deeds. And Allah's statement: **"And do not differ in the religion"**, i.e.-To enable you all to obtain and agree upon the fundamentals and sub-divisions of the religion, and be keen and eager that issues and problems do not divide you, and split you up into sects and groups. This leads to showing enmity towards each other while being in agreement upon the fundamentals of your religion."[3]

Verily, know that differing is definitely not 'mercy', and what some people have mentioned that the Prophet ﷺ said: 'The differing of my nation is mercy', is falsehood. This narration is fabricated, inauthentic, incorrect and a lie upon the Prophet Muhammad ﷺ.[4] For verily Allah has made mercy with the absence of differing and conflict.

Allah the Most Magnificent said:

﴿ وَلَوْ شَاءَ رَبُّكَ لَجَعَلَ ٱلنَّاسَ أُمَّةً وَٰحِدَةً ۖ وَلَا يَزَالُونَ مُخْتَلِفِينَ ۝ إِلَّا مَن رَّحِمَ رَبُّكَ ۚ وَلِذَٰلِكَ خَلَقَهُمْ ۗ وَتَمَّتْ كَلِمَةُ رَبِّكَ لَأَمْلَأَنَّ جَهَنَّمَ مِنَ ٱلْجِنَّةِ وَٱلنَّاسِ أَجْمَعِينَ ۝ ﴾

"And if your Lord had willed, He could have surely made mankind one nation, community, Muslims; but they will not cease to disagree-Except him on whom your Lord has bestowed His mercy and for that reason He created them. And

---

[1] -Tafsir ibn Kathir 4/140
[2] -**(TN)**He is Abu Abdullah Abdur Rahman ibn Naasir as Sa'dee, he was born in the city of Unayzah (Qaseem, Saudia Arabia) in the year 1307 hijri. He was a virtuous Imam, Scholar, Jurist, Judge, Teacher, Muhaddith adhering to the creed of Ahl Sunnah wal Jamaa'ah. He has many compilations and books. He died in 1367.
[3] -Tafsir as Sa'dee pg.754
[4] -see 'Silsilah al Ahadeeh ad Da'eefah #57

the word of your Lord has been fulfilled, His saying: 'Surely, I shall fill Hell with jinn and men all together." (Hud 11:118-119)

Mercy was made as the exception here in this verse and there are many similar verses which also prove this. Indeed, the Prophet ﷺ warned his followers from differing in numerous narrations:

On the authority of Abu Hurairah who said: the Messenger of Allah ﷺ said:

عَنْ أَبِى هُرَيْرَةَ قَالَ قَالَ رَسُولُ اللَّهُ -صلى الله عليه وسلم- « افْتَرَقَتِ الْيَهُودُ عَلَى إِحْدَى أَوْ ثِنْتَيْنِ وَسَبْعِينَ فِرْقَةً وَتَفَرَّقَتِ النَّصَارَى عَلَى إِحْدَى أَوْ ثِنْتَيْنِ وَسَبْعِينَ فِرْقَةً وَتَفْتَرِقُ أُمَّتِى عَلَى ثَلاَثٍ وَسَبْعِينَ فِرْقَةً »

"The Jews split up into seventy one or seventy two religious sects, and the Christians split up into seventy two religious sects, and this (Muslim) nation will split up into seventy three religious sects.[1]

Also on the authority of Mu'awiyyah that he said: *'The Prophet stood up amongst us and said:*

عَنْ مُعَاوِيَةَ بْنِ أَبِى سُفْيَانَ أَنَّهُ قَامَ فِينَا فَقَالَ أَلاَ إِنَّ رَسُولَ اللَّهِ -صلى الله عليه وسلم- قَامَ فِينَا فَقَالَ « أَلاَ إِنَّ مَنْ قَبْلَكُمْ مِنْ أَهْلِ الْكِتَابِ افْتَرَقُوا عَلَى ثِنْتَيْنِ وَسَبْعِينَ مِلَّةً وَإِنَّ هَذِهِ الْمِلَّةَ سَتَفْتَرِقُ عَلَى ثَلاَثٍ وَسَبْعِينَ ثِنْتَانِ وَسَبْعُونَ فِى النَّارِ وَوَاحِدَةٌ فِى الْجَنَّةِ وَهِىَ الْجَمَاعَةُ »

"Verily those nations who came before you from the People of the Book (Jews and Christians) split up into seventy two religious sects, and indeed this (Muslim) nation will split up into seventy three religious sects, seventy two in the hellfire and only one of them will be in the paradise, and it is the 'jama'ah'." In another narration:

زَادَ ابْنُ يَحْيَى وَعَمْرٌو فِى حَدِيثَيْهِمَا « وَإِنَّهُ سَيَخْرُجُ مِنْ أُمَّتِى أَقْوَامٌ تَجَارَى بِهِمْ تِلْكَ الأَهْوَاءُ كَمَا يَتَجَارَى الْكَلْبُ لِصَاحِبِهِ »

"Verily there will be people from amongst my nation who will appear and will allow desires and innovations to flow through them just as rabies flows through the sick one."

---

[1]-Abu Dawud in his Sunan, Book of the Sunnah, Chapter: Explanation of the Sunnah #4596 with a 'Hasan' good chain of narration.

Al 'I'tibaa'a

In another narration:

وَقَالَ عَمْرٌو «الْكَلْبُ بِصَاحِبِهِ لاَ يَبْقَى مِنْهُ عِرْقٌ وَلاَ مَفْصِلٌ إِلاَّ دَخَلَهُ».

"Just as rabies flows through the sick one, there will not remain a vein, nor joint except that the sickness with enter it."[1]

The previous narration has been transmitted with this meaning from numerous companions. Bukhari narrated on the authority of Abdullah ibn Mas'ud who said:

قَالَ: سَمِعْتُ عَبْدَ اللهِ، يَقُولُ: سَمِعْتُ رَجُلًا قَرَأَ آيَةً، سَمِعْتُ مِنَ النَّبِيِّ صَلَّى اللهُ عَلَيْهِ وَسَلَّمَ خِلَافَهَا، فَأَخَذْتُ بِيَدِهِ، فَأَتَيْتُ بِهِ رَسُولَ اللهِ صَلَّى اللهُ عَلَيْهِ وَسَلَّمَ فَقَالَ: «كِلَاكُمَا مُحْسِنٌ»، قَالَ شُعْبَةُ: أَظُنُّهُ قَالَ: «لاَ تَخْتَلِفُوا، فَإِنَّ مَنْ كَانَ قَبْلَكُمُ اخْتَلَفُوا فَهَلَكُوا»

"I heard a man recite a verse from the Quran, a verse which I heard the Prophet Muhammad ﷺ recite in a different manner. So I took the man by his hand and rushed to see the Prophet Muhammad ﷺ and mentioned what had occurred. I saw in the Prophet's ﷺ face dislike, and he said: "Both of you are good doers, do not differ, for verily those who came before you differed and were destroyed."[2]

Ibn Abee Aasim[3] narrated on the authority of Jabir and Abdullah ibn Mas'ud, and the wording is for Jabir who said:

عَنْ جَابِرِ بْنِ عَبْدِ اللهِ، قَالَ: كُنَّا جُلُوسًا عِنْدَ النَّبِيِّ صَلَّى اللهُ عَلَيْهِ وَسَلَّمَ فَخَطَّ خَطًّا هَكَذَا أَمَامَهُ فَقَالَ: «هَذَا سَبِيلُ اللهِ عَزَّ وَجَلَّ»، وَخَطَّ خَطًّا عَنْ يَمِينِهِ، وَخَطَّ خَطًّا عَنْ شِمَالِهِ، وَقَالَ: «هَذِهِ سُبُلُ الشَّيْطَانِ»، ثُمَّ وَضَعَ يَدَهُ فِي الْخَطِّ

---

[1]-(TN)The 'Jama'ah'(group) mentioned here means the ones who follow the Quran and Sunnah and upon the understanding of the companions of Allah's Messenger. These narrations can be found in Sunan Abee Dawud, Book of the Sunnah, Chapter: Explanation of the Sunnah, which Mu'awiyyah narrated #4597 was graded Hasan by al Albaani.

[2]-Saheeh Bukhari, Book of Quarrels, Chapter: What is mentioned about people, 5/70, #2410, also see al Bukhari #3476 and #5062.

[3]-(TN)He is Abu Bakr Ahmad bin `Amr bin Abee Aasim ad-Dahhaak bin Makhlad ash-Shaybaanee, famously known as ibn Abee Aasim. The Imaam, the Great Haafidh, the one who closely followed the narrations, author of many works and the Faqeeh. From amongst his works was 'Kitaab as-Sunnah' concerning the Attributes of Allaah as were understood by the Salaf. He was born in the year 206H and died in the year 287H.

Al 'I'tibaa'a

الْأَوْسَطِ، ثُمَّ تَلَا هَذِهِ الْآيَةَ ﴿ وَأَنَّ هَذَا صِرَاطِي مُسْتَقِيمًا فَاتَّبِعُوهُ وَلَا تَتَّبِعُوا السُّبُلَ فَتَفَرَّقَ بِكُمْ عَنْ سَبِيلِهِ ذَلِكُمْ وَصَّاكُمْ بِهِ لَعَلَّكُمْ تَتَّقُونَ ﴾

'We were sitting with the Prophet Muhammad ﷺ and he drew a line (like this) in front of him and said: "This is Allah's path", then he drew a line on the right of it and the left of it and said: "These are the Satan's paths". Then the Prophet ﷺ placed his hand on the middle line and read the verse from the Quran: "And verily this is my straight path, so follow it and do not follow the other paths, for they will deter you and lead you astray from His path. This is what you have been recommended with so that you may be pious....." (al An'am 6:153). This is a 'hasan' (good) narration.[1]

Many narrations from the Prophet ﷺ have reached us regarding this topic as well as numerous narrations from the companions, who were the people farthest away from differing. For this reason their methodology in times of differing about any affair or issue would be: 'whatever the authentic text from Allah and His Messenger ﷺ commanded with or prohibited from', while searching for these texts in the Quran and Sunnah. If they found that the Quran and Sunnah had stipulated something for the issue then they would judge according to the Quran and Sunnah and refer to both of them. If it so happened that they didn't find the Quran and Sunnah stipulated something for the issue, then they would consult, seek advice and ask the other companions what they knew or memorized from the Quran or Sunnah regarding the issue. This understanding is made clear by Allah's saying:

﴿ فَسْـَٔلُوٓا۟ أَهْلَ ٱلذِّكْرِ إِن كُنتُمْ لَا تَعْلَمُونَ ۝ ﴾

"So ask the people of reminder if you do not know" (al Anbiyaa'a 21:7)

The companions were one hundred percent sincere in Allah's religion without being bigoted or fanatical about their own opinions nor were they bigoted or fanatical about the opinions of others.

The first instance of differing which occurred between the companions after the death of the Prophet Muhammad ﷺ was the differing of Umar ibn al Khattab regarding the death of the Prophet Muhammad ﷺ. Umar used to swear by Allah saying: "I swear by Allah the Prophet ﷺ did not die!'

---

[1] -'as Sunnah' by Ibn Abee Aasim 1/13, #16-17, also see Tafsir ibn Kathir 2/261-262

Al 'I'tibaa'a

Al Bukhari narrated on the authority of Abdullah ibn Abaas who said:

عَنْ عَبْدِ اللَّهِ بْنِ عَبَّاسٍ، أَنَّ أَبَا بَكْرٍ خَرَجَ وَعُمَرُ بْنُ الْخَطَّابِ يُكَلِّمُ النَّاسَ فَقَالَ: اجْلِسْ يَا عُمَرُ، فَأَبَى عُمَرُ أَنْ يَجْلِسَ، فَأَقْبَلَ النَّاسُ إِلَيْهِ، وَتَرَكُوا عُمَرَ، فَقَالَ أَبُو بَكْرٍ: " أَمَّا بَعْدُ فَمَنْ كَانَ مِنْكُمْ يَعْبُدُ مُحَمَّدًا صَلَّى اللهُ عَلَيْهِ وَسَلَّمَ، فَإِنَّ مُحَمَّدًا قَدْ مَاتَ، وَمَنْ كَانَ مِنْكُمْ يَعْبُدُ اللَّهَ فَإِنَّ اللَّهَ حَيٌّ لاَ يَمُوتُ، قَالَ اللهُ: (وَمَا مُحَمَّدٌ إِلَّا رَسُولٌ قَدْ خَلَتْ مِنْ قَبْلِهِ الرُّسُلُ أَفَإِنْ مَاتَ أَوْ قُتِلَ انْقَلَبْتُمْ عَلَى أَعْقَابِكُمْ وَمَنْ يَنْقَلِبْ عَلَى عَقِبَيْهِ فَلَنْ يَضُرَّ اللَّهَ شَيْئًا وَسَيَجْزِي اللَّهُ الشَّاكِرِينَ) [آل عمران: 144]، وَقَالَ: وَاللَّهِ لَكَأَنَّ النَّاسَ لَمْ يَعْلَمُوا أَنَّ اللَّهَ أَنْزَلَ هَذِهِ الآيَةَ حَتَّى تَلاَهَا أَبُو بَكْرٍ، فَتَلَقَّاهَا مِنْهُ النَّاسُ كُلُّهُمْ، فَمَا أَسْمَعُ بَشَرًا مِنَ النَّاسِ إِلَّا يَتْلُوهَا " فَأَخْبَرَنِي سَعِيدُ بْنُ الْمُسَيِّبِ، أَنَّ عُمَرَ قَالَ: «وَاللَّهِ مَا هُوَ إِلَّا أَنْ سَمِعْتُ أَبَا بَكْرٍ تَلاَهَا فَعَقِرْتُ، حَتَّى مَا تُقِلُّنِي رِجْلاَيَ، وَحَتَّى أَهْوَيْتُ إِلَى الْأَرْضِ حِينَ سَمِعْتُهُ تَلاَهَا، عَلِمْتُ أَنَّ النَّبِيَّ صَلَّى اللهُ عَلَيْهِ وَسَلَّمَ قَدْ مَاتَ»

'Abu Bakr went out and Umar was talking to the people, so Abu Bakr said to him: 'Sit down Umar', but Umar refused to sit down. So the people suddenly gathered around Abu Bakr and left Umar, so Abu Bakr said: 'To proceed: 'Whoever used to worship Muhammad for verily Muhammad has died, and whoever worships Allah, for indeed Allah is Everlasting and does not die, Allah says in the Quran: "And what is Muhammad except a Messenger and indeed many Messengers have passed away before him. If he dies or is killed, will you then turn back on your heels as disbelievers? And he who turns back on his heels, no harm in the least will he do to Allah. And Allah will give reward to those who are grateful" (Ali Imran 3:144). Then the Ibn Abaas said: I swear by Allah, that it was as if the people didn't know that Allah revealed this verse until Abu Bakr recited it, so all of the people learned it from him, until the point that you wouldn't hear any person except that he was reading that verse.

Al 'I'tibaa'a

Muhammad ibn Muslim az Zhuri[1] said: 'Sa'eed ibn Musayyib[2] mentioned that Umar said: *'I swear by Allah that when I heard Abu Bakr reciting that verse, I was devastated and my legs could not support me until I fell down to the ground at the very moment of hearing Abu Bakr recite that verse, and I knew then that the Prophet had died."*[3]

After that some differing occurred between them regarding who would be the successor to the Prophet Muhammad ﷺ, and immediately the differing was resolved and settled by what they possessed of narrations from the Prophet Muhammad ﷺ who said:

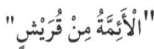

"The leaders are from Quraish"[4]

Ibn al Arabi[5] said: 'The Ansaar gathered together in the house of Bani Saa'idah consulting and advising each other and they could not come up with a solution. The news of this reached the 'Muhajireen' who said: We'll send them a message to come and see us. Abu Bakr as Sideeq replied: rather, we will walk to see them. So the Muhajireen left out to go see the Ansaar, from amongst the Muhajireen were: Abu Bakr, Umar, Abu Ubaidah so they recanted their speech. And some of

---

[1]-**(TN)** Muhammad ibn Muslim ibn Ubaydillah ibn Shihab al-Zuhri is regarded as one of the greatest authorities on hadeeth. He died in the year 124 hijri. The leading critics of hadeeth such as Ali ibn al-Madini, Ibn Hibban, Abu Hatim, adh-Dha'habi and Ibn Hajar al-Asqalaani are all agreed upon his indisputable authority. He received ahadeeeth from many of the companions and numerous scholars among the first and second generations after the Companions narrated from him.

[2]-**(TN)** Saa'eed Ibn Al-Musayyib ibn Hazn ibn Abee Wahb ibn Amru ibn Aa'idth al Qurashi al Makhzoomi, he lived in al Medina and was among the foremost authorities in hadith, 'fiqh' and Quranic interpretation among the Taba'een (generation succeeding the companions). He was born two years after the caliphate of Umar ibn al Khattab and died in the year 93 or 94 hijri.

[3]-Saheeh Bukhari 8/183, Book of Military Expeditions, Chapter: The sickness and death of the Prophet #4454

[4]-**(TN)** Ibnu Abee Shaybah transmitted this narration in his Musanaf #33055, Ibn Abee Aasim in as Sunnah #1120 and Imam Ahmed in his Musnad #'s 12307, 12900, 19777, and al Bukhari transmitted it in his Tarikh al Kabeer 2 ------(1875), 4 (2096), an Nisaa'ee also transmitted it by the way of Shu'bah #5942. The hadeeth is authentic rather 'mutawaatir' as almost forty of the companions narrated this hadeeth. See Fatul Baari 7/32 and at Talkhees al Habeer 4/42.

[5]-**(TN)** He is Muhammad ibn Abdullah ibn Muhammad al Ma'aafaree al Ishbeelee al Maliki, judge and from the memorizers of hadeeth. He was born in Spain in the year 468 hijri and he died in the year 543 hijri.

Al 'I'tibaa'a

the Ansaar said: 'A leader from us and a leader from you. Abu Bakr said many things which were plentiful and faultless, from the things he said: 'We are the commanders and you are the ministers, the Prophet ﷺ said: **"The leaders are from Quraish"**[1]

Then Abu Bakr said: "I advise you to be good with the Ansaar, accept from the good-doers and overlook the evil doers, Allah named us in the Quran as the 'truthful ones', and named you the 'successful ones', and Allah ordered you all to be with us wherever we are, as Allah said:

﴿ يَٰٓأَيُّهَا ٱلَّذِينَ ءَامَنُوا۟ ٱتَّقُوا۟ ٱللَّهَ وَكُونُوا۟ مَعَ ٱلصَّٰدِقِينَ ﴾

"O you who believe! Fear Allah and be with those who are truthful." (at Tawbah 9:119)".

Abu Bakr also made many other faultless statements and produced strong evidences. The Ansaar were reminded complied to this, then they all took the pledge of allegiance to Abu Bakr."[2]

After that some differing took place regarding the place where the Prophet ﷺ should be buried, and this was immediately resolved with the narration of the Prophet Muhammad ﷺ regarding the issue.

---

[1] -**(TN)** Ibnu Abee Shaybah transmitted this narration in his Musanaf #33055, Ibn Abee Aasim in as Sunnah #1120 and Imam Ahmed in his Musnad #'s 12307, 12900, 19777, and al Bukhari transmitted it in his Tarikh al Kabeer 2 (1875), 4 (2096), an Nisaa'ee also transmitted it by the way of Shu'bah #5942. The hadeeth is authentic rather 'mutawaatir' as almost forty of the companions narrated this hadeeth. See Fatul Baari 7/32 and at Talkhees al Habeer 4/42.

[2] -al Awaasim min al Qawaasim pg. 45. Sheikh Wasiullah says: 'I didn't find this story with the same wording, as for the hadeeth "The leaders are from Quraish" , then this is an authentic well known narration, rather 'mutawatir', al Bukhari narrated it with its meaning from the words of Abu Bakr, on the authority of Abdullah ibn Abaas. Abu Bakr said to the Ansaar: **"All the good which you have mentioned, you deserve, but this command is only for the people of Quraish. They are from the best of the Arabs in their abode and lineage. I am pleased for you that you that you take one of these two men and give allegiance to whomever of them you wish. "He took the hand of Umar ibn al Khattab and the hand of Abu Ubaydah ibn al Jarrah who was sitting with us....etc...**(Saheeh Bukhari) 12/174, The Book of Punishments, Chapter: Stoning of the pregnant woman who commited fornication #6830

Al 'I'tibaa'a

As at-Tirmidthi narrated on the authority of Aa'isha who said:

عَنْ عَائِشَةَ، قَالَتْ: لمَّا قُبِضَ رَسُولُ الله صَلَّى الله عَلَيْهِ وَسَلَّمَ اخْتَلَفُوا في دَفْنِهِ، فَقَالَ أَبُو بَكْرٍ: سَمِعْتُ مِنْ رَسُولِ الله صَلَّى اللهُ عَلَيْهِ وَسَلَّمَ شَيْئًا مَا نَسِيتُهُ، قَالَ: "مَا قَبَضَ اللهُ نَبِيًّا إلاَّ في المَوْضِعِ الَّذِي يُحِبُّ أَنْ يُدْفَنَ فيهِ، ادْفِنُوهُ في مَوْضِعِ فِرَاشِهِ."

'When the Prophet ﷺ passed away, they differed regarding his burial, so Abu Bakr said: I heard the Messenger of Allah ﷺ say and I didn't forget it, he said: **"Allah never took the life of a Prophet except in the place in which he loves to be buried in," so bury him in the place of his bed."**

At Tirmidthi said: 'This narration is 'ghareeb' (scarce), and Abdurahman ibn Abee Bakr al Mulaykee is weak in his memorization.

This narration has also been transmitted with other chains of narration, Ibn Abaas narrated it on the authority of Abu Bakr from the Prophet ﷺ also.[1]

A short time after that some differing took place between Ali ibn Abee Talib, Abaas and Fatimah and between Abu Bakr after he became the successor, so once again the differing was resolved with the narrations of the Prophet Muhammad ﷺ.

Al Bukhari narrated: "On the authority of Urwah ibn az Zubayr who said that Aa'isha told him that after the death of the Prophet Muhammad ﷺ, Fatimah- the daughter of the Prophet Muhammad ﷺ - asked Abu Bakr as Siqeeq to give her, her share of inheritance from what The Prophet Muhammad ﷺ had left of the 'fay'-the war booty gained without fighting-which Allah had given him. Abu Bakr replied to her saying:

فَقَالَ لَهَا أَبُو بَكْرٍ: إِنَّ رَسُولَ اللهِ صَلَّى اللهُ عَلَيْهِ وَسَلَّمَ قَالَ: «لَا نُورَثُ، مَا تَرَكْنَا صَدَقَةٌ»

'Allah's Messenger ﷺ said: "Our property is not inherited, whatever we (prophets) leave behind is to be used for charity."

---

[1] -Jami at Tirmidthi pg.242, Book of Funeral Prayers, Chapter: What came concerning the burial of the Prophet Muhammad when he passed away, #1018 and al Albaani said it is Saheeh. This narration also has many other authentic chains of narration which Sheikh al Albaani mentioned in 'Ahkaam al Janaa'iz' pg. 137

So upon hearing this Fatimah became upset and angry and stopped speaking to Abu Bakr and continued upon this until she died. Fatimah lived six months after the death of Allah's Messenger ﷺ. Aa'isha said: Fatimah used to ask Abu Bakr for her share from the property of Allah's Messenger ﷺ which he left at Khaibar and Fadak, and his property in al Madinah. But Abu Bakr refused to give her anything and said: 'I am not one who will abandon anything that Allah's Messenger ﷺ used to do, I will do exactly as he ﷺ did. For verily I'm afraid that if I abandon anything from the Prophet's ﷺ affairs (Sunnah) that I will indeed go astray. As for the Prophet's ﷺ property in al Madinah than Umar gave it to Ali and Abaas, but he withheld the properties of Khaibar and Fadak in his custody and said: 'These two properties are what the Prophet ﷺ used to use for his expenditures and urgent needs. Now their management is to be entrusted to the ruler." Az Zuhri said: 'They have been managed in this way up until today'.' Then the mention of Ali and Abaas regarding this affair was transmitted.'[1]

The examples of these situations, occurrences, new issues, and calamities- in which the companions differed are many. However, the companions used to look closely, analyze, ask and search for the proofs and evidences from the Quran and the Sunnah to resolve them. If they came across a proof then the differing was resolved immediately. Certainly, the companions truly believed and implemented, Allah's statement:

﴿ فَإِن تَنَٰزَعۡتُمۡ فِى شَىۡءٍ فَرُدُّوهُ إِلَى ٱللَّهِ وَٱلرَّسُولِ ﴾

"And if you differ in anything amongst yourselves, than refer it back to Allah and His Messenger" (an Nisa 4:59)

Many occurrences have proved that if one of them could not recall or did not remember the proofs and evidences for a specific matter then he would remain silent, and he would ask other companions. This methodology is what the 'tabi'oon' (the predecessors of the companions) and those who follow their example in goodness, tread upon and this will remain until the Day of Resurrection.

Ibnul Qayyim said: "When the techniques of learning and acquiring the religion from the Prophet Muhammad ﷺ were of two types: indirectly and directly. The companions were fortunate because they learned and acquired their religion

---

[1]-Saheeh Bukhari 6/241-243, Book, Chapter: One fifth of the war booty, #3092-3094

Al 'I'tibaa'a

from the Prophet ﷺ directly and they were the forerunners and achieved the best, and the companions seized and captured the time and opportunity. Then the companions taught the 'tabi'oon' everything they learned from the lantern of prophethood-pure and unaltered. Their source and chain of narration was from the Prophet from the angel Jibreel from the Lord of all of creation, an authentic and lofty chain of narration with few narrators. The companions said to their students: This is the covenant of our Prophet ﷺ for us, and verily we have entrusted you with it, and this is the legacy of our Lord, and His obligation upon us, and it is His recommendation and obligation for you all. So the 'tabi'oon' (the righteous successors of the companions) tread upon the companions true methodology, and they imitated and followed the footsteps upon the straight path.

Then after them came the 'tabi tabi'oon' (the tabi'oon's successors) who tread on this very same path of guidance, as Allah says:

$$\textoverset{ }{ \text{﴿ وَهُدُوٓا۟ إِلَى ٱلطَّيِّبِ مِنَ ٱلْقَوْلِ وَهُدُوٓا۟ إِلَىٰ صِرَٰطِ ٱلْحَمِيدِ ﴾} }$$

"And they are guided in this world unto good speech and they are guided to Allah's path (Islamic Monotheism) which is most praiseworthy." (al Hajj 22:24)

The 'tabi'oon and those who proceeded them were compared with those who came before them as Allah the Most Truthful said:

$$\text{﴿ ثُلَّةٌ مِّنَ ٱلْأَوَّلِينَ ۝ وَقَلِيلٌ مِّنَ ٱلْآخِرِينَ ﴾}$$

"A multitude of those will be from the previous generations-and a few of those will be from the later generations." (al Waqi'ah 56:13-14)[1]

So the generation of the companions, the 'tabi'oon', the 'tabi tabi'oon', and the 'fiqh' scholars remained upon this methodology and they adhered to and remained firm upon this methodology in their manner of learning 'fiqh'. They would never be compelled or forced to use personal views nor 'qiyas' nor 'ijtihaad' except if they lacked or didn't possess any proof or evidence and they were incapable of searching for the proof.

---

[1]-I'laam al Muwaqa'een 1/6

Al 'I'tibaa'a

Ibnul Qayyim mentioned after his previous statement: 'Then the scholars of the fourth generation came onto the scene, as it has been mentioned in an authentic narration which Abee Sa'eed al Khudri, Abdullah ibn Mas'ud, Abu Hurairah, Aa'isha, and Imran ibn Husayin mentioned.[1] So these fourth generation scholars treaded upon the companion's and tabi'een's path as narrators who learned and acquired their light and knowledge from the lantern of the earlier predecessors. Verily, the religion of Allah was the most exalted and noble thing within their hearts and essence. To the point where it should never be imagined that they would give priority to their own opinions, logic, desire to be personal imitated, or 'qiyas'. So they became famous and renowned with praise throughout the world, and Allah made their statements truthful amongst the later generations.

The students of the fourth generation scholars treaded upon their path, and the successful ones from their followers adopted their practices and methodologies also, being indifferent and never became bigoted to any men, always standing with the proofs and evidences. They moved with the truth wherever it went, and they were independent with that which was correct wherever it went. If the proofs and evidences become apparent to him, he would grasp it with the snare and act hastily to take possession of it-individually and collectively. The authentic texts from the Quran and the Sunnah were the most exalted and glorified things within their hearts and essences. The Quran and Sunnah where so glorified to them that they would never give priority to a saying from the people, or let their personal opinions or 'qiyas' contradict or conflict with the Quran and Sunnah.[2]

I say: this is the situation during the era of the Prophet Muhammad ﷺ, the companions and those who strictly and completely emulated them. They never were bigoted or gave preference to anyone's saying regardless of his status. Rather, if they came across someone's statement and it was contrary to the proofs and evidences, they would reject it and refute it with wisdom and the best of manners. Certainly, all wisdom is in mentioning the texts from the Quran and the Sunnah when refuting. The religion of Allah was the greatest thing

---

[1]-**(TN)** Ibnul Qayyim is referring to the narration in which the Prophet Muhammad ﷺ: **"The best of generations is my generation (companions) then the generation which proceeds it (tabi'een), then the generation which proceeds that generation (atbaa at Tabi'een)..."** which Bukhari, Muslim and others transmitted with authentic chains of narration. Bukhari see #2652, 3651, 6429, and Muslim #2533 on the authority of Ibn Mas'ud; Saheeh Muslim #2534 from Abu Hurairah; Saheeh Bukhari # 2897, 3594, 3649, and Muslim #2532 on the authority of Abee Sa'eed al Khudri; Saheeh Bukhari# 2651, 3650, 6428, 6695 on the authority of Imran ibn Husein; Saheeh Muslim #2536 on the authority of Ai'isha

[2]-I'laam al Muwaqa'een 2/9-10

within their hearts, more magnificent than any great, noble, and venerable person.

Even to the extent that some of them may have disagreed with the ruler or leader when they found the leader's saying or action contrary to the Sunnah, and the leader's prestige and veneration did not affect them to the least, nor were they worried about the criticism of the critics. Imam Bukhari narrated on the authority of Abu ash Sha'thaa'a that he said:

عَنْ أَبِي الشَّعْثَاءِ أَنَّهُ قَالَ: «وَمَنْ يَتَّقِي شَيْئًا مِنَ الْبَيْتِ؟» وَكَانَ مُعَاوِيَةُ يَسْتَلِمُ الأَرْكَانَ، فَقَالَ لَهُ ابْنُ عَبَّاسٍ رَضِيَ اللهُ عَنْهُمَا: إِنَّهُ لَا يُسْتَلَمُ هَذَانِ الرُّكْنَانِ، فَقَالَ: «لَيْسَ شَيْءٌ مِنَ الْبَيْتِ مَهْجُورًا» وَكَانَ ابْنُ الزُّبَيْرِ رَضِيَ اللهُ عَنْهُمَا «يَسْتَلِمُهُنَّ كُلَّهُنَّ»

'Who is weary or cautious about touching the Ka'bah?". Mu'awiyyah used to touch all four corners of the Ka'bah, so Ibn Abbaas said to him: 'These two corners should not be touched'. Mu'awiyyah replied: 'None of the Ka'bah should be neglected.' Also Ibn az Zubayr used to touch all the corners of the Ka'bah.'"[1]

Imam Ahmed narrated in his 'Musnad' and at Tirmidthi in his 'Sunan':

حَدَّثَنِي أَبُو الطُّفَيْلِ، أَنَّهُ رَأَى مُعَاوِيَةَ رَضِيَ اللهُ عَنْهُ يَطُوفُ بِالْكَعْبَةِ وَعَنْ يَسَارِهِ عَبْدُ اللهِ بْنُ عَبَّاسٍ وَأَنَا أَتْلُوهُمَا فِي ظُهُورِهِمَا أَسْمَعُ كَلَامَهُمَا، فَطَفِقَ مُعَاوِيَةُ يَسْتَلِمُ رُكْنَيِ الْحِجْرِ فَيَقُولُ لَهُ ابْنُ عَبَّاسٍ: " إِنَّ رَسُولَ اللهِ صَلَّى اللهُ عَلَيْهِ وَسَلَّمَ لَمْ يَكُنْ يَسْتَلِمُ هَذَيْنِ الرُّكْنَيْنِ " فَيَقُولُ مُعَاوِيَةُ: يَا ابْنَ عَبَّاسٍ، فَإِنَّهُ لَيْسَ شَيْءٌ مِنْهَا مَهْجُورًا "

On the authority of Abee at Tufail that he saw Mu'awiyyah going around the Ka'bah and on his left side was Abdullah Ibn Abaas and I was trailing behind them, listening to their conversation when Mu'awiyyah began to touch the two corners of the 'Hijr'[2], so Ibn Abaas said to him: 'Verily the Messenger of Allah ﷺ did not touch those two corners', so Mu'awiyyah replied: 'O Ibn Abaas there is nothing from the Ka'bah which should be neglected.'"[3]

---

[1] -Saheeh Bukhari 3/603, Book of Hajj, Chapter: Whoever doesn't touch anything except the two Yemeni corners #1608

[2] -(TN) Hijr Ismaa'eel

[3] -Musnad Imam Ahmed 1/372,# 6384 and Jami/Sunan at Tirmidthi 3/213. The chain of narration is authentic

Also Imam Ahmed and at Tirmidthi narrated a similar narration in which the wording in it is:

فَقَالَ ابْنُ عَبَّاسٍ رَضِيَ اللهُ عَنْهُمَا: ﴿لَقَدْ كَانَ لَكُمْ فِي رَسُولِ اللهِ أُسْوَةٌ حَسَنَةٌ﴾ " قَالَ: صَدَقْتَ "

'Ibn Abaas said to Mu'awiyyah, Allah's statement: *"Verily you have a fine example within the Messenger of Allah"* (al Ahzab 33:21) *and Mu'awiyyah replied: 'You are correct'*.[1] Also Imam Ahmed narrated with a 'hasan'(good) chain of narration

عَنْ أَبِي الطُّفَيْلِ قَالَ رَأَيْتُ مُعَاوِيَةَ يَطُوفُ بِالْبَيْتِ عَنْ يَسَارِهِ عَبْدُ اللهِ بْنُ عَبَّاسٍ وَأَنَا أَتْلُوهُمَا فِي ظُهُورِهِمَا أَسْمَعُ كَلَامَهُمَا فَطَفِقَ مُعَاوِيَةُ يَسْتَلِمُ رُكْنَ الحِجَرَ فَقَالَ لَهُ ابْنُ عَبَّاسٍ إِنَّ رَسُولَ اللهِ صَلَّى اللهُ عَلَيْهِ وَسَلَّمَ لَمْ يَسْتَلِمْ هَذَيْنِ الرُّكْنَيْنِ فَيَقُولُ مُعَاوِيَةُ دَعْنِي مِنْكَ يَا ابْنَ عَبَّاسٍ فَإِنَّهُ لَيْسَ مِنْهَا شَيْءٌ مَهْجُورٌ فَطَفِقَ ابْنُ عَبَّاسٍ لَا يَزِيدُهُ كُلَّمَا وَضَعَ يَدَهُ عَلَى شَيْءٍ مِنَ الرُّكْنَيْنِ قَالَ لَهُ ذَلِكَ "

On the authority of Abee at Tufail who said: 'I saw Mu'awiyyah going around the Ka'bah and on his left side was Abdullah ibn Abaas and I was trailing behind them, listening to their conversation. Then Mu'awiyyah began to touch the corner of the 'Hijr', then Ibn Abaas said to him: Verily the Messenger of Allah ﷺ did not touch those two corners. Mu'awiyyah replied: 'leave me alone O Ibn Abaas, for verily there is nothing from the Ka'bah which should be neglected. So Ibn Abaas would repeat this to Mu'awiyyah every time he touched those two corners of the Ka'bah.'[2]

In closing, it is clear that the 'fatwa'(legal opinions) of the companions and the tabi'een were based upon evidences from the Quran and the Sunnah. So they laid down the precepts and foundations of knowledge and 'fatwa' based upon the Quran and Sunnah. It wasn't known amongst the companions to ascribe themselves to another person of knowledge or school of 'fiqh', nor did they ascribe themselves to a particular 'madth'hab' while feuding with and opposing their opponents, while firmly supporting and patronizing their allies.

---

[1]-This wording is from 'Sharh Ma'aani al Athaar' by at Tahaawee # 3854, Musnad Imam Ahmed 1/217, and Sunan at Tirmidthi 3/213. The chain of narration is authentic
[2]-Musnad Imam Ahmed 1/246 #2210

Al 'I'tibaa'a

Part Nine

The changing of affairs after the best of generations[1]

The previous section explained the condition of the Muslims within the first generation. These conditions continued up until it reached a stage where the people started following and adhering to sayings of other individuals which held no evidential or legislative significance. The people made it obligatory and incumbent upon the other Muslims to strictly follow and adhere to the sayings of Imam's and prohibited them from abandoning any of their statements. Furthermore, whoever said: 'I do not specifically follow a particular 'fiqh' scholar and I follow all of the scholars in whatever they say as long as it is in agreement and coincides with the evidences and proofs' (Quran and Sunnah), then this is considered as a defect and shortcoming in that person's Islam. Then this person is labeled as someone who doesn't follow a madthaab and he is described as being a fool, charlatan, bigoted, silly, and misguided, or he is working for the colonizers or government and a hidden hand is behind his actions.'[2]

Certainly, the 'tabi'oon' and their successors from the four scholars of 'fiqh' and others were upon what the companions were upon regarding following the proofs, while they were known to be from 'Ahlul Hadeeth' (people of hadeeth). For verily four Imam's had all prohibited their students from being bigoted to anyone and did not allow any of their students to follow or imitate anyone in specific.

These great Imams never ordered anyone to blindly follow them or to be bigoted to their statements or actions! Indeed the four Imams were the ones who lived and implemented the Quran and the Sunnah in their lives. This made it easy for

---

[1]-(TN)**First Three Generation.** A generation (قرن) in Arabic has various meanings: It can mean a group of people existing in one era who are gathered together upon a certain affair, religion, action, 'madth'hab'. Also it can mean a period of time, this is something which the scholars have differed in regarding how much time is considered as a generation. The opinions regarding this issue are many the most famous of these statements is that a generation is one-hundred years. Some scholars mentioned the first generation is considered to be from the time of the Prophet Muhammad's prophethood until the death of the last companion, who was Abu Tufail who lived between 110-120 years. So the first generation ended at the time of the last companions death, the second generation ended at the time of the last 'tabi'oon's death, and the third generation ended at the last 'tabi tabi'oon's death. This is what Sheikh Wasiullah views to be correct and Allah knows best. See 'Fathul Baari' vol. 7/9 Dar as Salam for further details

[2]-see 'Bidah at Ta'asub al Madth'habee' by Eid al Abaasee pg.8-9

Al 'I'tibaa'a

them to sincerely follow the Quran and Sunnah and made it easy for the Quran and Sunnah to mix and unify with their bones and blood. They were constantly acting upon the Quran and Sunnah and implementing it in all their worldly affairs, may Allah have mercy upon all of them.

Verily the great scholar Muhammad Naasirud Deen al Albaani mentioned the sayings of the four scholars of 'fiqh' from their main sources and their references, I will mention them here.

The first of them is Abu Haneefah Nu'maan ibn Thaabit[1], whose companions and students have narrated various statements from him with different wordings, all of them leading to one conclusion: the obligation to accept the hadeeth, and to give up following the opinions of the Imaams which contradict it:

He said:

(إِذَا صَحَّ الحَدِيثُ فَهُوَ مَذْهَبِي)

1. "When a hadeeth is found to be saheeh, then that is my madhhab."[2]

He also said:

(لاَ يَحِلُّ لِأَحَدٍ أَنْ يَأْخُذَ بِقَوْلِنَا مَا لَمْ يَعْلَمْ مِنْ أَيْنَ أَخَذْنَاهُ)

2. "It is not permissible for anyone to accept our views if they do not know from where we took them from."[3]

---

[1]-(TN)He is Nu'maan ibn Thaabit at Taymee al Koofee, the jurist of Iraq and the imam of the people of opinions. He was born in the year 80 hijri and grew up in al Koofa (Iraq). He is considered to be from the 'tabi tabi'een' and others have said he is from the 'tabi'een and he met some of the companions of Allah's messenger. One of his famous compilations is 'al Fiqh al Akbar' which is a book of aqeedah. He died in the year 150.

[2]-Hashiyatu ibn Aabideen 1/63, and in his letter 'Rasam al Mufti' 1/4 from the collection of Ibn Aabideen's letters, and Sheikh Salih al Fulaani in 'Eeqaath al himam pg. 62, and others.

[3]-Ibn Abdul Barr in 'al Intiqaa'a' pg. 145, and Ibnul Qayyim in 'I'laam al Muwa'qaeen 2/309, also Ibn Aabideen in his 'Commentary on al Bahr ar Raa'iq' 6/293 and in 'Rasam al Mufti pg.29-32. Also as Shi'raani in 'al Meezan' with an second and third chain of narration, which Abaas ad Dooree narrated in 'at Tarikh' by Ibn Ma'een 6/77/1 with an authentic chain of narration on the authority of Zufr, and similar to this narration was transmitted by Zufr, Abu Yusuf and Aafiyatu ibn Yazeed as was mentioned in 'Eeqath' pg. 52. And Ibnul Qayyim declared the authenticity of the narration from Abu Yusuf 2/244

Al 'I'tibaa'a

(حَرَامٌ عَلَى مَنْ لَمْ يَعْرِفْ دَلِيلِي أَنْ يُفْتِيَ بِكَلَامِي)

In one narration, "It is prohibited for someone who does not know my evidence to give verdicts on the basis of my words."

زاد في رواية: (فَإِنَّنَا بَشَرٌ نَقُولُ القَوْلَ اليَوْمَ وَنَرْجِعُ عَنْهُ غَدًا)

Another narration adds, "... for verily we are mortals: we say something today, and take it back the tomorrow."

He also said:

(وَيْحَكَ يَا يَعْقُوبُ (هو أبو يوسف) لَا تَكْتُبْ كُلَّ مَا تَسْمَعُ مِنِّي فَإِنِّي قَدْ أَرَى الرَّأْيَ اليَوْمَ وَأَتْرُكُهُ غَدًا و أَرَى الرَّأْيَ غَدًا وَأَتْرُكُهُ بَعْدَ غَدٍ)

In another narration, "Woe to you, O Ya'qub! Do not write down everything you hear from me, for verily it could so happen that I hold one opinion today and leave it off tomorrow, or hold one opinion tomorrow and leave it the day after tomorrow."

He also said:

(إِذَا قُلْتُ قَوْلاً يُخَالِفُ كِتَابَ اللهِ تَعَالَى وَخَبَرَ الرَّسُولِ صَلَّى اللهُ عَلَيْهِ وَسَلَّمَ فَاتْرُكُوا قَوْلِي)

3. "If I say something contradicting the Book of Allaah or a narration from the Messenger ﷺ then ignore my saying."[1]

The second great scholar of 'fiqh' is Imaam Maalik ibn Anas[2], who said:

(إِنَّمَا أَنَا بَشَرٌ أُخْطِئُ وَأُصِيبُ فَانْظُرُوا فِي رَأْيِي فَكُلُّ مَا وَافَقَ الكِتَابَ وَالسُّنَّةَ فَخُذُوهُ وَكُلُّ مَا لَمْ يُوَافِقْ الكِتَابَ وَالسُّنَّةَ فَاتْرُكُوهُ)

1. "Truly I am only a mortal: I make mistakes (sometimes) and I am correct (sometimes). Therefore, look into my opinions: all that agrees with the Book and

---

[1] -Salih al Fulaani in 'Eeqath al himam' pg. 50, and attributed this statement to Imam Muhammad also.

[2] -(TN) He is Malik ibn Anas ibn Abee Aamir ibnul Harith al Asbahee al Humayree Abu Abdullah al Madani, he was born in the year 93 hijri, he was the Imam of al Madinah in his time. He authored his famous book 'al Muwa'taa'a' which contains his narrations of hadeeth, views and juristic opinions. He died 179 hijri.

the Sunnah, accept it; and all that does not agree with the Book and the Sunnah, ignore it."[1]

He also said:

(لَيْسَ أَحَدٌ بَعْدَ النَّبِي صَلَّى اللهُ عَلَيْهِ وَسَلَّمَ إِلَّا وَ يُؤْخَذُ مِنْ قَوْلِهِ وَيُتْرَكُ إِلَّا النَّبِيُّ صلى الله عليه وسلم)

2. "There is no one after the Prophet Muhammad ﷺ except that his sayings are accepted and rejected –with the exception of the Prophet Muhammad ﷺ."[2]

He also said:

قَالَ ابْنُ وَهْبٍ: سَمِعْتُ مَالِكًا سُئِلَ عَنْ تَخْلِيلِ أَصَابِعِ الرِّجْلَيْنِ فِي الوُضُوءِ فَقَالَ: لَيْسَ ذَلِكَ عَلَى النَّاسِ. قَالَ: فَتَرَكْتُهُ حَتَّى خَفَّ النَّاسُ فَقُلْتُ لَهُ: عِنْدَنَا فِي ذَلِكَ سُنَّةٌ فقال: وما هي قُلْتُ: حَدَّثَنَا اللَّيْثُ بْنُ سَعْدٍ و ابنُ لَهِيعَةَ وعَمْرُو بْنُ الحَارِثِ عَنْ يَزِيدَ بْنِ عَمْرُو المَعَافِرِي عَنْ أَبِي عَبْدِ الرَّحْمَنَ الحُبُلِيُّ عَنِ المَسْتَوْرَدَ بْنُ شَدَّادٍ القُرَشِي قال: رَأَيْتُ رسولَ الله صلى الله عليه وسلم يدْلِك بِخِنْصَرِه ما بَيْنَ أَصَابِعِ رِجْلَيْهِ. فقال: إنَّ هذا الحديثَ حَسَنٌ وما سَمِعْتُ به قَطُّ إلَّا السَّاعَةَ ثُمَّ سَمِعْتُهُ بَعْدَ ذلك يُسْأَلُ فَيَأْمُرُ بِتَخْلِيلِ الأَصَابِعِ"

3. Ibn Wahb said: "I heard Maalik being asked about cleaning between the toes during ablution. He said, 'The people do not have to do that.' So I left him until the crowd had lessened, then I said to him, 'We know of a Sunnah about that.' He said, 'What is it?' I said, 'Laith ibn Sa'd, Ibn Lahee'ah and 'Amr ibn al-Haarith narrated to us from Yazeed ibn 'Amr al-Ma'aafiri from Abu 'Abdur-Rahman al-Hubuli from Mustawrid ibn Shaddaad al-Qurashi who said, '**I saw the Messenger of Allah ﷺ rubbing between his toes with his little finger.**' Malik replied:'This hadeeth is good; I have not heard of it at all up until now.' Afterwards, I heard

---

[1]-Ibn Abdul Barr in 'al Jami' 2/32 and on the authority of Ibn Abdul Barr, Ibn Hazm in 'Usool al Ahkam' 6/149, also al Fulaani pg.72

[2]-This statement has been attributed to Imam Malik amongst the later scholars, and Ibn Abdul Haadi authenticated it in 'Irshaad as Saalik' 1/277, Ibn Abdul Barr narrated it in 'al Jami' 2/91 and Ibn Hazm in 'Usool al Ahkam' 6/145-179 from the statement of al Hakam ibn Utaybah and Mujahid, also Taqi ad Deen as Subkee in his 'Fataawa' 1/148 from the statement of Ibn Abaas praising its goodness, then he said:' Mujahid took this statement from Ibn Abaas and Malik took it from both of them and it became famous from Malik. Sheikh Wasiullah said: 'then Imam Ahmed took the statement from them, indeed Abu Dawud said in his 'Masaa'il al Imam Ahmed',pg.276: 'I heard Ahmed say: There is no one except that his opinions are accepted and rejected, except for the Prophet Muhammad.'

Al 'I'tibaa'a

him being asked about the same thing, on which he ordered with the cleaning between the toes."[1]

As for the third noble scholar of 'fiqh' for he is Imaam ash Shaafi'ee[2], the quotations from him are numerous and beautiful, and his followers were the best in adhering and following his sayings: He said:

(مَا مِنْ أَحَدٍ إِلَّا وتَذْهَبُ عَلَيهِ سُنَّةٌ لِرَسُولِ اللهِ صلى الله عليه وسلم وتَعْزِبُ عَنْهُ فَمَهْمَا قُلْتُ مِنْ قَولٍ أَوْ أَصَّلْتُ مِنْ أَصْلٍ فِيهِ عَنْ رسولِ اللهِ صلى الله عليه وسلم خِلافٌ ما قُلْتُ فَالقَوْلُ ما قَالَ رسولُ اللهِ صلى الله عليه وسلم وهو قَوْلِي)

1."There doesn't exist anyone except that some of the narrations of the Messenger of Allah don't reach him, or one is oblivious to some of them. So whenever I voice my opinion, make a statement, or formulate a principle; whenever something contrary to my saying exists on the authority of the Messenger of Allaah then the correct saying is what the Messenger of Allah has said, and whatever the Messenger of Allah has said is my saying."[3]

He also said:

(أَجْمَعَ المُسْلِمُونَ عَلَى أَنْ مَنْ اسْتَبَانَ لَهُ سُنَّةٌ عَنْ رَسولِ اللهِ صلى الله عليه وسلم لَمْ يَحِلّ لَهُ أَنْ يَدَعَهَا لِقَوْلِ أَحَدٍ)

---

[1]-'Introduction of al Jarh wa Ta'deel' by Ibn Abee Haatim pgs.31-32 and al Bayhaqi narrated it in full in his 'Sunan' 1/76

[2]-(TN)He is Abu Abdullah Muhammad ibn Idrees ibnul Abbaas ibn Uthmaan ibn Haashim ibn Abdul Muttalib al Qurashi al Mattalibi. The great Imam and example for the Muslims, he was born in Gaza (Philistine) 150 hijri and was carried to Makkah when he was two years old. He used to give religious verdicts when he was 15 years old, and it is said that he memorized 'al Muwa'taa'a' of Imam Malik when he was ten years old. He studied under Imam Malik and also the students of Abu Haneefah. He learned hadeeth and the knowledge of hadeeth from Imam Malik ibn Anas and Sufyaan ibn Uyaynah in al Madinah. Then he traveled to Iraq and learned 'fiqh' from Muhammad ibnul Hasan, the student of Abu Haneefah. He benefited from the two schools of thought 'People of Hadeeth' and the 'People of opinions' and this is one of the factors which made him one of the outstanding Imam's. Imam Ahmed ibn Hanbal is one of his students. He authored many compilations and books, which the most famous of them are 'ar Risalah' and 'al Umm' which contain many of his 'fiqh' principles and opinions. He died in the year 204 hijri.

[3]-al Haakim narrated it with a connected chain to Imam ash Shaafi'ee as it came in 'Tarikh Damascus' by Ibn Asaakir 15/1/3, also 'I'laam al Muwa'qaeen' 2/363-364 and 'Eeqath' pg.100

2. "The Muslims are unanimously agreed that if a Sunnah of the Messenger of Allaah ﷺ is made clear to someone, then it is not permissible for him to leave it for the statement of anyone else."[1]

He also said:

(إِذَا وَجَدْتُم فِي كِتَابِي خِلَافَ سُنَّةِ رَسُولِ اللهِ صلى الله عليه وسلم فَقُولُوا بِسُنَّةِ رَسُولِ اللهِ صلى الله عليه وسلم وَدَعُوا مَا قُلْتُ)

3. "If you find in my book something contrary to the Sunnah of the Messenger of Allaah ﷺ, then mention the Sunnah of the Messenger of Allaah ﷺ and leave what I have said."

(وفي رواية (فَاتَّبِعُوهَا وَلَا تَلْتَفِتُوا إِلَى قَوْلِ أَحَدٍ)

In another narration: "... then follow it (the Sunnah), and do not turn your head to anyone else's statement."[2]

He also said:

(إِذَا صَحَّ الحَدِيثُ فَهُوَ مَذْهَبِي)

4. "When a hadeeth is found to be authentic, then that is my 'madth'hab."[3]

He also said:

(أَنْتُم أَعْلَمُ بِالحَدِيثِ وَالرِّجَالِ مِنِّي فَإِذَا كَانَ الحَدِيثُ الصَّحِيحُ فَأَعْلَمُونِي بِهِ أَيُّ شَيْءٍ يَكُونُ: كُوفِيًّا أَوْ بَصْرِيًّا أَوْ شَامِيًّا حَتَّى أَذْهَبَ إِلَيْهِ إِذَا كَانَ صَحِيحًا)

---

[1] -Ibnul Qayyim 2/361 and Al Fulaani pg.68

[2] -al Harwee in 'Dhem al Kalam' 3/47/1 and al Khateeb in 'al Ihtijaaj bish Shafi'ee 2/8, Ibn Asaakir 15/9/1, an Nawawi in 'al Majmoo' 1/63, Ibnul Qayyim 2/361, al Fulaani pg.100, and another narration for Abee Nu'aym in 'al Hilyah 9/107, and Ibn Hibbaan in his 'Saheeh' 3/284 with an authentic chain from him.

[3] -an Nawawi in al Majmoo' and ash Shi'raani 1/57 and referred it to al Haakim and al Bayhaqi, al Fulaani pg.107, and ash Shi'raani said: 'Ibn Hazm said: i.e.-it is authentic in his view and other scholars views

5. "You[1] are more knowledgeable about Hadeeth and the narrators then me, so when a hadeeth is authentic, inform me of it, whether it is from Kufah, Basrah or Syria, so that I may take the view of the hadeeth, as long as it is saheeh."

He also said:

(كُلُّ مَسْأَلَةٍ صَحَّ فِيهَا الخَبَرُ عَنْ رَسُولِ اللهِ صلى الله عليه وسلم عِنْدَ أَهْلِ النَّقْلِ بِخِلَافِ مَا قُلْتُ فَإِنَّا رَاجِعٌ عَنْهَا فِي حَيَاتِي وَبَعْدَ مَوْتِي)

6. "Every issue in which there is an authentic narration from the Messenger of Allaah ﷺ amongst the people of hadeeth, which is contrary to what I have said, then I take my saying back, whether during my life or after my death."[2]

(إِذَا رَأَيْتُمُونِي أَقُولُ قَوْلًا وَقَدْ صَحَّ عَنِ النَّبِيِّ صلى الله عليه وسلم خِلَافُهُ فَاعْلَمُوا أَنَّ عَقْلِي قَدْ ذَهَبَ)

7. "If you see me saying something, and contrary to it is something authentically reported from the Prophet ﷺ then know that I have lost my intellect."[3]

He also said:

(كُلُّ مَا قُلْتُ فَكَانَ عَنِ النَّبِي صلى الله عليه وسلم خِلَافُ قَوْلِي مِمَّا يَصِحُّ فَحَدِيثُ النَّبِي أَوْلَى فَلَا تُقَلِّدُونِي)

8. "For everything I say, if there is something authentic from the Prophet ﷺ contrary to my saying, then the hadeeth of the Prophet ﷺ is given precedence, so do not imitate or blind follow me."[1]

---

[1]-This is directed towards al Imam Ahmed ibn Hanbal, Ibn Abee Haatim mentioned it in 'Adaab ash Shafi'ee pg.94-95, Abu Nu'aym in al Hilyah 9/106, al Khateeb in 'al Ihtijaaj bish Shafi'ee'1/8 and from him Ibn Asaakir 15/9/1 and Ibn Abdul Barr in 'al Intiqaa'a' pg.75, Ibn Jawzee in 'Manaqib al Imam Ahmed' pg.499 and al Harwee 2/47/2 from three different chains of narration on the authority of Abdullah ibn Ahmed ibn Hanbal from his father that ash Shafi'ee said to him....It is authentic from him, and for this reason Ibnul Qayyim attributed it to him in 'I'laam' 2/325, and al Fulaani in 'Eeqaath' pg. 152, then he said: 'al Bayhaqi said: for this reason ash Shafi'ee accepted and took many of the ahadeeth, and he took the hadeeth from the people of Hijaaz, ash Shaam, Yemen and Iraq. And he took all of the narrations he viewed to be authentic without prejudice or bias, also without leaning towards or being influenced by what the followers of the 'madth'hab of that city used to see as correct.....

[2]-Abu Nu'aym in al Hilyah 9/107, Al Harwee 1/47, Ibnul Qayyim in 'I'laam al Muwaqa'een 2/363 and al Fulaani pg.104

[3]-Ibn Abee Haatim in 'Adaab ash Shafi'ee pg. 93 and Abul Qaasim as Samarqundi in 'al Amaali' as it is in 'al Muntaqaa and also for Abee Hafs al Mu'adab 1/234, and Abu Nu'aym in al Hilyah 9/106 and Ibn Asaakir 15/10/1 with an authentic chain

Al 'I'tibaa'a

He also said:

(كُلُّ حَدِيثٍ عَنِ النَّبِي صلَّى الله عليه وسلم فَهُوَ قَوْلِي وَإِنْ لَمْ تَسْمَعُوهُ مِنِّي)

9. "Every narration on the authority of the Prophet ﷺ is my view, even if you do not hear it from me."[2]

As for the last of the great scholars of 'fiqh' according to time, than he is Imaam Ahmad ibn Hanbal[3] who was the foremost among the Imaams in collecting the Sunnah and adhering to it, so much so that he even "disliked that a book consisting of deductions and personal opinions be written."[4] Because of this he said:

(لَا تُقَلِّدْنِي وَلَا تُقَلِّدْ مَالِكًا وَلَا الشَّافِعِيَ وَلَا الأَوْزَاعِيَ وَلَا الثَّوْرِي وَخُذْ مِنْ حَيْثُ أَخَذُوا)

1. "Do not follow me; nor Maalik, nor Shaafi'i, nor Awzaa'i, nor Thawri, but take from where they took."[5]

(لَا تُقَلِّدْ دِينَكَ أَحَدًا مِنْ هَؤُلَاءِ مَا جَاءَ عَنِ النَّبِي صلى الله عليه وسلم وَأَصْحَابِهِ فَخُذْ بِهِ ثُمَّ التَّابِعِينَ بَعْدُ الرَّجُلُ فِيهِ مُخَيَّرٌ)

In one narration: " Do not imitate anyone of these people in your religion, but whatever comes from the Prophet ﷺ and his Companions, take it; and proceeding them are their successors (tabi'oon), where a man has a choice."

---

[1]-Ibn Abee Haatim pg.93, and Abu Nu'aym and Ibn Asaakir 15/9/2 with an authentic chain of narration.
[2]-Ibn Abee Haatim pg. 93-94
[3]-(TN)He is Abu Abdullah Ahmed ibn Muhammad ibn Hanbal ibn Hilal ibn Asad Al Maazinee ash Shaybaani. He was born in the year 164 hijri in Baghdaad. He traveled many places seeking knowledge and hadeeth. He is known to be the Imam of the People of the Sunnah and Ahlus Sunnah wal Jamaa'ah. He was tortured by the misguided leader of Iraq regarding the issue of the creation of the Quran. He remained firm in the trials and tribulations which he faced and was an example for the Muslims of that time and today. He compiled an enormous compilation of hadeeth which is called the 'Musnad' which contains over 30,000 narrations from the Prophet and his companions, etc...He died in Baghdaad 241 hijri. One of his most famous students is Imam al Bukhari who is the author of 'Saheeh Bukhari' (The biographies for the four Imams were taken from 'Tabaqaat al Huffadth, Hilyatul Awliyaa'a, Tabaqaat al Fuqahaa'a, Tadthkirah al Huffadth, Sifatu Safwa, al Bidayah wan Nihayah)
[4]-Ibnul Jawzee in 'al Manaqib' pg.192
[5]-al Fulaani pg. 113, and Ibnul Qayyim in 'I'laam' 2/302

# Al 'I'tibaa'a

Once he said:

(الِاتِّبَاعُ أَنْ يَتَّبِعَ الرَّجُلُ مَا جَاءَ عَنْ النَّبِي صلى الله عليه وسلم وَعَنْ أَصْحَابِهِ ثُمَّ هُوَ مِنْ بَعْدَ التَّابِعِينَ مُخَيَّرٌ)

"Al It'ibaa'a' (Following) means that a man follows what comes from the Prophet ﷺ and his Companions; then after the Successors, he has a choice."[1]

He also said:

(رَأْيُ الْأَوْزَاعِي وَرَأْيُ مَالِكٍ وَرَأْيُ أَبِي حَنِيفَةَ كُلُّهُ رَأْيٌ وَهُوَ عِنْدِي سَوَاءٌ وإنَّمَا الحُجَّةُ في الآثَارِ)

2. "The opinion of Awzaa'i, the opinion of Maalik, the opinion of Abu Haneefah: all of it is opinion, and it is all equal in my eyes. However, the proof is in the narrations (from the Prophet ﷺ and his Companions)."[2]

He also said:

(مَنْ رَدَّ حَدِيثَ رَسُولِ اللهِ صلى الله عليه وسلم فَهُوَ عَلَى شَفَا هَلَكَةٍ)

3. "Whoever rejects a statement of the Messenger of Allah ﷺ is on the brink of destruction."[3]

If you are astonished and amazed about these statements, than more astonishment and wonder should be given to the blind followers of the 'madthaa'hib' who strictly adhere to and are bigoted towards their scholars in the subsidiary issues while verily the ones they follow-the Imam's of their specific school of 'fiqh'- have prohibited them from following themselves and other than them.

Meaning of 'Fiqh'

As for 'al fiqh' [4] in creed- which is the more important type of 'fiqh', comparatively, to the 'fiqh' of subsidiary issues. Verily, you find that the blind followers of the 'madtha'hib' are in opposition to the great Imams in their

---

[1] -Abu Dawud in 'Masaa'il al Imam Ahmed' pgs.276-277
[2] -Ibn Abdul Barr in 'al Jami' 2/149
[3] -Ibnul Jawzee pg. 182, and see the Introduction to The Description of the Prophet's Prayer by al Alaamah al Albaani may Allah have mercy upon him pgs. 46-53
[4] -**(TN)**Fiqh also means understanding, comprehension and to have knowledge of something

Al 'I'tibaa'a

creed[1]. The majority of the followers of these 'madtha'hib' are in opposition to the Imam's that they ascribe themselves to as being followers of them. The majority of them have followed the 'madth'hab' of the 'al Ash'ariyyah'[2] and others in their creed, except the followers of Imam Ahmed. As for the followers of Imam Ahmed, then they served as the symbol for the authentic and correct creed of as-Salifiyyah throughout previous centuries, except for a very few of them.

As for the other three 'madtha'hib' then the majority of the followers were adhering to other methods and ideologies contrary to that of the salaf (righteous predecessors). This is the reality which is well known and only an arrogant person, or someone who has no knowledge about the history of Islam and the Islamic schools of 'fiqh' would deny this fact.

Some of the scholars transmitted statements attributed to the great Imam-Abu Haneefah-in issues of creed, which Abu Haneefah himself disagrees with and views that which is contrary to the majority of those who blindly follow him.

Ibnu Taymiyyah said:'In the book 'al Fiqh al Akbar'[3], the well known book amongst the companions and students of Abu Haneefah in which they have narrated from him on the authority of Abee Matee' al Hakam ibn Abdullah al Balkhee who said: 'I asked Abu Haneefah about 'al Fiqh ul Akbar', and he replied: 'Do not call or consider anyone a disbeliever if they commit a sin, and do not negate faith from the one who commits a sin, enjoin the good and forbid the

---

[1] -see the statement of Ibn Abee Izz al Hanafee in the Explanation of the Creed of at Tahawiyyah pg. 65, he named the knowledge of the fundamental principles of the religion 'fiqh al akbar' and 'fiqh al ahkam' (understanding of 'fiqh' rulings) as 'fiqh al furoo' (fiqh of subsidiary issues)

[2] -(TN)The Ash'arees are the followers of Abul Hasan Al-Ash'aree (d.324). The Ash'arees deny all of Allah's attributes except 7, and they make ta'weel (figurative interpretations) in the Attributes of Allaah. For example, the change the meanings of the Attributes from their apparent meanings (i.e, to say Allaah's Hand means Allaah's --------power).The seven attributes they (the Ash'arees) affirm for Allaah are; Living, Knowing, Speech, Will, Hearing, Seeing and Ability (Power). The Ash'arees perform Ta'weel (an interpretation not in accordance with the way of the Salaf) with the attributes they deny. Examples of such ta'weel is saying Allaah's Hand means power, Allaah's Face means reward, or Allaah's Eyes to mean knowledge, or His Pleasure to mean His rewards etc. Other deviations of the Ash'arees are: they claim that Allaah will not be seen in the hereafter, they claim that one cannot point up when being asked where Allaah is, they claim that the speech of Allaah is without sound and is an internal speech, and many other misguided beliefs which are contrary to what the Prophet and his companions believed. Please refer to glossary for more information.

[3] -Fiqhul Akbar: is the understanding of the creed and beliefs

evil. And know that whatever you have been afflicted by was bound to reach you, and whatever has not affected you will never afflict you. Do not renounce, or free yourselves from any of the companions of Allah's Messenger ﷺ, and do not patronize or support anyone while excluding others. And the affair of Uthmaan ibn Affaan and Ali ibn Abee Taalib, refer it back to Allah the Most High...'until Abee Matee' said: Then Abu Haneefah said about the one who says: "I don't know whether my Lord is in (above) the sky or on the earth" has apostated and disbelieved, for verily Allah says:

﴿ ٱلرَّحْمَٰنُ عَلَى ٱلْعَرْشِ ٱسْتَوَىٰ ۝ ﴾

"The Most Merciful Allah rose over the Mighty Throne (in a manner which suits His majesty)" (Taha 20:5).

Then I said: 'if the person says': "Allah is above His Throne" but he says : "I don't know whether the Throne is in (above) the heavens or in the earth?". Abu Haneefah replied: He is a disbeliever, because he denied that fact that Allah and His Throne are in (above) the sky, Allah is above the highest part of the heavens and Allah is supplicated to and called upon while being in the heavens not below.

In another wording: 'I asked Abu Haneefah about the one who says: "I don't know whether my Lord is in(above) the sky or on the earth", Abu Haneefah replied: He has disbelieved, because Allah says: **"The Most Merciful rose above His Throne.."** and Allah's Throne is above the seven heavens. He said: for if he says: 'Above the Throne', but he doesn't know if the Throne is in (above) the heavens or in the earth. Abu Haneefah replied: 'If he denies that it is in (above) the sky, then he has disbelieved."In these words of Abu Haneefah, which are well known amongst his followers, is the statement of his which he said that the one who hesitates saying: 'I don't know whether my Lord is in the sky or on the earth, is a disbeliever and apostate'. So how can the one who says Allah's Throne is not in (above) the sky, or they are not in(above) the sky nor the earth; only be considered one who denies and negates this fact!?[1]

Furthermore, Ibn Abee Izz al Hanafee, the commentator on 'Aqeedah at Tahawiyyah' said: 'There are many statements from the salaf concerning the

---

[1]-Also Imam adh Dhaha'bee mentioned the same story in his book 'Mukhtasar al Uloow lil'Alee'e al Gaffaar', pg. 136, who transmitted the story from the author of 'al Farooq'.

Al 'I'tibaa'a

establishment of Allah's characteristic of exaltedness, elevation, being above everything. From amongst these statements is what has been narrated from Sheikhul Islam Abu Ismaa'eel al Ansaari in his book 'al Farooq', with his chain of narration up to Matee al Balkhee that he asked Abu Haneefah about the one who says: 'I don't know whether my Lord is in (above) the sky or on the earth, Abu Haneefah replied: He has disbelieved, because Allah says: *"The Most Merciful rose above His Mighty throne"*, and His Throne is above the seven heavens.....[1]

In addition, all disregard should be given to the ones who deny this fact, from amongst those who ascribe themselves to the 'madth'hab' of Abu Haneefah. Verily some of the sects of the 'Mu'tazilah'[2] have ascribed themselves to Abu Haneefah, when in reality they are in complete opposition to the majority of Abu Haneefah's beliefs in 'aqeedah' (creed). Unfortunately, the same has been done with Imam Malik, Imam ash Shafi'ee and Imam Ahmed where many of the so called followers of these 'madtha'hib' (schools of thought) are in complete opposition and contradiction to these great Imam's in many issues of 'aqeedah'.[3]

Similarly, if we recall the famous story of Abu Yusuf[4] –when Bishr al Mareesee[5] was seeking repentance for his denial of Allah being above His Great Throne and what happened in that incident. Imam adh Dha'habee mentioned this incident in the book 'al Uloow' stating: Bashaar ibn Musa al Khaffaaf said: Bishr ibn al Waleed al Kindee came to the great judge-Abu Yusuf. So he said to Abu Yusuf: 'You prohibit me from speaking while Bishr al Mareesee and Ali al Ahwal are speaking?', Abu Yusuf replied: 'what are they saying?'. He said: 'They are saying that Allah is everywhere'. Abu Yusuf replied: 'I will deal with them', so they were

---

[1] -(see previous statement from Ibn Taymiyyah)

[2] -(TN)A deviant sect whose beliefs center around five fundamentals: negating Allah's attributes, rejecting 'al Qadaa and al Qadr', believing that whoever commits a major sin is doomed to the hellfire, and that such a person is considered asnot being a disbeliever nor a believer but between the two, also they believe that it is permissible to rebel against Muslim rulers.

[3] -Explanation of Aqeedah at Tahawiyyah pgs.322-323

[4] -(TN)A well known student of Abu Haneefah

[5] -(TN)He is Abu Abdurahman Bishr ibn Giyaath al Mareesee born 138 Hijri and died 218 Hijri. His father was a Jew and he learned 'fiqh' from Abu Yusuf and it is said he was the founder of the 'Jahmiyyah' and he was from the influential members of the 'Mu'tazilah', he used to say that the Quran was created from the time of ar Rasheed and continued propagating this innovation for forty years up until the time of al Ma'moon where he was one of his closest companions and responsible for teaching this innovation to al Ma'moon. Many of the scholars of hadeeth of Baghdaad of that time refuted Bishr al Mareesee, from them is Imam ad Daaraamee in his book 'ar radd ala Bishr al Mareesee.

Al 'I'tibaa'a

brought to Abu Yusuf. Bishr al Mareesee stood up and ran away and then Ali al Ahwal was brought with another sheikh. Abu Yusuf said to them-and looked at the sheikh-'If it wasn't for the fact that you possess some manners and courtesy I would have hurt you and tortured you with extreme pain. So Abu Yusuf ordered that he be imprisoned and whipped Ali al Ahwal and brought him around the city for the people to see.'[1]

However the 'Mu'tazilah' and the 'Asha'irah' who ascribe to the Hanafee school of thought interpret the word 'al Istiwaa'a' (to rise above or over or upon) to mean 'al'Isteelaa'a' (to seize, capture, take possession of).

Al Ash'aree Abul Hasan said in his book 'Maqaalatul Islaamiyeen': 'The Mu'tazilah say: 'Indeed Allah rose above His Throne, meaning that He seized and captured it.'[2]

Furthermore, within Abul Hasan's letter to Ahlul Thagar he said: 'Allah's rising above His Throne is not his seizing and capturing of it, as the people of 'Al Qadr'[3] say, for verily this is because Allah is still the occupier and has possession of everything.'[4]

This reached a point until the corrupted meaning of the word 'al istiwaa'a' (isteelaa'a) captured and seized the intellects of the linguists of the 'Ashaa'irah'. They introduced new things into the Arabic language which the previous generations and the 'salaf' were unfamiliar with. Al Jawharee and ar Raazi said: 'Istiwaa'a' (rising above) the sky, means: he intended and rose, i.e.: seized and captured and made himself apparent. One of the Arabic Poets said:

$$\text{قَدْ اسْتَوَى بِشْرٌ عَلَى الْعِرَاقِ مِنْ غَيْرِ سَيْفٍ وَدَمٍ مَهْرَاقِ}$$

Verily Bishr rose above Iraq-without a sword or bloodshed[5]

---

[1] -Mukhtasar al Uloow pg. 100, from the narration of Ibn Abee Haatim who said: We heard from al Hasan ibn Ali ibn Mlhran, who said: we heard from Bashaar this narration. In this chain of narration is Bashaar ibn Musa who is a weak narrator, who makes many mistakes. However that was the creed of Abu Yusuf according to what at Tahawee mentioned in the introduction of 'Aqeedah at Tahawiyyah'
[2] -Maqaalatul Islaamiyeen 1/254
[3] -(TN)The ones who denied 'al Qadr' (pre-decree), please see glossary for further information.
[4] -Letter to Ahlul Thagar pg. 232-236
[5] -as Sihaah 6/2385, tahqeeq Ahmed Abdul Gafoor Ataar, 'Mukhtaar as Sihaah' pg.335

Al 'I'tibaa'a

Similarly many of the followers of the 'Maliki' school of thought are in opposition and believe contrary to what Imam Malik used to believe in many issues of creed.

Furthermore, Abdullah ibn Imam Ahmed ibn Hanbal narrated in his 'Sunnah' with his chain of narration on the authority of Malik ibn Anas that he said: 'Allah is above the heavens and His knowledge is everywhere, nothing is void of His knowledge.'[1]

Al Bayhaqi mentioned with an authentic chain of narration on the authority of Abee ar Rabee' ar Rushdaynee from Ibn Wahb who said: "I was with Imam Malik and a man entered upon us and said: O Abu Abdullah (Malik), (Allah's saying): *"The Most Merciful (Allah) has risen above His Great Throne"*. So Imam Malik remained silent, bowed his head, and began to sweat severely. Then he lifted his head and said: 'The Most Merciful has risen above His Great Throne", as He has describe Himself, and don't ask-How? The knowledge of 'How' is unknown, and you are a person of innovation, then he ordered to take him out of the gathering.

Also Yahyaa ibn Yahyaa at Taymee , Ja'far ibn Abdullah, and others said: 'A man came to Imam Malik and said: 'O Abu Abdullah: *"The Most Merciful has risen above His Great Throne"*, how did Allah rise above it? The narrator mentioned: I never saw Imam Malik become more furious or angry than from what this man had said. Then Imam Malik started to sweat, and the people remained silent until he spoke angrily saying: 'How' is not understood, and the fact that Allah rose above His throne is something not unknown, and asking questions about it is an innovation, and I fear that you are misguided', then he ordered that the man be removed from the gathering."[2]

Similarly the followers of the 'Shafi'ee' school of thought opposed and differed with Imam ash Shafi'ee in many issues of creed.

Imam ash Shafi'ee said: "The statement regarding the Sunnah which I follow, and that which I saw the people following like: Sufyaan ibn Uyaynah and Malik ibn Anas and others. They all declared the testimony of faith 'La ilaha Illa Allah' (No deity worthy of worship except Allah) and that Muhammad is the Messenger of Allah, and that Allah is above His Throne in (above) the heavens, and He comes close to His creation, as He likes and is befitting to His Majesty. Allah also

---

[1] -**(TN)**Abdullah ibn Imam Ahmed narrated it in 'as Sunnah' #11, (1/106)
[2] -Mukhtasar al Uloow pgs.140-141

descends to the lowest part of the heavens (closest to Earth) as He wills," and then ash Shafi'ee mentioned the rest of his beliefs and creed.'[1]

On the authority of Yunus ibn Abdul A'laa who said: I heard ash Shafi'ee say: 'Allah The Most High possesses beautiful names and attributes, it is impossible for anyone whom the proofs have reached him can deny this'. And in 'al Mukhtasar' there is additional wording which states: 'If one differs regarding this matter, after the proofs and evidences have been established then he is a disbeliever, as for prior to establishing the proofs, then he is excused for his ignorance and lack of knowledge. Because knowledge of this is not realized with the intellect nor meditation or reflection.

These attributes are established and all similarities are negated from them, as Allah negated from Himself any similarities in His saying:

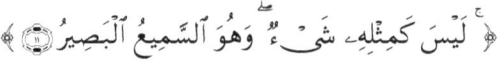

"There is nothing similar to Him (Allah) and He is the All Hearer All Seeing" (ash Shura 42:11)

It is well known that Imam ash Shafi'ee was from those who used to dispraise 'Kalam' (theological rhetoric) and its people. He was well known and very keen and serious in following the 'athaar' (narrations of the Prophet Muhammad ﷺ and the Companions) in the fundamental issues of the religion as well as the subsidiary issues.

As for Imam Ahmed ibn Hanbal, many statements have been transmitted from him regarding creed and articles of belief while reinforcing his statements with authentic narrations from the Prophet ﷺ and companions, while never changing the meanings of Allah's names and attributes. He is the flag bearer of the Sunnah, the one who showed extreme patience in the trials and tribulations he underwent to revive the Sunnah. It is well known from him that whoever talked about the Quran being created, he considered them to be disbelievers. He also established all of Allah's names and attributes, established that Allah's exaltedness is above the heavens, as well as established Allah's predestination of all things. Imam Ahmed also considered Abu Bakr and Umar to be the first two rightly guided caliph's after the Prophet Muhammad ﷺ. He also believed that

---

[1]-Mukhtasar al Uloow pg. 176

faith increases and decreases and many other issues in the religion which may be too lengthy to mention here."[1]

History has proven and bares witness to the fact that the followers of Imam Ahmed served as the symbol of those who corrected and rectified the matters of creed throughout the passing of numerous generations. However there have been found amongst them, some who have taken the views of those who oppose the correct creed such as the 'Ashaa'irah' and others.

This is the total opposite of the other three schools of thought (Hanafee, Maliki, ash Shafi'ee) as the majority of them are upon 'madtha'hib' which are not 'Salafi' in their creed and beliefs. There were very few amongst them who were upon the creed of 'as Salafiyyah' after the spreading of the 'madtha'hib' in the fourth century. As regards to the followers of the 'madtha'hib' before the fourth century and the spreading of the 'madtha'hib', then all of them were apparently upon the creed of the companions and the righteous predecessors. This is evident by observing what we mentioned previously regarding the story of Abu Yusuf-may Allah have mercy upon him- and his creed. Then observing what was narrated about those who ascribed themselves to Abu Haneefah such as at Tahaawee, Ibn Abee Izz, and others, while not excluding the other schools of thought.

As it is obvious to anyone who has studied the books of 'aqeedah' especially the book of Imam al Laalikaa'ii 'Explanation of the Fundamentals of Creed of Ahl Sunnah wal Jamaa'ah'[2], as well as the books of Ibn Taymiyyah, Ibnul Qayyim and adh Dha'habee.

Ibn Taymiyyah said: 'Many sects and groups from the people of innovations and desires have ascribed themselves to the Four Imam's in the subsidiary issues of 'fiqh'. While these groups oppose the Four Imam's in the fundamental issues (such as creed), and the great Imam's are free from those who claim they are their followers. This is well known, as there were many people from the 'Jahmiyyah, 'al Qadariyyah, al Mutazilah and others who all ascribed themselves to Abu Haneefah and his school of thought in the subsidiary issues of 'fiqh'. While Abu Haneefah and his companions were completely in opposition to the

---

[1]-Al Uloow lil Alee'e el Gafaar,pg. 130 and the summarized version of the book pg.189

[2]-This book is considered one of the main resources in regards to knowing and understanding the creed of the salaf. Imam al Laalikaa'ii died in the year (416 hijri).It has been printed by 'Dar Taybah' in five volumes and the texts have been verified by Dr. Ahmed ibn Sa'd ibn Hamdaan al Ghamdee, ustaadh at University Umm al Qura, Makkah al Mubarakah

Al 'I'tibaa'a

views and creed of the Mutazilah, and their statements regarding this issue is well known.

Even to the extent that Abu Haneefah said: May Allah curse Amru ibn Ubaid[1], who opened up the doors for people to speak about such things..'

Nuh al Jami' said: 'I asked Abu Haneefah about what the people have invented regarding speech about 'al A'raad and al Ajsaam'[2], so Abu Haneefah replied: 'This is philosophical speech, adhere to the Quran and the Sunnah and leave off what he people have invented and introduced for verily it is an innovation.' Then Abu Yusuf said: 'Whoever seeks knowledge with theological rhetoric than he will become a disbeliever or atheist.

In addition, Abu Yusuf wanted to punish Bishr al Mareesee when he started to talk about 'ta'teel'[3] until he fled and ran away.

Muhammad ibnul Hasan[4] said: 'The scholars of the East and West have agreed upon the fact that believing in Allah's attributes the way He described Himself, or the Messenger of Allah ﷺ describe them, and they are mentioned and talked

---

[1] -(TN)One of the well known Mu'tazilah who used to propagate and spread their teachings and was one of the earliest leaders in the theological movement of the Mu'tazilis, which was founded by Wasil ibn Ataa'a.

[2] -(TN)Speech about Allah's essence, His names and attributes and striking similarities between Allah and His creation. Comparing the limbs and organs of humans to that which Allah possesses and other than this. And we seek refuge in Allah from this type of misguidance.

[3] -(TN) saying Allah's attributes have no meaning/disabling their meanings

[4] -(TN) Muḥammad ibn al-Ḥasan ash-Shaybānī was a disciple of Abu Haneefah and Abu Yusuf,. He was born in Wāsiṭ, Iraq, in soon after he moved to Koofa, the home town of Abū Ḥanīfa, and grew up there. He began studying in Koofa as a pupil of Abu Hanifa. When al-Shaybani was 18 however, Abu Hanifa died after having taught him for only two years. Shaybani then began training with Abū Yūsuf, his senior, and the leading disciple of Abu Hanifa. He also had other prominent teachers as well: Sufyan al-Thawrī and al-Awzā'ī. he also later visited al Medinah, and studied for two to three years with Malik ibn. Anas. Thus, as a result of his education, al-Shaybani became a jurist at a very early age. According to Abu Hanifa's grandson Ismail, he taught in Kufa at age twenty. Ash-Shaybānī moved to Baghdad, where he continued his learning. He was so respected that Caliph Harun al-Rashid appointed him (judge) of his capital city Ar-Raqqah. After being relieved of his position as judge he returned to Baghdad and resumed his educational activities. It was during this period he exerted his widest influence. He taught Muhammad ibn Idris ash-Shafi`ee the most prestigious of his pupils. Even later, when ash-Shafi'ee disagreed with his teacher and wrote the book al-Radd 'alā Muḥammad b. al-Ḥasan ("Refutation of Muḥammad b. al-Ḥasan [al-Shaybānī]"), he still maintained immense admiration for his teacher. He died 189 hijri.

about as they came in the texts-without changes or alterations... Then he mentioned some other speech which I don't recall.

The scholars of 'fiqh' (Abu Haneefah) and their companions and students(Abu Yusuf, Muhammad ibnul Hasan) continued to abandon, rebuke, and refute the Mu'tazilah and the other misguided people of innovations and desires. Bishr al Mareesee who was the leader of the 'Jahmiyyah' and Ahmed ibn Ibee Du'aad the head judge-their counterparts from the Jahmiyyah and the Mu'tazilah and others previous to them and after them- all used to ascribe themselves to Abu Haneefah and his school of thought regarding the subsidiary issues of 'fiqh'.

They were the ones who ignited the fire of conflict until the well known trials and tribulations about 'disabling the meanings of Allah's attributes' and the conflict about the' creation of the Quran took place.[1]

This continued up until the generations in which the (ahlul Hadeeth) People of Hadeeth and the ones adhering to 'Aqeedah as Salifiyyah' were few and disgraced amongst their fellow Muslims. This should be of no surprise, because verily the Prophet Muhammad ﷺ -the Most truthful and trustworthy one- informed us that :

«إِنَّ الْإِسْلَامَ بَدَأَ غَرِيبًا وَسَيَعُودُ غَرِيبًا كَمَا بَدَأَ، فَطُوبَى لِلْغُرَبَاءِ» . قُلْنَا: «مَنْ هُمْ يَا رَسُولَ اللَّهِ؟» قَالَ: «الَّذِينَ يُصْلِحُونَ حِينَ يُفْسِدُ النَّاسُ»

'Indeed Islam started as something strange and will return to being something strange, so glad tidings to the strangers,' then it was asked: 'O Messenger of Allah who are the strangers?' So he replied: 'They are the ones who rectify the affairs when the people become corrupt.'[2]

---

[1]-ad Daleel ala Batlaan at Tahleel' by Ibn Taymiyyah, verification by Hamdi Abdul Majeed as Salafi, Maktabul Islamee 1418 hijri, also see: 'Muqadimah as Sulmaasee died.550, in his book 'Manazil al l'imatul al Arba'ah by Yahya ibn Ibrahim as Sulmaasee, verification done by: Dr. Mahmoud ibn Abdurahman Qadh, Islamic University of al Madinah

[2]-Abu Amru ad Daani narrated this hadeeth with similar wording with an authentic chain from Muhammad ibn Adam al Maseesee, who said Hafs ibn Giyath said to us on the authority of al A'amash from Abee Salih from Abee al Ahwas from Abdullah ibn Mas'ud who said: The Messenger of Allah said... Also at Tirmidthi and Muslim (1/130 #233) narrated it without the question 'Who are the strangers...?"Imam al Laalikaa'ee mentioned it in 'Sharh I'tiqaad ahl Sunnah. #173.

Al 'I'tibaa'a

The situations, occurrences, and extent of bigotry and group partisanship to specific 'madthaa'hib' in creed and 'fiqh' reached to such an extent that the ones who were adhering to the creed of 'as Salafiyyah' were prohibited to reveal, disclose and make public their beliefs. Similarly, the ones who used to study and teach the books of the Sunnah-rather than the books of 'fiqh'-upon which many of the laws of the country was formed and established upon and which the scholars of that country were blindly following-they were harmed and sometimes tortured.[1]

What was the harm which was brought to Imam Ahmed ibn Hanbal and his companions except from the hands of those in opposition to the creed of the salaf and the bigoted followers of specific 'madthaa'hib'?!

What was the injury, harassment and damage which Ibn Taymiyyah and his students underwent except at the hand of those bigoted fanatics who, whenever they gained power and authority they never considered nor thought about protecting and safeguarding their Muslim brothers.?!

For this reason, it is obligatory upon the Muslims- if they want unity and power- to hold firmly to and strictly adhere to the 'sincere religion', in their beliefs and actions. This must be done in accordance to what the first three and best of generations were upon, and specifically what the companions of Allah's Messenger ﷺ were upon. Keeping in mind that before Islam the companions used to oppose, differ, fight and kill one another. But Allah, out of his extreme mercy, reconciled between them and brought their hearts together with this 'sincere religion' of Islam. While blessing them with the complete adherence to the religion in all affairs, creed, 'fiqh', fundamentals and the subsidiary issues.

The first obligation regarding this issue falls upon the shoulders of the Muslim scholars from every 'madth'hab'. It is also obligatory upon the general population of Muslims to fear Allah regarding their religion. They must know and understand that there is no religion except that which was completed and perfected in the time of the Prophet Muhammad ﷺ, and that which his noble companions were adhering to. In addition, know that Allah and the Prophet Muhammad ﷺ were completely pleased and satisfied with the companions and their religion at the time of the Prophet's ﷺ death.

---

[1]-see introduction of this book

Al 'I'tibaa'a

It is also obligatory upon the Muslims to never be bigoted to anyone except Allah and His Messenger. Likewise one should never support nor oppose anyone except that it is based upon Allah's and His Messenger's commandments- do this so that you will be the successful ones in the sight of Allah.

Ibn Taymiyyah said: 'The most deserving people who should be considered to be from the 'al firqatul Najiyyah' (Successful Sect) are 'Ahlul Hadeeth' (People of Hadeeth) and Sunnah. They are the ones who have no one to follow nor be bigoted to, except the Messenger of Allah. They are the most knowledgeable people of the Prophet's sayings, actions and affairs. They are also the best ones who can distinguish between the authentic and inauthentic narrations, while their scholars are legal experts regarding it. They possess knowledge of the meanings of these texts and they are the ones who follow and adhere to the Sunnah out of pure love, belief, and confirmation of it. They support and patronize all who support the Sunnah and they oppose all those who oppose it. They are the ones who refer all the abstract sayings back to what has come in the Quran and the Sunnah. They never erect, post, or nominate sayings and make these statements principals in their religion if they are not established and proven to be authentic from what the Prophet Muhammad ﷺ came with. Rather they make what the Prophet Muhammad ﷺ came with -in the Quran and Sunnah- to be the foundations and principals which they depend upon, referring back to them constantly, and sincerely believing in them."[1]

Just as the earlier scholars and Imam's followed the creed of the 'salaf', they were also adherent to the way of the salaf regarding Islamic legislations (fiqh) pertaining to actions of worship, as well as dealings and transactions. They were strictly adherent to the Quran and Sunnah as the companions were in their generation and the Quran and Sunnah were given precedence over all things. These great Imam's would also follow the consensus of the companions and the narrations related from them. Furthermore,'qiyas' (if needed) would be made upon the proofs from the Quran, Sunnah and narrations of the companions even if there was consensus or individual statements from them.

There never existed 'madthaa'hib' or schools of thought which were ascribed or attributed to certain companions of the Prophet Muhammad ﷺ, as we never find

---

[1]-Majmoo' Fataawa Ibn Taymiyyah 3/347

any one of them saying: I'm Bakree, or Umaree, or Uthmaanee, or Abaasee, or Mas'udee[1] attaching or ascribing oneself to their particular 'fiqh' rulings.

In every city and country there were Islamic scholars who directed and guided the people with their knowledge and religious verdicts, wherever they settled or traveled. The people would ask the scholars of that particular city about 'fiqh' and religious verdicts without particularization or designation of a specific 'madth'hab', and without restricting or limiting themselves to a particular person.

It is a well known fact that the student is affected by the ideas, sayings and creed of his 'sheikh'. A student would be known to be from the students or companions of a particular 'sheikh' by constantly staying with and accompanying that 'sheikh' and/or studying with him. It would be said: 'he is a companion or student of Imam Abu Haneefah and he is from the companions or students of Malik, ash- Shafi'ee and Ahmed.

However the students and disciples never showed bigotry towards the opinions of their teachers except if their opinions were in agreement and in accordance to the evidences from the Quran and Sunnah. Many times the students opposed and differed with their teachers, and the respected, honorable, and noble minded 'sheikh' would never feel offended, discomforted, nor embarrassed by the opposition of his students. Rather, you may find that he would retract his statement and take the statement of his student while praising him for differing and opposing him. This issue does not need proofs because it is well known to all.

Furthermore, Abu Yusuf and Muhammad ibnul Hasan differed with Abu Haneefah in one-third of his 'madth'hab' and a third is a large amount![2]

The different books of 'fiqh' according to the 'madtha'hib' can bear witness to this, to the extent that many of the diligent scholars of the 'madthaa'hib' would

---

[1]-**(TN)** Saying one is Bakree means that he follows Abu Bakr as Siqeeq, Umaree-Umar ibn al Khattab, etc...

[2]-see 'Hashiyatu Ibn Aabideen 1/62 and 'an Nafi' al Kabeer' by Laknawee pg. 93, this has been taken from 'The Description of the Prophet's Prayer pg. 55. **(TN)** This statement is taken from what the Prophet Muhammad ﷺ mentioned regarding bequeathing one third of the deceased person's wealth and he replied: 'leave his one third and one third is a lot.' Saheeh Muslim, the Book of Wills, Chapter: Bequething one third #'s 4209-4218.

Al 'I'tibaa'a

sometimes say: 'the 'fatwa' (religious verdict) is according to the students in opposition to the Imam.'[1]

Abu Shamah[2] said: 'al Muzanee[3] mentioned in his book named 'al Jamiul Kabeer' regarding the one who has made 'tayamum' and started praying, then he sees water: 'That ash Shafi'ee forbid people from imitating him, as advice for you. He will receive reward from what you are correct in and he is free and innocent from your mistakes, and your advice is accepted from him.

Also Sheikh Abu Ali as Sinjee in his book 'at Talkhees' said: 'Verily al Muzanee mentioned this statement regarding this issue because it was the first issue in which he opposed ash Shafi'ee in his 'al Jamiul Kabeer'. Whereas al Muzanee took the opinion of the scholars of 'al Koofah' which states that: 'one should exit the prayer and make ablution then resume the prayer. So al Muzanee explained the excuse for his opposing ash- Shafi'ee in this issue, which is that ash- Shafi'ee prohibited the peope from the imitation and blind following of himself as well as others.

Abu Shamah said: 'So here we observe that al Muzanee verily abided by and complied to the order of his 'sheikh' (teacher) regarding the prohibition of blind following and imitating him. Al Muzanee opposed his teacher in this issue because of what became apparent to him by his observations and reflections over the evidences, accompanied with his reasoning and personal opinion. So what would one suspect of the individual if he came across a narration (Quran and Sunnah) which bluntly stated and declared that which was in opposition to his statement, for certainly he would be the hastiest and quickest of people to oppose the statement of his teacher, even if the statement was in agreement and not in opposition to it. For verily he was ordered with: 'if he finds a hadeeth which contradicts or conflicts with ash Shafi'ee's statement than ash Shafi'ee's statement should be abandoned'. So if you are interested and you have desire to research this issue, and are concerned about the clarification and manifestation of the truth, then know that you will find that many of the people of knowledge and especially the authors of the Shafi'ee school of thought, have aided,

---

[1]-see 'al Hidayah' and the other books of the various schools of 'fiqh' thought

[2]-(TN)He is Abdur Rahman ibn Ismaa'eel ibn Ibrahim ibn Uthmaan, the great scholar and jurist al Maqdisi ash Shafi'ee, he was born 596 hijri and died in the year 665H.

[3]-(TN)He is Imam, the jurist, Abu Ibrahim Ismaa'eel ibn Yahyaa ibn Ismaa'eel ibn Amru ibn Muslim al Muzanee, the Egyptian, the great student of Imam ash Shafi'ee. He was born 175 hijri and died 264 hijri. He was known for his advocacy and propagation of the Shafi'ee madth'hab.

supported and advocated ash Shafi'ee's true school of thought. Furthermore, they all adhered and complied to what ash Shafi'ee ordered them to do in opposing his statements: 'It is correct to use the authentic narrations as proofs, this is what Allah has commanded us with, even if ash Shafi'ee doesn't mention it.'[1]

Furthermore, we must search for the rulings and legislations in 'fiqh' using the fundamentals and principals of the companions, while adhering to their methodology in doing so. The reason for this is because the companions learned and received the entire religion-creed, rulings, regulations, and subsidiary issues- directly from the Prophet Muhammad ﷺ. They believed in it and accepted it all without distinguishing between articles of faith, 'fiqh' rulings, regulations and subsidiary issues. This is al Iti'baa'a, and this is the meaning of Allah's statement:

﴿ ٱتَّبِعُواْ مَآ أُنزِلَ إِلَيۡكُم مِّن رَّبِّكُمۡ وَلَا تَتَّبِعُواْ مِن دُونِهِۦٓ أَوۡلِيَآءَۗ قَلِيلٗا مَّا تَذَكَّرُونَ ۞ ﴾

"Say O Muhammad: 'Follow what has been sent down unto you from your Lord (Quran and Sunnah) and do not follow any protectors, helpers (who order you with polytheism) besides Allah. Little do you remember!" (al A'raf 7:3)

---

[1]-'Khutbatul Mu'amal' pg. 112

Chapter Two

Learning the Religion and the 'Fiqh' of the Salaf

Al 'I'tibaa'a

Part One

Obligation of learning the religion

It is obligatory upon every Muslim to learn his or her religion and all the issues related to the worship of Allah, which is the sole purpose of their creation, as Allah says:

﴿ وَمَا خَلَقْتُ ٱلْجِنَّ وَٱلْإِنسَ إِلَّا لِيَعْبُدُونِ ۝ ﴾

"And I (Allah) did not create the jinn and mankind except that they should worship Me" (Adh Dhariyat 51:56)

Verily Allah urged and exhorted us with reading and learning the religion in the very first verses which He revealed to His Prophet Muhammad ﷺ, as Allah says:

﴿ ٱقْرَأْ بِٱسْمِ رَبِّكَ ٱلَّذِى خَلَقَ ۝ خَلَقَ ٱلْإِنسَـٰنَ مِنْ عَلَقٍ ۝ ٱقْرَأْ وَرَبُّكَ ٱلْأَكْرَمُ ۝ ٱلَّذِى عَلَّمَ بِٱلْقَلَمِ ۝ عَلَّمَ ٱلْإِنسَـٰنَ مَا لَمْ يَعْلَمْ ۝ ﴾

"Read! In the name of your Lord who has created all that exists-He has created man from a clot-Read! And your Lord is the Most Generous-Who has taught writing by the pen-He has taught man that which he knew not" (al Alaq 96:1-5)

In the very first verses of revelation, the Lord (Allah) emphasizes the command to read. These verses also contain an indication that one of the greatest tools for learning is the pen and with it knowledge is transmitted and related to others. These verses also contain an indication that knowledge is the most noble and honorable thing in the sight of Allah and definitely the most respected in light of the fact that Allah from his graciousness and generosity bestows not only his favors upon the person with knowledge but also by giving him/her the tools of knowledge.

Allah also ordered the people from the nation of Muhammad ﷺ (Muslims) to go out and learn their religion wherever they expect to find it, while making great efforts in learning as much as they can.

Al 'I'tibaa'a

As Allah said:

$$\bullet\ \text{وَمَا كَانَ ٱلْمُؤْمِنُونَ لِيَنفِرُواْ كَآفَّةً ۚ فَلَوْلَا نَفَرَ مِن كُلِّ فِرْقَةٍ مِّنْهُمْ طَآئِفَةٌ لِّيَتَفَقَّهُواْ فِى ٱلدِّينِ وَلِيُنذِرُواْ قَوْمَهُمْ إِذَا رَجَعُوٓاْ إِلَيْهِمْ لَعَلَّهُمْ يَحْذَرُونَ} \text{﴿١٢٢﴾}$$

"And it is not proper for the believers to go out to fight all together. Of every group of them, a party should go out, that they who are left behind may be taught their religion, and that they may warn their people when they return to them, so that they may beware of evil." (At Tawbah 9:122)

The Prophet Muhammad ﷺ also urged us to seek knowledge as he said:

«مَنْ يُرِدِ اللهُ بِهِ خَيْرًا يُفَقِّهْهُ فِي الدِّينِ، وَإِنَّمَا أَنَا قَاسِمٌ وَاللهُ يُعْطِي، وَلَنْ تَزَالَ هَذِهِ الأُمَّةُ قَائِمَةً عَلَى أَمْرِ اللهِ، لاَ يَضُرُّهُمْ مَنْ خَالَفَهُمْ، حَتَّى يَأْتِيَ أَمْرُ اللهِ»

'Whoever Allah wants goodness for, He gives him understanding of the religion, and verily I am a distributor, and Allah gives and bestows what He wills. Also this Muslim nation will remain firm upon their religion, they will not be harmed by those who oppose them, until Allah's command is given (last day).'[1]

What is meant by 'al fiqh' in the religion, as will be mentioned soon is: understanding the religion, understanding the creed, the rulings, the fundamentals and the subsidiary issues. There is no distinction between creed and actions or between fundamentals and subsidiary issues. 'Fiqh' regarding the creed means understanding everything that is associated and related to: 1- Allah's essence and His attributes, 2- The Messengers and everything related to them, 3-Understanding the issues related to the unseen affairs such as the angels, also the Divine Revelations and Holy Books which Allah revealed to His Messengers, as well as understanding (what happens on) the Last Day, and understanding (and believing) in Allah's Decree of everything-the good and the bad.

In addition, understanding everything (mentioned in the Quran and Sunnah) regarding the affairs which are unseen from the occurrences of death and the

---

[1]-Saheeh Bukhari 1/217, Book of Knowledge, Chapter: Whoever Allah wants good for, #71 from the hadeeth of Mu'awiyyah ibn Sufyan

grave, the awakening from the graves and the resurrection after death. This type of 'fiqh' according to the terminology of the later generations is called : knowledge of as Sunnah, or 'Aqeedah' (creed) or 'Tawheed' (monotheism). Amongst the 'khalaf' (ones who oppose the salaf) this knowledge is called: knowledge of 'kalaam' (theological rhetoric). So 'kalaam' and the knowledge of it was not accepted by the salaf because it is a newly invented matter in Allah's religion, and whoever innovates an affair which is not from our religion than it is rejected.

Similarly, seeking knowledge of 'fiqh' related to the rulings, legislations and the subsidiary issues is obligatory upon the Muslim. He must seek this knowledge in accordance to the methodology of the companions of Allah's Messenger. Solely because the companions are the ones who learned and took all of the religion from the Prophet Muhammad directly, they learned the religion with complete acceptance without distinguishing and differentiating between creed, acts of worship and 'fiqh' rulings and legislations.

In addition, it is obligatory upon all Muslims to learn the issues of their religion which will enable every single one of them to know their Lord, their religion and their Messenger Muhammad. These are the three questions which every person will be asked when he is in his grave, and upon these three issues the whole religion is based: **Who is your Lord?**, **What is your religion?** **Who is your Prophet?**[1] Allah said:

﴿ وَمَا خَلَقْتُ ٱلْجِنَّ وَٱلْإِنسَ إِلَّا لِيَعْبُدُونِ ﴾

"Verily I did not create the jinn and mankind except to worship Me alone" (adh Dhariyaat 51:56) from the time of Adam until the Day of Resurrection.

So how can one know how to worship Allah? There is no way to worship Allah except by the way of the Messengers and the last of them was Muhammad.

Al 'I'tibaa'a

It has been narrated that Prophet Muhammad ﷺ said:

$$\text{"طَلَبُ الْعِلْمِ فَرِيضَةٌ عَلَى كُلِّ مُسْلِمٍ"}$$

'Seeking knowledge is obligatory upon every Muslim' [1]

Al Khateeb al Baghdaadi[2] commented on this narration stating: 'To know the fasting, the prayer, the prohibited matters, the prescribed punishments, and the rulings.'

Al Khateeb also narrated from al Hasan ibn ar Rabee' who said: 'I asked Abdullah ibnul Mubaarak saying : **'Seeking knowledge is obligatory upon every Muslim'**, what is the explanation of this? He said: 'It is not that which you are seeking or thinking. Verily the seeking of knowledge which is obligatory is when something occurs or happens to someone in his religion he asks about the issue until he knows the answer.'

On the authority of al Hasan ibn Shaqeeq who said: I asked Abdullah ibnul Mubaarak: 'What is obligatory upon the people in regards to learning and seeking knowledge? He said: 'That a man should not move forward or proceed except with knowledge, by asking and learning, this is what is obligatory upon the people to learn of knowledge. Then he explained this by saying: 'if a man does not possess wealth than it is not obligatory upon him to learn about 'Zakat', but if he possesses two hundred dirham than it becomes obligatory upon him to know when and how much charity he must give from that wealth, also who receives it and where does he place this charity, etc...'[3]

Imam ash Shafi'ee said in the Chapter of Knowledge from his book 'ar Risalah': someone said to me: 'what is knowledge? And what is obligatory upon the people regarding knowledge?

---

[1]-An authentic narration which many of the scholars of hadeeth mentioned, from the hadeeth of Anas, Abdullah ibn Umar, Abu Sa'eed al Khudri, Abdullah ibn Abaas, Abdullah ibn Mas'ud and Ali ibn Abee Talib. See 'Takhreej Ahadeeth Mushkilah al Faqr' by al Albaani pgs.48-62. Ibn Majah narrated it #224 and al Albaani said it is Saheeh.

[2]-(TN)He is al Hafidth al Imam Muhaddith of Sham and Iraq, the historian of Baghdaad Abu Bakr Ahmed ibn Ali ibn Thabit ibn Ahmed ibn Mahdee al Baghdaadi. He was born in 392 hijri and died in 463 hijri. He has numerous compilations and books related to hadeeth and the sciences of hadeeth.

[3]-al Faqeeh wal Mutafaqih 1/42

Al 'I'tibaa'a

Ash Shafi'ee said to him: 'Knowledge is of two types: general knowledge which is impossible for the mature adult-whose intellect is sound-to be ignorant of.' It was said: like what?

Ash Shafi'ee responded:' like the five daily prayers, the fact that Allah has made it obligatory upon the people to fast the Month of Ramadan and make Hajj for those who have ability to do so. Also to give the obligatory charity (Zakat), and that Allah prohibited them from committing fornication, killing, stealing, drinking alcohol. And all the other things which Allah has instructed the Muslims to understand, comprehend, and act upon. By sacrificing and giving from their selves, their wealth, and to avoid and stay away from the things which they were prohibited from...Then he mentioned the specific knowledge.'[1]

Imam Abdullah ibn Ahmed ibn Hanbal said: I asked my father about what is obligatory upon the man to seek of knowledge, he replied: 'He should know that in which he can establish the prayers and other affairs of his religion like the fasting and obligatory charity, he should definitely have knowledge of these things.'[2]

Al Khateeb al Baghdaadi stated: 'It is obligatory upon every single person to seek that which is necessary for him to know regarding the affairs which Allah has made obligatory upon him. All of this according to his ability and personal efforts. Every mature, intelligent Muslim, male or female, free or slave, is obliged to knowing the way to purify oneself, to pray, and to fast. It is necessary that every Muslim becomes familiar with this knowledge.

It is also obligatory upon every Muslim to know and distinguish between what is permissible and prohibited from amongst the foods, drinks, clothing, genitals, blood, money. It is not permissible for anyone to be ignorant of any of these things as Allah has made it obligatory upon them to take the necessary steps to learning these issues until they reach puberty and they are Muslims, or after they accept Islam and reach sexual maturity.

It is also mandatory upon the leaders and the Imams to teach the women all that has been mentioned.

It is also obligatory upon the Imam to assist the people in learning and arrange for them sittings in which the ignorant can learn. They should be given provisions

---

[1]-ar Risalah pg. 357-358 and the proceeding pages
[2]-'Masaa'il Abdullah ibn Ahmed pg. 439

Al 'I'tibaa'a

from the community savings, and it is obligatory upon the scholars to teach the ignorant so that the laymen can distinguish between the truth and the falsehood.'[1]

Al Salmaasee[2] said: 'As for the religion, than it is obligatory upon the person to know all that concerns him. All mature adults who have reached puberty, it is obligatory upon them to have knowledge of 'taharah' (purification), knowledge of the prayer and fasting and knowledge of what is permissible and impermissible to eat. It is also obligatory upon the wealthy person to have knowledge of 'zakat', and the one who possesses the ability to make 'hajj'- to know the rituals of 'hajj'. Whoever has desire to get married than it is obligatory upon him to know what is permissible regarding the concubines and marriage and what is prohibited and permissible. Similarly it is obligatory upon the ones involved in buying and selling to know what is permissible and prohibited from business transactions and contracts. It is also obligatory upon the governors and leaders to know the religious rulings, the politics of war and battling, the rulings pertaining to war, fighting and the spoils of war. It is also obligatory upon everyone to memorize 'ummul Quran' (surah al Fatihah) as the Prophet ﷺ said:

"لَا صَلَاةَ إِلَّا بِفَاتِحَةِ الْكِتَابِ"

'There is no prayer except with the suratul Fatihah'[3], and memorize something from the Quran.'[4]

Furthermore, it has been made obligatory upon some-fard kifayah-(collective duty)[5] to learn the 'fiqh' rulings and legislations while expanding and increasing in their knowledge until they have the ability to guide the people and give religious verdicts. So that they may provide answers for their incidents, issues,

---

[1]-look al Faqeeh wal Mutafiqih 1/43-46

[2]-(TN) He is Muhammad ibn Hibatullah ibn Abdullah as Salmaasee the Shafi'ee jurist. He died in the year 574 hijri

[3]-This wording has been narrated by al Bukhari in 'al Qiraa'ah khalf al Imam' #55 on the authority of Ubadah ibn as Saamit. The wording which the six is mentioned in the six books of hadeeth is لا (صلاة لمن لم يقرأ بفاتحة الكتاب). See Saheeh Bukhari #756, Muslim #394, Abu Dawud #822, at Tirmidthi #247, an Nisaa'ee 2/137 Book of 'Iftitaah, Chapter: Obligation of reading al Fatihah in the prayer, Ibn Majah #837.

[4]-'Manaazil al a'Imatul Arba'ah pg.134-135

[5]-(TN)If some of the Muslims perform it than it is sufficient and it becomes desirable for the rest of the Muslims

Al 'I'tibaa'a

situations and calamities, as was mentioned previously in Allah's statement:

﴿ ۞ وَمَا كَانَ ٱلْمُؤْمِنُونَ لِيَنفِرُواْ كَآفَّةً فَلَوْلَا نَفَرَ مِن كُلِّ فِرْقَةٍ مِّنْهُمْ طَآئِفَةٌ لِّيَتَفَقَّهُواْ فِى ٱلدِّينِ وَلِيُنذِرُواْ قَوْمَهُمْ إِذَا رَجَعُوٓاْ إِلَيْهِمْ لَعَلَّهُمْ يَحْذَرُونَ ۝ ﴾

"And it is not proper for the believers to go out to fight all together. Of every group of them, a party should go out, that they who are left behind may be taught their religion, and that they may warn their people when they return to them, so that they may beware of evil." (At Tawbah 9:122)

Ibn Kathir said: 'Allah says that at least a group from every district or neighborhood and a group of people from every tribe should go out for fighting if all of them do not go. This is so that those who went with the Messenger ﷺ would gain instruction and at the same time would learn from the divine revelation that was being descended upon the Prophet ﷺ. Then they would warn their people about that battle and the enemies when they returned to them. So the group that went with the Prophet ﷺ would achieve two goals (fighting with the Prophet ﷺ and learning their religion from him at the same time). After the time of Prophet ﷺ there should always remain and exist a group from every tribe or neighborhood who should seek religious knowledge or fight for the sake of Allah, for verily fighting is required from at least one group of people from every Muslim community. The verse preceeding this one mentioned the obligation of fighting with the Prophet Muhammad ﷺ if he went out to battle.'[1]

This is what Sufyaan ibn Uyaynah meant when he explained the Prophet's ﷺ statement: **'Seeking knowledge is obligatory'**.

On the authority of Mujahid ibn Musa who said: 'We were with ibn Uyaynah and this (above) hadeeth was mentioned, Ibn Uyaynah said: 'It is not obligatory upon every Muslim, if some of them seek knowledge than it is sufficient for all. Like the funeral prayer, if some of them perform it than that is sufficient for all, or something similar to that.

Al Khateeb al Baghdaadi mentioned this narration and commented on it saying: 'What was intended by Ibn Uyaynah was: the knowledge of the 'fiqh' rulings that are related to the subsidiary issues in the religion. As for the fundamentals, which are : knowledge of Allah, His 'tawheed', His attributes, the truthfulness of

---

[1] -Tafsir ibn Kathir 2/543

Al 'I'tibaa'a

His Messengers- all of these things are from amongst the things which are obligatory upon everyone to have knowledge of, and it is not correct for anyone to act or believe on someone's behalf regarding these issues.'[1]

Ibn Abdul Barr[2] said: 'The scholars have come to consensus that there is some knowledge which is obligatory upon every single Muslim to know (fard- ayn), and other knowledge which is 'fard kifayah'-if some of them perform it than it is no longer obligatory upon the others.'[3]

In light of this, it is obligatory upon the scholars of Islam to teach the general population of Muslims as well as the students of knowledge. As for the general masses, than the scholar should summarize for them the issues of creed, the pillars of Islam, and the manners with which a Muslim should live his life, while knowing his Lord, his religion and his Prophet.

As for the students of knowledge, then the scholar should teach them so as to increase them in knowledge and understanding of the 'fiqh' issues, rulings and legislations related to the religion. So that these students will graduate from studying underneath these great scholars and become proficient and well versed judges, guides, and leaders for all the Muslims.

Furthermore, the 'fiqh' principals and fundamentals that the Muslims were upon in the time of the Prophet, the companions and the era of the great 'fiqh' scholars is as follows:

---

[1]-al Faqeeh wal Mutafaqih pg. 44-45

[2]-**(TN)** He is Abu Umar Yusuf ibn Abdullah ibn Muhammad ibn Abul Barr, the Spainard, al Maliki. The great historian and author of many great and important compilations. He was a judge, muhaddith, and jurist. He was born 368 hijri and died 463 hijri. He was known to follow the 'Thahiree' madth'hab, then he started following the Maliki madth'hab. He was a great an noble Imam and a scholar from Ahl Sunnah. He has many works from them: Al-Tamhîd limâ fîl-Muwatta' min al-Ma`ânî wal-Asânîd ("The Facilitation to the Meanings and Chains of Transmission Found in Mâlik's Muwatta'"), Al-Istidhkâr li Madhhab `Ulamâ' al-Amsâr fîmâ Tadammanahu al-Muwatta' min Ma`ânî al-Ra'î wal-Athâr ("The Memorization of the Doctrine of the Scholars of the World Concerning the Juridical Opinions and the Narrations Found in Mâlik's Muwatta'"); Jâmi` Bayân al-`Ilmi wa-Fadlihi wamâ Yanbaghî fî Riwâyatihi wa Hamlih ("Compendium Exposing the Nature of Knowledge and Its Immense Merit, and What is Required in the Process of Narrating it and Conveying it") and many others.

[3]-Jami' Bayaan al Ilm wa Fadlihi 1/10

Al 'I'tibaa'a

Imam an Nisaa'ee narrated with an authentic chain of narration:

عَنْ عَبْدِ الرَّحْمَنِ بْنِ يَزِيدَ، قَالَ: أَكْثَرُوا عَلَى عَبْدِ اللَّهِ ذَاتَ يَوْمٍ فَقَالَ عَبْدُ اللَّهِ: " إِنَّهُ قَدْ أَتَى عَلَيْنَا زَمَانٌ وَلَسْنَا نَقْضِي، وَلَسْنَا هُنَالِكَ، ثُمَّ إِنَّ اللَّهَ عَزَّ وَجَلَّ قَدَّرَ عَلَيْنَا أَنْ بَلَغْنَا مَا تَرَوْنَ، فَمَنْ عَرَضَ لَهُ مِنْكُمْ قَضَاءٌ بَعْدَ الْيَوْمِ، فَلْيَقْضِ بِمَا فِي كِتَابِ اللَّهِ، فَإِنْ جَاءَ أَمْرٌ لَيْسَ فِي كِتَابِ اللَّهِ، فَلْيَقْضِ بِمَا قَضَى بِهِ نَبِيُّهُ صَلَّى اللَّهُ عَلَيْهِ وَسَلَّمَ، فَإِنْ جَاءَ أَمْرٌ لَيْسَ فِي كِتَابِ اللَّهِ، وَلَا قَضَى بِهِ نَبِيُّهُ صَلَّى اللَّهُ عَلَيْهِ وَسَلَّمَ، فَلْيَقْضِ بِمَا قَضَى بِهِ الصَّالِحُونَ، فَإِنْ جَاءَ أَمْرٌ لَيْسَ فِي كِتَابِ اللَّهِ، وَلَا قَضَى بِهِ نَبِيُّهُ صَلَّى اللَّهُ عَلَيْهِ وَسَلَّمَ، وَلَا قَضَى بِهِ الصَّالِحُونَ، فَلْيَجْتَهِدْ رَأْيَهُ، وَلَا يَقُولُ: إِنِّي أَخَافُ، وَإِنِّي أَخَافُ، فَإِنَّ الْحَلَالَ بَيِّنٌ، وَالْحَرَامَ بَيِّنٌ، وَبَيْنَ ذَلِكَ أُمُورٌ مُشْتَبِهَاتٌ، فَدَعْ مَا يَرِيبُكَ إِلَى مَا لَا يَرِيبُكَ " قَالَ أَبُو عَبْدِ الرَّحْمَنِ: «هَذَا الحَدِيثُ جَيِّدٌ جَيِّدٌ»

> On the authority of Abdullah ibn Mas'ud who said: Abdurahman ibn Yazeed said: 'The people were numerous and frequently asking Abdullah ibn Mas'ud questions that day, so Abdullah ibn Mas'ud said: 'Verily much time has passed us by, and we cannot judge between the people[1], and we don't possess the status nor ability to judge between the people. Furthermore, Allah has placed us in the position which we have reached as is apparent to all of you. So after today, whoever is presented with an issue which needs a religious verdict or ruling; then let him give his verdict with what is in the Book of Allah (Quran) and if an issue presents itself which is not mentioned in the Quran, then let him give his verdict with what the Prophet Muhammad ﷺ judged[2] in the issue. If an issue presents itself which is not mentioned in the Quran nor did the Prophet Muhammad ﷺ pass judgment in the issue than let him give his verdict in agreement with what the righteous people [3]judged. If an issue presents itself which is not mentioned in the Quran, nor did the Prophet Muhammad ﷺ clarify it, nor did the righteous people make a judgment in the issue, then let him exert his 'ijtihaad' in the issue.[4] And he should not say : "I'm scared or I'm worried, for verily the permissible things have been made clear and the impermissible things have also been made clear, and between the them are doubtful things, so leave off that which causes you doubt for that which does not cause you doubt."

---

[1]-(TN)They have what is sufficient for them: Quran, Sunnah, Narrations of the Prophet and Companions
[2]-(TN)The Prophetic Sunnah which is the Prophet's ﷺ descriptions, sayings, actions and approvals
[3]-(TN)The companions of the Prophet Muhammad ﷺ
[4]-(TN)This is for the ones who possess knowledge and have the ability

Al 'I'tibaa'a

An Nisaa'ee said: 'This narration is 'jayed jayed' [1] Also ibn Abee Khaythamah[2] narrated this with an authentic chain which contains the wording:

"فَإِنْ لَمْ يُحْسِنْ فِلْيَقُمْ و لا يَسْتَحِي"

'If he is not good at this than let him get up and leave, and not be shy or timid about it.'[3] Also ad Daramee[4] narrated with his chain of narration:

عَنْ عَلِيِّ بْنِ مُسْهِرٍ، عَنْ أَبِي إِسْحَاقَ، عَنِ الشَّعْبِيِّ، عَنْ شُرَيْحٍ، أَنَّ عُمَرَ بْنَ الْخَطَّابِ كَتَبَ إِلَيْهِ: " إِنْ جَاءَكَ شَيْءٌ فِي كِتَابِ اللهِ، فَاقْضِ بِهِ وَلَا تَلْفِتْكَ عَنْهُ الرِّجَالُ، فَإِنْ جَاءَكَ مَا لَيْسَ فِي كِتَابِ اللهِ فَانْظُرْ سُنَّةَ رَسُولِ اللهِ صَلَّى اللهُ عَلَيْهِ وَسَلَّمَ، فَاقْضِ بِهَا، فَإِنْ جَاءَكَ مَا لَيْسَ فِي كِتَابِ اللهِ وَلَمْ يَكُنْ فِيهِ سُنَّةٌ مِنْ رَسُولِ اللهِ صَلَّى اللهُ عَلَيْهِ وَسَلَّمَ، فَانْظُرْ مَا اجْتَمَعَ عَلَيْهِ النَّاسُ فَخُذْ بِهِ، فَإِنْ جَاءَكَ مَا لَيْسَ فِي كِتَابِ اللهِ وَلَمْ يَكُنْ فِي سُنَّةِ رَسُولِ اللهِ صَلَّى اللهُ عَلَيْهِ وَسَلَّمَ، وَلَمْ يَتَكَلَّمْ فِيهِ أَحَدٌ قَبْلَكَ. فَاخْتَرْ أَيَّ الْأَمْرَيْنِ شِئْتَ: إِنْ شِئْتَ أَنْ تَجْتَهِدَ بِرَأْيِكَ ثُمَّ تَقَدَّمَ فَتَقَدَّمْ، وَإِنْ شِئْتَ أَنْ تَتَأَخَّرَ، فَتَأَخَّرْ، وَلَا أَرَى التَّأَخُّرَ إِلَّا خَيْرًا لَكَ "

On the authority of Ali ibn Mushir, from Abee Ishaaq, from ash Sha'bee, from Shurayh, that Umar ibnul Khattab wrote to him saying: 'If your presented with any issue which (the ruling) is in the Quran than make your judgment with it and pay no attention to what the people say or think, and if your presented with any issue which is not mentioned in the Quran then look in the Sunnah of Allah's Messenger ﷺ and make your judgment with it. And if you are presented with any issue which is not mentioned in the Quran, nor the Sunnah and no one who preceded you spoke about the issue; then choose one of these two choices: 1.If you want to exert your efforts with your personal opinion and become one who gives verdicts then do so,if you want to leave it, then leave it. And I see that leaving this off is better for you."[5]

---

[1] -Sunan an Nisaa'ee pg.811, Book Manners of the Judges, Chapter: Verdict with the agreement of the scholars, #5397, also see 'al Faqeeh wal Mutafaqih' 1/219, also 'Jami' Bayan Uloom wa Fadlihi' , ad Daramee 1/61 and Wakee' ibn Khalaf in 'Akhbaar al Qudaat 1/76. This narration is an authentic narration from the statements of Abdullah ibn Mas'ud, may Allah be pleased with him.

[2]-(TN) He is Abu Bakr Ahmed ibn Abee Khaythamah, the author of 'at Tarikh al Kabeer'. He died in the year 279 h

[3]-Ibnul Qayyim mentioned it with his chain of narration in 'I'laam al Muwa'qaeen 2/118

[4]-(TN)He is Abu Muhammad Abdullah ibn AbdirRahman ad Daramee at Tameemee. He compiled a book called 'Sunan ad Daramee' which contains over 3550 narrations. He died in 255 hijri.

[5]-(TN)This is regarding the issues in which the person has doubt about knowing the correct proofs and evidences.' Sunan Ad Daramee 1/55, also Wakee mentioned this narration in 'Akhbaar al Qudaat' 2/189 with many chains of narration from Sufyaan ath Thawree, from ash Shaybaani Sulaymaan ibn Abee Sulayman from Shurayh, with an authentic chain of narration.

Al 'I'tibaa'a

Part Two

'Fiqh' in the religion

'Fiqh' in the religion, creed, and actions is the complete religion of Islam and all goodness. The Prophet Muhammad ﷺ said:

«مَنْ يُرِدِ اللَّهُ بِهِ خَيْرًا يُفَقِّهْهُ فِي الدِّينِ، وَإِنَّمَا أَنَا قَاسِمٌ وَاللَّهُ يُعْطِي، وَلَنْ تَزَالَ هَذِهِ الأُمَّةُ قَائِمَةً عَلَى أَمْرِ اللَّهِ، لاَ يَضُرُّهُمْ مَنْ خَالَفَهُمْ، حَتَّى يَأْتِيَ أَمْرُ اللَّهِ»

'Whoever Allah wants good for He gives him fiqh (understanding) of the religion, and verily I am a distributor, and Allah gives and bestows what He wills. Also this Muslim nation will continue to remain firm upon their religion, they will not be harmed by those who oppose them, until Allah's command is given (i.e. the last day).'[1]

The Prophet Muhammad ﷺ also said:

قَالَ: «تَجِدُونَ النَّاسَ مَعَادِنَ، خِيَارُهُمْ فِي الجَاهِلِيَّةِ خِيَارُهُمْ فِي الإِسْلاَمِ، إِذَا فَقِهُوا...»

'You will find the people of many different backgrounds, the best of them in 'jahiliyyah'[2] are the best in Islam, if they gain understanding (of the religion).'[3]

'Fiqh' is divided into two divisions:

1. **Fiqh ul Akbar (The Greater 'fiqh')**: It is related to the affairs of creed and the fundamentals of the religion
2. **Fiqh ul Furoo'**: It is that which is related to the rulings, legislations, dealings, and business transactions. Perhaps we may call it the (The Lesser 'fiqh') and both of these divisions are from the religion of Islam. Furthermore this type of division (Fiqh ul Akbar and Fiqh ul Furoo) was not known at the time of the companions, and never did they differentiate or make this type of separation between creed and the rulings.

---

[1] Saheeh Bukhari 1/217, Book of Knowledge, Chapter: Whoever Allah wants good for, #71 from the hadeeth of Mu'awiyyah ibn Sufyan
[2] -(TN)Times of ignorance before the sending of Allah's Messenger ﷺ
[3] -Saheeh Bukhari 6/652, Book of Manaaqib, Chapter: Allah's statement (O Mankind....) #3493, from the hadeeth of Abu Hurairah

Al 'I'tibaa'a

Similarly they never made distinctions as to where these two divisions of 'fiqh' were taken from. Certainly they were taken from the Quran and the Sunnah. One of the prime examples of this is Abu Haneefah's book regarding creed named 'Fiqh ul Akbar'.

' Fiqh ul Akbar' is known as knowledge of 'tawheed' and creed, it is understanding everything related to Allah, His names and His attributes. Understanding the affairs of the unseen (from the Quran and Sunnah) and what Allah and His Messenger informed us about these things from the angels and the divine revelations which Allah revealed to His Messengers, as well as believing in all the Messengers who informed us about all of these things. Understanding the events of the Last Day, the good and bad of the pre-decree. Everything related to what Allah and His Messenger ﷺ informed us about regarding the situations and occurrences of the previous nations. In addition, what is unapparent to us from the affairs of death and what happens to the deceased when one dies and what occurs when one goes to one's grave, what happens when one is resurrected and awakened from his grave, etc...

It is obligatory upon the Muslim to believe in all of these things, in the way that Allah wants and intends for us to believe in them. We must also believe in all of these things in accordance to the way the companions understood them from the Prophet ﷺ directly without intermediaries or interceders. Upon this understading- the religion was completed and Allah's blessings and favors were bestowed upon the nation of Muhammad ﷺ. The companions living in the era of the Prophet Muhammad ﷺ agreed and came together upon these beliefs and ways, and even after the Prophet Muhammad ﷺ had passed away the people came together and remained steadfast upon what the companions and those who followed them with goodness were upon. Successively, the 'tabioon' followed the companions, then the 'tabi tabi'een' proceeded them following in their footsteps. These generations were the best of generations which whom the consensus was concluded. So it is obligatory upon every Muslim to believe and understand the way that those righteous, pious predecessors understood and believed, without negating anything or interpreting falsely, disabling meanings, or asking 'how'[1]. All Muslims must believe in the Islamic articles of creed without striking similarities between Allah's attributes and the creation and other than these issues from the affairs of creed and faith.

---

[1]-(TN)asking 'how' about Allah's names and attributes, which is an innovation

Al 'I'tibaa'a

Furthermore, that which emerged from the innovations of 'at tashay'u'[1], 'al khurooj', 'an nasb'[2], and 'al qadr'[3] was found only amongst the perverted deviants from the Muslims at the time of the Prophet Muhammad ﷺ. The scholars of 'fiqh' as well as the entire Muslim nation considered them to be deviants and considered them to be in opposition to the Prophet Muhammad. These misguided deviants were renounced, rejected, abandoned and forsaken by all of the companions, scholars and all the Muslims of that time.

In addition, it is not permissible for the Muslims to differ regarding this issue. As indeed the consensus was made by the best people after the Prophet Muhammad ﷺ (companions). Meaning that if consensus was made in any issue at the time of the companions then it is not permissible to have differences regarding it at any time or in any place.

Consequently, Allah the Most High decreed to make apparent some of the misguided groups regarding their false creed which started to emerge throughout the Muslim lands after the era of the first three generations. From these misguided groups: Mu'tazilah, Jahmiyyah, Ash'ariyyah, Maturidiyyah,[4] and these so called 'intellectual' groups-as they claim- introduced philosophical terminologies into their beliefs and 'madthaa'hib' such as: classifying and dividing things into categories referring to them as being essential and nonessential, certain knowledge and presumptive knowledge, striking similarities between Allah and His creation, denying all similarities from Him while nullifying the meanings of Allah's attributes, and many other ideas which distorted the image of the pure, unadultered, decisive, authentic Isamic creed. The creed which even the nomadic bedouins living far out in the desert understood in the time of the Prophet ﷺ and the companions. The creed in which nothing was found to be ambiguous, problematic or difficult to understand. By right the companions were absolutely the best of generations

---

[1]-(TN)The methodology and beliefs of the 'Shia'a' which originated from Abdullah ibn Saba' and spread during the conflict of Uthmaan ibn Affan and Ali ibn Abee Talib. Abdullah ibn Saba' spread false beliefs about Ali which led many people astray and into misguidance.

[2]-(TN) al khurooj: referring to the methodology and beliefs of the 'Khawarij', whose origins go back to Dhul Khuwaysirah and those with him from amongst the people who rebelled against Uthmaan ibn Afaan, and also the ones who rebelled against Ali ibn Abee Talib. An nasb: referring to the ones who showed extreme hatred and disobedience to Ali and his rulings in the time of conflict.

[3]-(TN)Referring to those who denied Allah's decree

[4]-(TN)One of the misguided sects, please see glossary for further information.

Al 'I'tibaa'a

because of their complete and perfect Islam and their complete faith in Allah the Most High.

Furthermore, the deviant ones named knowledge of 'tawheed' as knowledge of 'kalaam' (theological rhetoric). Perhaps this was because many of the misguided sects and groups introduced a large amount of theological rhetoric and controversy around this subject in their debates and arguments.[1] All of this was introduced after the time of the companions, who weren't familiar with anything except listening to the Prophet Muhammad ﷺ and being obedient to what he ﷺ ordered them with or prohibited them from.

In addition, as 'taqleed'[2] in 'fiqh' related to rulings and legislations began to spread, similarly the blind following of people also began to spread. The creed of the deviants became predominate over the creed of as-Salafiyyah and the ones who were adhering to the creed of the deviants became boastful and bragged about their creed stating that it was the creed of the majority. As a result of this they made it seem as though 'the majority' and large groups of followers was the sign and defining characteristic that showed that they were upon the truth. However based upon what the Prophet Muhammad ﷺ informed us:

«لَا تَزَالُ طَائِفَةٌ مِنْ أُمَّتِي قَائِمَةً بِأَمْرِ اللهِ، لَا يَضُرُّهُمْ مَنْ خَذَلَهُمْ أَوْ خَالَفَهُمْ، حَتَّى يَأْتِيَ أَمْرُ اللهِ وَهُمْ ظَاهِرُونَ عَلَى النَّاسِ»

"A group from my nation will continue to live by the command of Allah and they will not be harmed by those who oppose them, until the decree of Allah comes while they are still prevailing over the people." [3]

For this reason the scholars of the Sunnah have taken it upon themselves to refute, disprove, rebut and reject all false ideologies, methodologies and creeds which are in opposition to that of the companions. The scholars of the Sunnah's numerous invaluable books and compilations have reached the far and distant regions throughout the entire world clarifying the authentic creed of the salaf and refuting the falsehood-May Allah have mercy upon them.

---

[1]-**(TN)** This took place when some of the Muslims started translating Greek books on philosophy, astronomy, mathematics and other sciences into Arabic, until some of the Muslims became influenced by these ideas which eventually led to them being misguided.

[2]-**(TN)** Acting upon a saying or action from someone whose sayings and actions are not authoritative sources or evidences in the religion

[3]-Saheeh Muslim 3/1524, Book of Leadership, Chapter: the Prophet's saying: A group of my nation will continue

Part Three

Subsidiary Divisions 'Fiqh'[1]

This section is based upon the understanding that 'Fiqh ul Akbar' (The Greater Fiqh)-creed-is only taken from that which is established from Allah and His Messenger ﷺ, since it does not accept 'ijtihaad' nor 'qiyas'.

As for 'fiqh' of the rulings, legislations and subsidiary issues of 'fiqh' then this type of 'fiqh' accepts 'ijtihaad' and 'qiyas'. So upon this we say:

The subsidiary 'fiqh' is restricted and limited to the proofs and evidences contained in the Quran and the Sunnah, they are the two fundamental sources.

Proceeding them (Quran and the Sunnah) is what has been unanimously agreed upon based upon the Quran and Sunnah collectively or individually. Subsequently following the Quran and Sunnah is 'qiyas' based upon them both or individually.

With this in mind we now divide this type of 'fiqh' into different divisions:

First division: The division in which there exists a clear-cut, decisive text from the authentic Quran or Sunnah.

In this division of 'fiqh' there is no place nor right for anyone's 'ijtihaad', 'madth'hab', or personal statement solely because of the obligation upon all people to follow this type of 'fiqh'. If someone exerts himself using his 'ijtihaad' and gives a religious verdict while not knowing or recalling the text, then remembers the text or becomes it apparent to him, it is obligatory upon him to leave off the opposing verdict which he gave and he must follow the authentic text. As Allah says:

﴿ وَمَا كَانَ لِمُؤْمِنٍ وَلَا مُؤْمِنَةٍ إِذَا قَضَى ٱللَّهُ وَرَسُولُهُۥٓ أَمْرًا أَن يَكُونَ لَهُمُ ٱلْخِيَرَةُ مِنْ أَمْرِهِمْ ﴾

"It is not for a male or female believer when Allah and His Messenger have decreed a matter that they should have any option in their decision..." (al Ahzab 33:36)

---

[1]-**(TN)** Also known as 'Fiqhul Furoo'

Second division: This division is that in which there exists no specific text regarding the particular issue, or there exists an authentic text from the Quran and Sunnah however it is not recalled and one scholar doesn't know it with the exclusion of other scholars. In this type of 'fiqh' it is permissible to use 'ijtihaad'. It may also be obligatory upon the scholar who gives numerous verdicts using 'qiyas'.

If he gives a religious verdict and afterwards the text becomes apparent to him, then it is obligatory upon him to return back to the text; this goes for the one giving the verdict as well as the one seeking the verdict.

Third division: The division in which there exists a text however its purport and meaning is undefined regarding a specific ruling and there is possibility and potential for more than one meaning. In this division it is also permissible and/or obligatory to use 'ijtihaad' in regards to specifying and determining the particular meaning or directing and/or correcting the various and different meanings, so the issue becomes one of many meanings and significances.

Fourth division: The division in which there exists texts that are apparently contradictory and seem to be in opposition to each other. In this division it is also permissible and/or obligatory to use 'ijtihaad' to combine and reconcile between the texts if possible, and/or searching for and discovering the abrogation of one of them, and/or giving preference to one of the texts, or finally refraining from making a decision or ruling on either texts.

Al 'I'tibaa'a

Fifth division: The division in which there exists a text from the Prophet Muhammad ﷺ however it is not established from him, or the chain of narration is inauthentic. In this division the 'mufti' could make a statement in agreement with a weak hadeeth according to what has been mentioned by some of the scholars,[1] or he can use 'ijtihaad', but he must indicate that the hadeeth is weak and clarify its weakness if he chooses to act upon it.

The meaning of 'al ijtihaad' is: The action which the scholar or jurist engages in by exerting all of his (intellectual, physical) efforts and doing everything in his ability to gain knowledge of a religious ruling which contains no text, by the way of deductive and inferential reasoning.

The scholar and jurist should look and consider the conditions of 'ijtihaad' which are agreed upon and the conditions which the scholars have differences of opinions about in the books of 'Usool Fiqh'(Principles of Fiqh). Indeed the scholars have differed concerning many of the conditions of 'ijtihaad'.

The righteous predecessors and those who proceeded them tread upon this methodology in the subsidiary 'fiqh' issues.

Ibn Taymiyyah said: 'Some of the scholars of 'fiqh' from the Hanafee 'madth'hab' came to me and said: 'I need your consultation in an issue'. I replied to him: 'What is it?', He said: 'I want to leave and change my 'madth'hab', so I said to him: Why? He replied: 'I have come to find that many authentic narrations

---

[1] -As has been mentioned in 'al Faqeeh wal Mutafaqih' on the authority of Imam Ahmed ibn Hanbal. -see 'al Faqeeh wal Mutafaqih' 1/220 and it contains: 'Perhaps there may be a hadeeth from the Prophet Muhammad ﷺ and within the chain of narration is some defect, so he takes it/uses it if there comes nothing stronger in opposition to it. Like the hadeeth of Amru ibn Shu'ayb, and like the hadeeth of Ibrahim al Hajree, and sometimes he would use the 'mursal' (the narration which the successors of the companions narrate from the Prophet ﷺ) if there comes nothing contrary to it.' End of quote. Also Ibnul Qayyim said: 'The meaning of 'da'eef'(weak) intended by Imam Ahmed is not that which is false nor 'munkar' (one which contains serious errors, or is an open sinner), nor does the chain of narration contain one who has been accused of lieing whereas it is not permissible to use it and act upon it. Rather a 'da'eef' (weak) hadeeth in Imam Ahmed's view the opposite of a 'saheeh' (authentic) hadeeth, as the 'da'eef' hadeeth is a type of 'hasan' (good) narration. As Imam Ahmed did not divide the narrations into 'saheeh', 'hasan' or 'da'eef', rather he divided them into two categories 'saheeh' and 'da'eef'(see I'laam al Muwa'qaeen' 2/55-56). This is also what Ibn Taymiyyah affirmed in his 'Majmoo al Fatawa 1/252, 18/125. That which becomes apparent is: that what is intended by 'da'eef' narrations which Imam Ahmed uses, is equivalent to the 'hasan' narrations amongst the later scholars.' (see 'Irshaad al Fuhool pg.250)

Al 'I'tibaa'a

oppose my 'madth'hab', so I consulted some of the scholars of the 'Shafi'ee' 'madth'hab' and they said to me: 'if you leave off your 'madth'hab' then this will not affect the 'madth'hab because the 'madth'hab' will remain and has been established, and your leaving it or returning back to it is of no benefit. Then some of the Sufi scholars advised me to manifest my extreme need of Allah and earnestly humble myself to Him by supplicating to Him and asking Him to grant me guidance to what He loves and is pleased with. So what do you advise me with?

I replied to him: 'Make your 'madthaa'hib' three divisions:

A division in which the truth is clearly apparent and coincides with what is in the Quran and Sunnah, make your ruling with this while being complacent and having an open heart.

A division 'marjooh'[1] which contains weaker or less preponderant evidence, that in which the opposing party possesses the stronger proofs and evidences. Do not give religious verdicts with this type of evidence, nor make judgments with it, and stay away from it.

A division which contains the affairs of 'ijtihaad' consisting of proofs and evidences that are inseparable, if you would like to give a religious verdict with it than do so, and if you would like you can abandon it.' Then the man responded: 'May Allah reward you with good'[2]

It is obligatory upon the one giving religious verdicts to observe, study and consider the situations in which 'ijtihaad' was used amongst the scholars of 'fiqh', and then give his religious verdict with that which is the closest to the evidences in the Quran and Sunnah, and that which is easiest for the Muslims.

These are the fundamentals and foundations upon which the 'fiqh' of the companions and their religious verdicts were based upon. As we previously mentioned some evidences which proved that in the instances or issues in which they differed, they would return and refer back to the texts, or ask each other about the texts if they didn't know them or recall them, or they would consult

---

[1]-Marjooh: means less preponderant or weaker, and Rajih: means preponderant or stronger
[2]-'I'laam al Muwaqa'een 6/165-166

each other as to what view is the closest to the truth. Abdur Razzaq[1] narrated with an authentic chain of narration

عَنْ عَلْقَمَةَ قَالَ: أُتِيَ عَبْدُ اللَّهِ بْنُ مَسْعُودٍ، فَسُئِلَ عَنْ رَجُلٍ تَزَوَّجَ فَلَمْ يَفْرِضْ لَهَا وَلَمْ يَمَسَّهَا حَتَّى مَاتَ فَفَرَضَ لَهُمْ، ثُمَّ قَالَ: «إِنِّي أَقُولُ فِيهَا بِرَأْيِي، فَإِنْ كَانَ صَوَابًا فَمِنَ اللَّهِ، وَإِنْ كَانَ خَطَأً فَمِنِّي، أَرَى لَهَا صَدَاقَ امْرَأَةٍ مِنْ نِسَائِهَا، وَلَا وَكْسَ، وَلَا شَطَطَ، وَعَلَيْهَا الْعِدَّةُ، وَلَهَا الْمِيرَاثُ» ، فَقَامَ مَعْقِلُ بْنُ سِنَانٍ الْأَشْجَعِيُّ، فَقَالَ: «أَشْهَدُ لَقَضَيْتَ فِيهَا بِقَضَاءِ رَسُولِ اللَّهِ صَلَّى اللهُ عَلَيْهِ وَسَلَّمَ فِي بِرْوَعَ ابْنَةِ وَاشِقٍ امْرَأَةٍ مِنْ بَنِي رُؤَاسٍ مِنْ بَنِي عَامِرِ بْنِ رُؤَاسِ ابْنِ صَعْصَعَةَ،» وَبِهِ يَأْخُذُ سُفْيَانُ "

On the authority of Alqamah who said: someone came to Abdullah ibn Mas'ud and asked him about a man who got married and didn't give the woman her dowry, and he didn't touch or have sexual relations with her until he died, so they designated for her a dowry. Then Abdullah ibn Mas'ud said: 'Verily I speak about this issue based upon my personal opinion, if it so happens to be correct than it is from Allah, and if it is incorrect than it is from me. I view that in regards to this issue that the woman should be given a dowry similar to the dowry given to her female relatives or those women close to her, not less than nor in excess to what she deserves, and she must observe the prescribed waiting period of the women whose husband has died, and she also inherits from him'. So then Ma'qal ibn Sinaan al Ashja'ee stood up and said: 'Verily I bear witness that you have indeed judged in accordance with the judgment of the Messenger of Allah ﷺ regarding the affair of Bir'wah' bint Washiq, the woman from the tribe of 'Ru'aas from Aamir ibn Ru'aas ibn Sa'sa'at. Sufyaan ath Thawree also holds this view.[2]

It is not permissible for anyone to give religious verdicts while being ignorant of the Quran and Sunnah. The scholar is considered to be the one who inherits knowledge from the Messenger ﷺ just as the Prophet Muhammad ﷺ would not speak except with divine revelation, similarly it is not permissible for the inheritor of the Prophet ﷺ to speak with anything except divine revelation. This

---

[1]-(TN) He is Abu Bakr Abdur Razzaq bin Hammam bin Nafi as Sanani. The author of the great book 'Musanaf Abdur Razzaq' which contains numerous narrations from the Prophet Muhammad, his companions and their successors. He was born 126H and died in the month of Shawwal, 211H in Sanaa Yemen.
[2]-Musanaf Abdur Razzaq 6/294 #10898

is what the Prophet ﷺ left behind for us-in the form of the Quran and Sunnah, or consensus of the companions or 'qiyas' based upon the Quran and Sunnah.

Whoever gives religious verdicts without knowledge has indeed committed a great sin. Ad Daramee narrated with a good chain of narration on the authority of Abu Hurairah who said: 'The Prophet Muhammad ﷺ said:

عَنْ أَبِي هُرَيْرَةَ رضي الله عنه، عَنِ النَّبِيِّ صَلَّى اللهُ عَلَيْهِ وَسَلَّمَ: «مَنْ أُفْتِيَ بِفُتْيَا مَنْ غَيْرِ ثَبْتٍ، فَإِنَّمَا إِثْمُهُ عَلَى مِنْ أَفْتَاهُ»

"Whoever is given a religious verdict without proof, for verily the sin is upon the one who has given it."[1] Also ad Daramee narrated on the authority of **Abdullah ibn Abaas** who said:

عَنِ ابْنِ عَبَّاسٍ رضي الله عنه، قَالَ: «مَنْ أَفْتَى بِفُتْيَا يُعَمَّى عنها، فَإِثْمُهَا عَلَيْهِ»

'Whoever gives a religious verdict without knowledge than the sin of it is upon him.'[2]

Similarly it is not permissible for anyone to seek a religious verdict from anyone based upon the saying, opinion, 'madth'hab' of another person. Hence, the one seeking religious verdicts are required and instructed to ask the people of knowledge who are known to be people of knowledge and Sunnah. Allah The Most High says:

$$\text{﴿ فَسْـَٔلُوٓاْ أَهْلَ ٱلذِّكْرِ إِن كُنتُمْ لَا تَعْلَمُونَ ﴾}$$

"Ask the people of knowledge if you do not know" (an Nahl 16:43) and what is intended here by **'knowledge'** is : Quran and Sunnah, as Allah says in the following verse:

$$\text{﴿ وَأَنزَلْنَآ إِلَيْكَ ٱلذِّكْرَ لِتُبَيِّنَ لِلنَّاسِ مَا نُزِّلَ إِلَيْهِمْ ﴾}$$

"And We have sent down to you O Muhammad the 'Dhikr' (reminder, advice , Quran) that you may clarify to the people what was sent down to them..." (an Nahl 16:44).

---

[1] -ad Daaramee mentioned it in his Sunan 1/53 #161. Al Haakim mentioned it in 'al Mustadrik and said: 'Authentic , according to the conditions of Bukhari and Muslim, and they didn't mention it in their books, and it has no defect.(al Mustadrik 1/126) There is difference of opinion regarding al Haakim's statement 'according to the conditions of Bukhari and Muslim', because one of the narrators-Muslim ibn Yasaar-is not from the narrators mentioned in Saheeh Bukhari.

[2] -Sunan ad Daramee 1/53, #162 Muhammad ibn Ahmed informed us who said, Sufyaan ibn Uyaynah said on the authority of Abee Senaan (Dirar ibn Murrah) on the authority of Sa'eed ibn Jubayr from Ibn Abbaas...

Al 'I'tibaa'a

So the Quran and the clarification of it- is what the religion of Islam is based upon. This is not considered 'taqleed' rather it is called 'al it'ibaa'a'. In all actuality, 'taqleed' is not considered knowledge. The type of 'taqleed'[1] of a particular scholar who is not known as being from those who have knowledge of the Quran and Sunnah. This being based upon what we mentioned previously that 'a question directed to a scholar who knows the Quran and Sunnah is not considered 'taqleed'. The 'taqleed' which Allah and His Messenger ﷺ dispraised is: accepting the statement of one whose statement is not an authoritative source or evidence in the religion. Furthermore, the questioner about the authoritative sources and religious evidences from a scholar of the Quran and Sunnah is not considered a 'Muqallid' rather a 'Mu'tabi'.[2] At Tabaraani narrated in his 'Mu'jam al Kabeer' from Abee al Ahwas on the authority of Ibn Mas'ud, and narrated from Ibn Hazm in 'al Ihkaam' from Hubairah ibn Maryam and Abee al Ahwas both of them **on the authority of Ibn Mas'ud who said:**

وَقَالَ ابْنُ مَسْعُودٍ رَضِيَ اللهُ عَنْهُ: «أَلَا لَا يُقَلِّدَنَّ أَحَدُكُمْ دِينَهُ رَجُلًا إِنْ آمَنَ آمَنَ وَإِنْ كَفَرَ كَفَرَ، فَإِنَّهُ لَا أُسْوَةَ فِي الشَّرِّ»

'Do not blind follow anyone regarding the affairs of your religion, if he believes than he believes, if he disbelieves than he disbelieves, indeed there is no example to be followed in evil.'[3]

Then we come across all the statements of the four scholars of 'fiqh' regarding the impermissibility of 'taqleed' showing us the importance of this issue and the serious dangers of 'taqleed'. This is especially for those amongst the scholars who have the ability to know and understand the Islamic legislations and rulings with their proofs and evidences.

---

[1]-(TN)Technically it means: acting upon a saying or action from someone whose sayings and actions are not authoritative sources or evidences in the religion.

[2]-(TN)Muqallid is one who follows another person's sayings whose sayings are not proofs in the religion. Mutabi is the one who follows the divine revelation from Allah in the form of the Quran and Sunnah.

[3]-'Mu'jam al Kabeer 9/886 #8764, with the wording: ('**...If it is necessary for you to imitate someone, then imitate those who have passed away, for verily the living person is not safe from fitnah..**), also in 'al Ihkaam' by Ibn Hazm 6/97, 6/147, Ibn Abdul Barr mentioned it also in 'al Jami' 2/988 #1882 without a chain of narration. The narration also has another chain of narration from Ibn Hazm on the authority of Ibn Wahb who said: the people who heard from al Aw'zaa'ee informed me that he said: Abdah ibn Abee Lubabah mentioned on the authority of Ibn Mas'ud say: It was disliked.

Al 'I'tibaa'a

Part four

Fundamentals and principles 'fiqh' amongst the Companions

The fundamentals of 'fiqh' of the companions were:

1. **Quran**
2. **Sunnah of Allah's Messenger** ﷺ
3. **Statements of the companions, and the consultations which took place between them**
4. **'Qiyas'**

These fundamentals are in pursuance and in conformity with the texts of the Quran and Sunnah.

Ad Daramee narrated with his chain of narration on the authority of Ali ibn Mushir, from Abee Ishaaq, from ash Sha'bee, from Shurayh,

عَنْ عَلِيِّ بْنِ مُسْهِرٍ، عَنْ أَبِي إِسْحَاقَ، عَنِ الشَّعْبِيِّ، عَنْ شُرَيْحٍ، أَنَّ عُمَرَ بْنَ الْخَطَّابِ كَتَبَ إِلَيْهِ: " إِنْ جَاءَكَ شَيْءٌ فِي كِتَابِ اللَّهِ، فَاقْضِ بِهِ وَلَا تَلْفِتْكَ عَنْهُ الرِّجَالُ، فَإِنْ جَاءَكَ مَا لَيْسَ فِي كِتَابِ اللَّهِ فَانْظُرْ سُنَّةَ رَسُولِ اللَّهِ صَلَّى اللهُ عَلَيْهِ وَسَلَّمَ، فَاقْضِ بِهَا، فَإِنْ جَاءَكَ مَا لَيْسَ فِي كِتَابِ اللَّهِ وَلَمْ يَكُنْ فِيهِ سُنَّةٌ مِنْ رَسُولِ اللَّهِ صَلَّى اللهُ عَلَيْهِ وَسَلَّمَ، فَانْظُرْ مَا اجْتَمَعَ عَلَيْهِ النَّاسُ فَخُذْ بِهِ، فَإِنْ جَاءَكَ مَا لَيْسَ فِي كِتَابِ اللَّهِ وَلَمْ يَكُنْ فِي سُنَّةِ رَسُولِ اللَّهِ صَلَّى اللهُ عَلَيْهِ وَسَلَّمَ، وَلَمْ يَتَكَلَّمْ فِيهِ أَحَدٌ قَبْلَكَ. فَاخْتَرْ أَيَّ الْأَمْرَيْنِ شِئْتَ: إِنْ شِئْتَ أَنْ تَجْتَهِدَ بِرَأْيِكَ ثُمَّ تَقَدَّمَ فَتَقَدَّمْ، وَإِنْ شِئْتَ أَنْ تَتَأَخَّرَ، فَتَأَخَّرْ، وَلَا أَرَى التَّأَخُّرَ إِلَّا خَيْرًا لَكَ "

"That Umar ibnul Khattab wrote to him saying: 'If your presented with any issue that (the ruling) is in the Quran than make your judgment with it and pay no attention to what the people say or think, and if you're presented with any issue that is not mentioned in the Quran then look in the Sunnah of Allah's Messenger and make your judgment with it. And if you are presented with any issue that is not mentioned in the Quran, nor the Sunnah and no one who preceded you spoke about the issue; then choose one of these two choices: 1.If you want to exert your efforts with personal opinion and become one who gives verdicts then do so, 2. if you want to leave it off, then leave it. And I see that leaving this off is better for you."¹

Imam an Nisaa'ee narrated with an authentic chain of narration:

عَنْ عَبْدِ الرَّحْمَنِ بْنِ يَزِيدَ، قَالَ: أَكْثَرُوا عَلَى عَبْدِ اللَّهِ ذَاتَ يَوْمٍ فَقَالَ عَبْدُ اللَّهِ: " إِنَّهُ قَدْ أَتَى عَلَيْنَا زَمَانٌ وَلَسْنَا نَقْضِي، وَلَسْنَا هُنَالِكَ، ثُمَّ إِنَّ اللَّهَ عَزَّ وَجَلَّ قَدَّرَ عَلَيْنَا أَنْ بَلَغْنَا مَا تَرَوْنَ، فَمَنْ عَرَضَ لَهُ مِنْكُمْ قَضَاءٌ بَعْدَ الْيَوْمِ، فَلْيَقْضِ بِمَا فِي كِتَابِ اللَّهِ، فَإِنْ جَاءَ أَمْرٌ لَيْسَ فِي كِتَابِ اللَّهِ، فَلْيَقْضِ بِمَا قَضَى بِهِ نَبِيُّهُ صَلَّى اللهُ عَلَيْهِ وَسَلَّمَ، فَإِنْ جَاءَ أَمْرٌ لَيْسَ فِي كِتَابِ اللَّهِ، وَلَا قَضَى بِهِ نَبِيُّهُ صَلَّى اللهُ عَلَيْهِ وَسَلَّمَ، فَلْيَقْضِ بِمَا قَضَى بِهِ الصَّالِحُونَ، فَإِنْ جَاءَ أَمْرٌ لَيْسَ فِي كِتَابِ اللَّهِ، وَلَا قَضَى بِهِ نَبِيُّهُ صَلَّى اللهُ عَلَيْهِ وَسَلَّمَ، وَلَا قَضَى بِهِ الصَّالِحُونَ، فَلْيَجْتَهِدْ رَأْيَهُ، وَلَا يَقُولُ: إِنِّي أَخَافُ، وَإِنِّي أَخَافُ، فَإِنَّ الْحَلَالَ بَيِّنٌ، وَالْحَرَامَ بَيِّنٌ، وَبَيْنَ ذَلِكَ أُمُورٌ مُشْتَبِهَاتٌ، فَدَعْ مَا يَرِيبُكَ إِلَى مَا لَا يَرِيبُكَ " قَالَ أَبُو عَبْدِ الرَّحْمَنِ: «هَذَا الحَدِيثُ جَيِّدٌ جَيِّدٌ»

On the authority of Abdullah ibn Mas'ud who said: Abdurahman ibn Yazeed said: 'The people were numerous and frequently asking Abdullah ibn Mas'ud questions that day, so Abdullah ibn Mas'ud said: 'Verily much time has passed us by, and we cannot judge between the people², and we don't possess the status nor ability to judge between the people. Furthermore, Allah has placed us in the position which we have reached as is apparent to all of you. So after today, whoever is presented with an issue which needs a religious verdict or ruling; then let him give his verdict with what is in the Book of Allah (Quran) and if an issue presents itself which is not mentioned in the Quran, then let him give his verdict with what the Prophet Muhammad ﷺ judged³ in the issue. If an issue presents itself which is not mentioned in the Quran nor did the Prophet Muhammad ﷺ pass judgment in the issue than let him give his verdict in agreement with what the righteous people ⁴judged. If an issue presents itself which is not mentioned in the Quran, nor did the Prophet Muhammad ﷺ clarify

---

¹-This is regarding the issues in which the person has doubt about knowing the correct proofs and evidences. Sunan Ad Daramee 1/55, also Wakee mentioned this narration in 'Akhbaar al Qudaat' 2/189 with many chains of narration from Sufyaan ath Thawree, from ash Shaybaani Sulaymaan ibn Abee Sulaymaan from Shurayh, with an authentic chain of narration.

²-(TN)They have what is sufficient for them: Quran, Sunnah, Narrations of the Prophet and Companions

³-(TN)The Prophetic Sunnah which is the Prophet's ﷺ descriptions, sayings, actions and approvals

⁴-(TN)The companions of the Prophet Muhammad ﷺ

Al 'I'tibaa'a

it, nor did the righteous people make a judgment in the issue, then let him exert his 'ijtihaad' in the issue.[1] And he should not say : "I'm scared or I'm worried, for verily the permissible things have been made clear and the impermissible things have also been made clear, and between the them are doubtful things, so leave off that which causes you doubt for that which does not cause you doubt." An Nisaa'ee said: 'This narration is 'jayed jayed.'[2]

Also ibn Abee Khaythamah[3] narrated this with an authentic chain which contains the wording:

"فإِنْ لَمْ يُحْسِنْ فَلْيَقُمْ و لا يَسْتَحِي"

'If he is not good at this than let him get up and leave, and not be shy or timid about it.'[4]

Ad Daramee and al Bayhaqi both mentioned in their 'Sunan', as well as Ibnul Qayyim mentioned this on the authority of Abee Ubayd from the book 'al Qadaa'a':

عَنْ مَيْمُونِ بْنِ مِهْرَانَ، قَالَ: " كَانَ أَبُو بَكْرٍ رَضِيَ اللهُ عَنْهُ إِذَا وَرَدَ عَلَيْهِ خَصْمٌ (حُكْمٌ) نَظَرَ فِي كِتَابِ اللهِ، فَإِنْ وَجَدَ فِيهِ مَا يَقْضِي بِهِ قَضَى بِهِ بَيْنَهُمْ، فَإِنْ لَمْ يَجِدْ فِي الْكِتَابِ، نَظَرَ: هَلْ كَانَتْ مِنَ النَّبِيِّ صَلَّى اللهُ عَلَيْهِ وَسَلَّمَ فِيهِ سُنَّةٌ؟ فَإِنْ عَلِمَهَا قَضَى بِهَا، وَإِنْ لَمْ يَعْلَمْ خَرَجَ فَسَأَلَ الْمُسْلِمِينَ فَقَالَ: " أَتَانِي كَذَا وَكَذَا، فَنَظَرْتُ فِي كِتَابِ اللهِ، وَفِي سُنَّةِ رَسُولِ اللهِ صَلَّى اللهُ عَلَيْهِ وَسَلَّمَ، فَلَمْ أَجِدْ فِي ذَلِكَ شَيْئًا، فَهَلْ تَعْلَمُونَ أَنَّ نَبِيَّ اللهِ صَلَّى اللهُ عَلَيْهِ وَسَلَّمَ قَضَى فِي ذَلِكَ بِقَضَاءٍ؟ "، فَرُبَّمَا قَامَ إِلَيْهِ الرَّهْطُ فَقَالُوا: " نَعَمْ، قَضَى فِيهِ بِكَذَا وَكَذَا "، فَيَأْخُذُ بِقَضَاءِ رَسُولِ اللهِ صَلَّى اللهُ عَلَيْهِ وَسَلَّمَ ". قَالَ جَعْفَرٌ وَحَدَّثَنِي غَيْرُ مَيْمُونٍ أَنَّ أَبَا بَكْرٍ رَضِيَ اللهُ عَنْهُ كَانَ يَقُولُ عِنْدَ ذَلِكَ: " الْحَمْدُ لِلَّهِ الَّذِي جَعَلَ فِينَا مَنْ يَحْفَظُ عَنْ نَبِيِّنَا صَلَّى اللهُ عَلَيْهِ وَسَلَّمَ "، وَإِنْ أَعْيَاهُ ذَلِكَ دَعَا رُءُوسَ الْمُسْلِمِينَ وَعُلَمَاءَهُمْ، فَاسْتَشَارَهُمْ، فَإِذَا اجْتَمَعَ رَأْيُهُمْ عَلَى الْأَمْرِ قَضَى بِهِ. قَالَ جَعْفَرٌ: وَحَدَّثَنِي مَيْمُونٌ أَنَّ عُمَرَ بْنَ الْخَطَّابِ رَضِيَ اللهُ عَنْهُ كَانَ يَفْعَلُ ذَلِكَ،

---

[1] -(TN)This is for the ones who possess knowledge and have the ability

[2] -Sunan an Nisaa'ee pg.811, Book Manners of the Judges, Chapter: Verdict with the agreement of the scholars, #5397, also see 'al Faqeeh wal Mutafaqih' 1/219, also 'Jami' Bayan Uloom wa Fadlihi' , ad Daramee 1/61 and Wakee' ibn Khalaf in 'Akhbaar al Qudaat 1/76. This narration is an authentic narration from the statements of Abdullah ibn Mas'ud, may Allah be pleased with him.

[3] -(TN) He is Abu Bakr Ahmed ibn Abee Khaythamah, the author of 'at Tarikh al Kabeer'. He died in the year 279 h

[4] -Ibnul Qayyim mentioned it with his chain of narration in 'I'laam al Muwa'qaeen 2/118

Al 'I'tibaa'a

فَإِنْ أَعْيَا أَنْ يَجِدَ فِي الْقُرْآنِ وَالسُّنَّةِ، نَظَرَ: هَلْ كَانَ لِأَبِي بَكْرٍ رَضِيَ اللهُ عَنْهُ فِيهِ قَضَاءٌ؟ فَإِنْ وَجَدَ أَبَا بَكْرٍ رَضِيَ اللهُ عَنْهُ قَدْ قَضَى فِيهِ بِقَضَاءٍ قَضَى بِهِ، وَإِلَّا دَعَا رُءُوسَ المُسْلِمِينَ وَعُلَمَاءَهُمْ، فَاسْتَشَارَهُمْ، فَإِذَا اجْتَمَعُوا عَلَى الْأَمْرِ قَضَى بَيْنَهُمْ"

"On the authority of Maymoon ibn Mihraan who said: 'If any issue came across Abu Bakr as Siqeeq which needed a judgement or ruling he would first look in the Quran, and if he found evidence in the Quran with which he could give a verdict with than he would do so. If he didn't find evidence in the Quran then he would look in the Sunnah of Allah's Messenger ﷺ, and if he found within the Sunnah evidence for the issue he would give his verdict with the Sunnah. If he found no evidence in the Quran and Sunnah then he would go to the people and say: 'this issue and that issue were brought to my attention and I searched in the Quran and Sunnah for the answer, and I don't recall anything. Then he would ask the (companions): 'Do any of you know what the Prophet ﷺ judged or declared regarding this issue? Perhaps some of them would say:'Yes, The Prophet ﷺ judged with this and that regarding this affair, etc... Then Abu Bakr would implement and pass his judgement in according to what the companions told him. Ja'far said that other than Maymoon told us that Abu Bakr used to say: All praises to Allah who has allowed us to memorize everything which came from the Prophet Muhammad ﷺ. Finally, If Abu Bakr didn't recall or find a saying, action, or approval from the Prophet Muhammad ﷺ then he would gather the leaders and chiefs amongst the people and consult them. If their views and opinions were in agreement upon the issue than Abu Bakr would give his verdict according to what was agreed upon. Then Ja'far went on to say: We heard from Maymoon that he said Umar ibn Al Khattab used to do the same thing. If he didn't recall or know any evidences from the Quran and Sunnah he would ask and inquire if Abu Bakr passed a judgement in the issue. If he found that Abu Bakr passes a judgement in the issue he would pass his judgement in accordance to what Abu Bakr decided. If he didn't find any verdict from Abu Bakr he would gather with the leaders and scholars and consult them. If their views and opinions were in agreement upon the issue then Umar would give his verdict according to what was agreed upon.'[1]

---

[1]-(TN)This is the wording in Sunan al Kubra by al Bayhaqi 10/196, #20341; and ad Daramee in his Sunan #163 with a wording similar to this. The narrators of this narration are all trustworthy except for the fact that it is not established that Maymoon heard from Abu Bakr, so the chain is 'Munqat'i' (disconnected).

Al 'I'tibaa'a

Also Abdur Razzaq narrated with two chains of narration and ad Daramee also:

عَنِ الشَّعْبِيِّ، قَالَ: سُئِلَ أَبُو بَكْرٍ، عَنِ الْكَلَالَةِ فَقَالَ: " إِنِّي سَأَقُولُ فِيهَا بِرَأْيِي، فَإِنْ كَانَ صَوَابًا فَمِنَ اللهِ، وَإِنْ كَانَ خَطَأً فَمِنِّي وَمِنَ الشَّيْطَانِ: أُرَاهُ مَا خَلَا الْوَالِدَ وَالْوَلَدَ " فَلَمَّا اسْتُخْلِفَ عُمَرُ، قَالَ: «إِنِّي لَأَسْتَحْيِي اللهَ أَنْ أَرُدَّ شَيْئًا قَالَهُ أَبُو بَكْرٍ»

"On the authority of as Sha'bee who said: 'Abu Bakr was asked about the 'Kalaalah'[1], so he replied: 'Verily I will give you my opinion, if it is correct than it is from Allah and if it is incorrect than it is from myself and the satan. I view that it is someone without a father and a son. So when Umar became the succeeding caliph after Abu Bakr he said: 'I feel embarrassed and bashful in front of Allah to abandon anything that Abu Bakr said.'"[2]

Ad Daramee narrated with an authentic chain of narration:

عَنْ عُبَيْدِ اللهِ بْنِ أَبِي يَزِيدَ، قَالَ: كَانَ ابْنُ عَبَّاسٍ رَضِيَ اللهُ عَنْهُمَا، «إِذَا سُئِلَ عَنِ الْأَمْرِ فَكَانَ فِي الْقُرْآنِ، أَخْبَرَ بِهِ، وَإِنْ لَمْ يَكُنْ فِي الْقُرْآنِ وَكَانَ عَنْ رَسُولِ اللهِ صَلَّى اللهُ عَلَيْهِ وَسَلَّمَ، أَخْبَرَ بِهِ، فَإِنْ لَمْ يَكُنْ، فَعَنْ أَبِي بَكْرٍ وَعُمَرَ رَضِيَ اللهُ عَنْهُمَا - فَإِنْ لَمْ يَكُنْ، قَالَ فِيهِ بِرَأْيِهِ»

"On the authority of Ubaydullah ibn Abee Yazeed who said: 'If Abdullah ibn Abaas was asked about any issue and it was mentioned in the Quran he would pass his verdict with what was in the Quran. If the answer to the issue was not in the Quran and was mentioned in the Sunnah then he would pass his verdict with what was in the Sunnah. If the answer was not contained in the Sunnah then he would pass his verdict with what Abu Bakr and Umar declared, and if he didn't find any ruling or verdict given by Abu Bakr or Umar then he would state his personal opinion.'"[3]

---

[1]-(TN)Those who leave neither descendants neither ascendants as heirs
[2]-This is the wording in Sunan ad Daramee 2/264 #3015, it is also in Musanaf Abdur Razzaq 10/304,#19191 but within this narration is a defect: Ash Sha'bee did not hear from Abu Bakr,(meaning the narration is 'Munqat'i') except for the fact that the statement of Abu Bakr is well known to be from him. The rest of the narrators are trustworthy. Ibnul Qayyim mentioned it in 'I'laam al Muwa'qaeen' 2/118
[3]-Sunan ad Daramee 1/55, #168, also 'al Faqeeh wal Mutafaqih' 1/203

Al 'I'tibaa'a

Ad Daramee also narrated:

عَنْ أَبِي سُهَيْلٍ، قَالَ: كَانَ عَلَى امْرَأَتِي اعْتِكَافُ ثَلَاثَةِ أَيَّامٍ فِي الْمَسْجِدِ الْحَرَامِ، فَسَأَلْتُ عُمَرَ بْنَ عَبْدِ الْعَزِيزِ، وَعِنْدَهُ ابْنُ شِهَابٍ، قَالَ: قُلْتُ عَلَيْهَا صِيَامٌ. قَالَ ابْنُ شِهَابٍ: لَا يَكُونُ اعْتِكَافٌ إِلَّا بِصِيَامٍ. فَقَالَ لَهُ عُمَرُ بْنُ عَبْدِ الْعَزِيزِ: أَعَنِ النَّبِيِّ صَلَّى اللهُ عَلَيْهِ وَسَلَّمَ؟ قَالَ: لَا. قَالَ: فَعَنْ أَبِي بَكْرٍ؟ قَالَ: لَا؟ قَالَ: فَعَنْ عُمَرَ؟ قَالَ: لَا. قَالَ: فَعَنْ عُثْمَانَ؟ قَالَ: لَا. قَالَ عُمَرُ: مَا أَرَى عَلَيْهَا صِيَامًا. فَخَرَجْتُ فَوَجَدْتُ طَاوُسًا وَعَطَاءَ بْنَ أَبِي رَبَاحٍ، فَسَأَلْتُهُمَا، فَقَالَ طَاوُسٌ: كَانَ ابْنُ عَبَّاسٍ رَضِيَ اللهُ عَنْهُمَا، «لَا يَرَى عَلَيْهَا صِيَامًا إِلَّا أَنْ تَجْعَلَهُ عَلَى نَفْسِهَا» . قَالَ: وَقَالَ عَطَاءٌ: ذَلِكَ رَأْيِي"

On the authority of Abee Sahl who said: 'It was compulsory for my wife to make 'I'tikaaf'1for three days in the Masjid al Haraam, so I asked Umar ibn Abdul Aziz who was accompanied by Ibn Shihab I said: Is it necessary for her to fast?, Ibn Shihab replied: 'There is not 'I'tikaaf' except while fasting'. Suddenly Umar ibn Abdul Aziz said to Ibn Shihab: 'Is that on the authority of the Prophet Muhammad?, Ibn Shihab replied: no. Then Umar asked: 'on the authority of Abu Bakr?, he replied: no. Then Umar asked: 'on the authority of Umar ibn al Khattab?, he replied: no. Then Umar asked: 'on the authority of Uthmaan?, he replied: no. Then Umar ibn Abdul Aziz said: 'I view that she doesn't have to fast'. Then I left and I came across Tawoos and Ataa'a ibn Abee Rabaah so I asked them the same question. Tawoos said: 'Ibn Abaas used to have the view that she doesn't have to fast, except if she makes it compulsory upon herself.' Then Ataa'a said: 'And that is also my view'.2

---

[1]-(TN)Seclusion in the masjid for the purpose of worshipping Allah.
[2]-Sunan ad Daramee 1/54, #164 with an authentic chain of narration

Al 'I'tibaa'a

Part Five

The Fundamentals which the scholars of 'Fiqh' used to base their rulings upon

1. The Quran

2. The Sunnah

3. Consensus of the companions, or other than them

4. Narrations of the companions

5. 'Qiyas'

These are the fundamentals of 'fiqh' which the four Imam's of 'fiqh' used in each of their schools of thought, taking them directly from the texts of the Quran, Sunnah and narrations of the companions.

Although the majority of the jurists mention that the fundamentals of 'fiqh' are only four fundamentals, they do not include the narrations of the companions. If they want to include the narrations of the companions to be from the Sunnah than this is a great thing, if not then at least it is necessary that they include the narrations of the companions to be from the fundamentals of 'fiqh'.

Now we will mention what has been narrated about the four scholars of 'fiqh' regarding this issue:

As for Abu Haneefah an Nu'maan ibn Thaabit for indeed Yahya ibn Ma'een mentioned and also al Khateeb al Baghdaadi in their books of 'Tarikh' (history) on the authority of Yahya ibn   ad- Durays who said: 'I saw Sufyaan ath Thawree and a man came to him and said: 'Is there anything that you hold a grudge against Abu Haneefah?, he said: 'For what reason?'. Then the man said: 'I heard Abu Haneefah say: 'I take from the Quran, and whatever issue I don't find the answer in the Quran, then I take from the Sunnah, if I don't find it in the Quran or the Sunnah then I take from the sayings of the companions, I choose whatever statement I like from amongst them, and I do not exceed or abandon the companions statements for anyone else's statements.

However if the affair comes down to the statements of Ibrahim an Nakha'ee, ash Sha'bee, Muhammad ibn Sireen, al Hasan al Basree, Ataa'a ibn Abee Rabah, or Sa'eed ibnul Musayib, and he mentioned many other men (tabi'oon)...They all exerted their efforts 'ijtihaad', so I will exert my efforts and 'ijtihaad' as they all did."[1]

Al Bayhaqi and Ibn Abdul Barr also mentioned this fundamental from Abu Haneefah.

They also mentioned a statement of Abu Yusuf who said: 'I heard Abu Haneefah say: 'If a hadeeth of the Prophet Muhammad ﷺ reaches us by the way of trustworthy narrators then we take this hadeeth, and if a narration reaches us from the companions then we do not exceed their statements, and if a narration reaches us from the 'tabi'oon' then we are rivals to them.'[2]

Al-Hasan ibn Salih said: 'Abu Haneefah was very scrutinizing and investigative in searching for the 'nasikh' and 'mansookh'[3] ahadeeth. He would act upon the hadeeth if he saw it to be authentic from the Prophet ﷺ and from the companions. He was well versed and very knowledgeable about the hadeeth which came from the people of al Koofah[4], as well as their 'fiqh'. He was extremely adherent to what the people were following in his city, and he used to say: 'Verily there are texts in the Quran which are 'nasikh' and 'mansookh' and similarly there are texts amongst the ahadeeth with are 'nasikh' and 'mansookh''. He had memorized and always recalled the last action of the Prophet Muhammad ﷺ before his death, according to what was known by the people of his city.'[5]

Abu Haneefah also said: 'If the hadeeth is authentic than that is my 'madth'hab'.[6]

Also Abu Hamzah as Sukaree[1] said: 'I heard Abu Haneefah say: 'If a hadeeth reaches me with an authentic chain of narration then we take it, and if a

---

[1] -Tarikh Ibn Ma'een from ad Dowree's transmission 4/63, and from his chain al Khateeb al Baghdaadi mentioned it in 'Tarikh Baghdaad' 13/368, also mentioned in 'Akhbaar Abee Haneefah' by as Sumayree pg.10.
[2] -'al Madkhal' by al Bayhaqi 1/46 also see 'al Intiqaa'a' by Ibn Abdul Barr pg.143
[3] -(TN)Nasikh:The text which abrogates other texts, Mansookh: the text which has been abrogated
[4] -(TN)City in Iraq
[5] -Akhbaar Abee Haneefah by as Sumayree Husein ibn Ali (died 436) Hyderabad printing 1394 hijri.
[6] -Introduction to The Prophets Prayer, by al Albaani

Al 'I'tibaa'a

narration of the companions reaches me then we select a narration or narrations from them, if a narration reaches me from the 'tabi'oon' then we are rivals to them and we do not exceed their statements."[2]

Abdullah ibnul Mubarak said: 'I heard Abu Haneefah say: 'If a statement comes to me from the Prophet Muhammad ﷺ then it is upon my head and eyes[3], if a statement comes to me from the companions then we choose from amongst their sayings, and if a statement comes from the 'tabieen' then we are rivals to them.'[4]

Similarly was case with Imam Malik who the scholars and his students have transmitted the fundamentals of his 'fiqh' from his statements:

Abu Nu'aym narrated in 'al Hilyah'[5] on the authority of Mutarrif ibn Abdullah who said I heard Imam Malik say: 'The Prophet Muhammad ﷺ and those in authority after him legislated and established laws. Taking them is considered adherence to the Book of Allah, and complete obedience to Allah, and gives one strength in Allah's religion. It is not permissible for anyone to change or alter anything, nor is it permissible for anyone to look into nor consider anything which is in opposition to the Islamic laws. Whoever is guided by the Islamic laws then verily he is the guided one, and whoever seeks and turns to these laws for aid, then verily he will be aided. Likewise, whoever abandons it and follows a path other than the path of the believers, then verily he will stay upon the path he has chosen and be burned by the hellfire, what an evil destination.'

On the authority of Ishaq ibn Isa who said: ' Imam Malik said: "Has it reached the point that whenever an extremely argumentative man comes-being more

---

[1]-(TN) He is Imam, al Hujjah, Muhammad ibn Maymoon al Marwazee, Abu Hamzah as Sukaree (Sugar), they used to call him this because of the sweetness of his speech. He died in the year 167 hijri

[2]-al Intiqaa'a by Ibn Abdul Barr pg.144-145

[3]-(TN)This is an Arabic expression used to mean that something is given top priority, utmost importance, emphasis and focus upon

[4]-al Madkhal ila Sunan by al Bayhaqi 1/46 from the chain of Nu'aym ibn Hamaad from Ibnul Mubarak

[5]-Hilyah al Awliyaah wa Tabaqaat al Asfiyaah is a book which Abu Nu'aym al Asbahaani authored which contains over 800 biographies of the companions, the tabi'een and others while mentioning some of their narrations, statements and stories. In the introduction of this book he talks about the 'Awliyaah' and the 'Mutasawifaah' then he goes on to mention the biography of Abu Bakr as Sideeq and the remaining rightly guided caliphates.

Al 'I'tibaa'a

argumentative than the previous one-that we abandon that which Jibreel descended with upon the Prophet Muhammad ?!¹

Within the letter of al Laith ibn Sa'd to Imam Malik is clear evidence proving the strict and firm adherence of Imam Malik to the narrations of the companions and especially those from al- Madinah.'²

Imam Malik also said: "Truly I am only a mortal: I make mistakes and I am correct. Therefore, look into my opinions: all that agrees with the Book and the Sunnah, accept it; and all that does not agree with the Book and the Sunnah, ignore it."³

He also said: "'There is no one after the Prophet Muhammad except that his sayings are accepted and rejected –with the exception of the Prophet."⁴

As for Imam ash Shafi'ee Muhammad ibn Idrees than verily his fundamentals in 'fiqh' were clarified in his books and adorned his compilations extensively. Similarly the statements which the trustworthy narrators narrated from him relaying his beautiful and excellent fundamentals of 'fiqh'. Furthermore the differing, conflict, disagreement, and bigotry and fanaticism towards the statements of the scholars increased in the time of ash Shafi'ee and Imam Ahmed. So for this reason you find both of them showed great emphasis and importance to the issues related to 'al it'ibaa'a and 'taqleed'.

Imam ash Shafi'ee said: 'The foundation is the Quran and Sunnah, if the issue is not found within them then 'qiyas' is used being based upon them both. If there is a hadeeth from the Prophet Muhammad with an authentic and connected chain of narration, then this is considered a Sunnah. In addition, consensus of

---

[1] -al Hilyah 6/324
[2] -I'laam al Muwa'qaeen 3/107
[3] -Ibn Abdul Barr in 'al Jami' 2/32 and on the authority of Ibn Abdul Barr, Ibn Hazm in 'Usool al Ahkam' 6/149, also al Fulaani pg.72
[4] -This statement has been attributed to Imam Malik amongst the later scholars, and Ibn Abdul Haadi authenticated it in 'Irshaad as Saalik' 1/277, Ibn Abdul Barr narrated it in 'al Jami' 2/91 and Ibn Hazm in 'Usool al Ahkam' 6/145-179 from the statement of al Hakam ibn Utaybah and Mujahid, also Taqi ad Deen as Subkee in his 'Fataawa' 1/148 from the statement of Ibn Abaas praising its goodness, then he said:' Mujahid took this statement from Ibn Abaas and Malik took it from both of them and it became famous from Malik. Sheikh Wasiullah said: 'then Imam Ahmed took the statement from them, indeed Abu Dawud said in his 'Masaa'il al Imam Ahmed',pg.276: 'I heard Ahmed say: There is no one except that his opinions are accepted and rejected, except for the Prophet Muhammad.'

Al 'I'tibaa'a

the companions precedes the individual narrations (of companions), and the hadeeth should be taken based upon its apparent meaning. If it so happens that the hadeeth contains more than one meaning then the meaning which is most apparent should be given precedence. Furthermore, if the narrations are equivalent in meaning than the hadeeth with the strongest chain of narration is given precedence, and the 'munqati'[1] hadeeth is worthless except for the 'munqati' of Sa'eed ibn Musayib.'[2]

Imam ash Shafi'ee also said: 'It is never permissible for anyone to utter- saying that something is 'halaal' or 'haraam' (permissible and impermissible) except with knowledge, and 'with knowledge' means: from the Quran, Sunnah, consensus of the companions, or 'qiyas'.

He also said: 'Allah the Most High did not give anyone the right to say anything after the Prophet ﷺ except with the knowledge that preceded him. The knowledge which proceeds the Quran, Sunnah, and consensus is the narrations of the companions and that described from 'qiyas.'[3]

Imam ash Shafi'ee also said: 'Knowledge is two aspects 'it'ibaa'a' (following and imitation) and 'istinbaat' (deduction).

'It'ibaa'a is: Following the Quran, if it is not in the Quran, then the Sunnah, and if it is not in the Sunnah than the statements of the majority of our righteous predecessors, we don't know of any opposition to this amongst the scholars. If nothing is found than we use 'qiyas' based upon the Quran, and if nothing is found in the Quran than we use 'qiyas' based upon the Sunnah, if nothing is found in the Sunnah then we use 'qiyas' based upon the statements of the majority of our righteous predecessors and there is no opposition to this. In addition, it is not permissible to issue a statement except with 'qiyas', and if the jurists use their 'qiyas' and differ in the issue, then after exerting their 'ijtihaad' in the issue they can state the conclusion they came to. In this case the jurist does not follow or imitate anyone who made 'ijtihaad' regarding the issue and came to a conclusion in opposition to his. And Allah knows best.'[4]

Ash Shafi'ee also said: 'Verily the evidence is contained in the Quran and Sunnah or a narration from some of the companions of the Prophet Muhammad ﷺ, or a

---

[1] -(TN)A hadeeth which has a disconnected or detached chain of narration
[2] -al Faqeeh wal Mutafaqih 1/230
[3] -ar Risalah pg. 84-538, al Fath Publishers-ash Shariqah
[4] -al Umm 1/153

Al 'I'tibaa'a

statement of the majority of the Muslims (companions) in which there was no differing, or 'qiyas' which is included in some of this.'[1]

He also said: 'The statement which is accepted is that which is in the Quran, Sunnah, or an authentic hadeeth on the authority of one of the companions or their consensus.'[2]

Ash Shafi'ee also said: 'As long as the Quran and the Sunnah are present than there is no excuse for the one who hears them and he must follow them. If the issue is not found in the Quran and Sunnah then we look to the statements of the companions of Allah's Messenger ﷺ collectively or individually. Furthermore, 'taqleed' of the statements of Abu Bakr, Umar or Uthmaan is more beloved to us than 'taqleed' of anyone else.'[3]

Ash Shafi'ee also said: 'Verily we came to realize and found that the scholars started to ask about knowledge from the Quran and Sunnah regarding the issues in which they wanted to speak about. So they would speak about these issues, then they would be informed that their statement was in opposition to the Quran and the Sunnah. Subsequently, they would never refrain, be hesitant, nor abstain from taking back their statements. This was mainly because of their extreme piety, righteousness and virtue. So if it was not found amongst the statements of the scholars then verily the companions of the Prophet Muhammad ﷺ are in a position in which we take their statements, and the following and imitation of the companions takes precedence over following those who come after them. And knowledge is of many degrees and categories:

1. The Quran and Sunnah, if the Sunnah is established and authentic

2. Consensus upon that which is not contained in the Quran and Sunnah

3. A statement of the some of the Prophet's ﷺ companions and we do not find any opposition to their statements

4. The various and different statements of the companions regarding that issue

---

[1] -al Umm 2/31
[2] -al Umm 2/434
[3] -al Umm by ash Shafi'ee 7/265

5. 'Qiyas' based upon some of these categories, and you should not look to other than the Quran and Sunnah as long as they are present.[1] Imam ash Shafi'ee used to use 'qiyas' only when it was extremely necessary.

He also said: 'We pass our ruling according to the consensus then proceeding this is 'qiyas' and 'qiyas' is weaker than consensus, but it is sometimes necessary. Solely because it is not permissible to use 'qiyas' with the existence of a narration, just as when traveling and there is a lack of water. So in this case 'tayammum' is only used as the means of purification when there is a lack of water, and if water exists than 'tayammum' is not used as a means of purification. So 'tayammum' is only used when there is a lack of water. Similarly that which is subsequent to the Sunnah is an authoritative evidence when there is a lack of or doesn't exist a narration from the Sunnah."[2]

Imam ash Shafi'ee has many statements, emphasizing this issue in many of his books and also in many of the books of those who narrated these statements from him regarding the arrangement and systematical organization of the fundamentals of 'fiqh'.[3]

Likewise we find many of the scholars mentioned and implemented the statements of Imam Ahmed ibn Hanbal in his fundamentals of 'fiqh.

Al Khateeb al Baghdaadi narrated on the authority of al Athram who said: 'I saw Abu Abdullah Ahmed ibn Hanbal in the issues which we heard from him saying: 'If there exists a hadeeth from the Prophet ﷺ in an issue no one should take the statement of a companion nor anyone proceeding them which is in opposition to that statement. And if there is an issue in which there exists differing statements from the companions then we choose from amongst their statements, and we do not exceed their statements by taking statements of those who proceed them. If there doesn't exist a hadeeth from the Prophet ﷺ nor a statement from the companions then we select a statement from the 'tabi'een'. Perhaps there may be a hadeeth from the Prophet Muhammad ﷺ in which the chain of narration contains a defect, if this is the case then we take this hadeeth if there isn't a narration that contradicts it that is stronger than it, like the hadeeth of

---

[1] -al Umm 7/265, also see 'ar Risalah pg.596-598, and 'al Faqeeh wal Mutafaqih' 1/220
[2] -ar Risalah 599-600
[3] -See 'Adaab ash Shafi'ee and Manaaqibuhu' by Ibn Abee Haatim, also see Munaaqib ash Shafi'ee and Ma'rifatus Sunan wal Athaar by al Bayhaqi, and al Faqeeh wal Mutafaqih by al Khateeb al Baghdaadi

Al 'I'tibaa'a

Amru ibn Shu'ayb and Ibrahim al Hijri, and perhaps one may take a 'mursal' hadeeth if there exist no opposing narrations.[1]

Sheikh al Imam Abu Muhammad Rizqullah Abdul Wahaab ibn Abdul Aziz at Tameemee, the Hanbali jurist of his time said about the of Imam Ahmed's fundamentals of 'fiqh': 'He (Imam Ahmed) used to view that Allah's proofs and evidences in the religious legislations and the incidents which do not fall under the category of essential knowledge are all taken from five fundamentals or sources:

1. The Quran and he would recite Allah's saying:

$$\text{﴿ مَّا فَرَّطْنَا فِى ٱلْكِتَٰبِ مِن شَىْءٍ ﴾}$$

"We haven't neglected anything in the Book (Quran)" (al An'am 6:38)

2. The Sunnah of Allah's Messenger and he would recite Allah's saying:

$$\text{﴿ فَإِن تَنَٰزَعْتُمْ فِى شَىْءٍ فَرُدُّوهُ إِلَى ٱللَّهِ وَٱلرَّسُولِ ﴾}$$

"If you differ in anything amongst yourselves refer to Allah and His Messenger" (an Nisa 4:59) i.e. referring back to the Messenger after his death, is referring back to his Sunnah, as the Prophet said: *"Hold firmly unto my Sunnah..."*[2] then recite Allah's saying:

$$\text{﴿ وَمَآ ءَاتَىٰكُمُ ٱلرَّسُولُ فَخُذُوهُ وَمَا نَهَىٰكُمْ عَنْهُ فَٱنتَهُواْ ﴾}$$

"Whatsoever the Messenger gives you, then take it, and whatever he forbids you from then leave it and abstain from it." (al Hashr 59:7)

3. Consensus of the scholars of a certain time period, the people of knowledge, the leaders and those in authority if they come to agreement, even if one of them is in disagreement then it is not considered consensus. Similarly if a statement issued by some of them becomes popular or widespread and all of

---

[1] -al Faqeeh wal Mutafaqih 1/221
[2] -(TN)Abu Dawud, Book of the Sunnah, Chapter: Holding onto the Sunnah, # 4607, At Tirmidthi #2676, and others. It is an authentic narration.

them have knowledge of this statement, and no one denies, disclaims, or disproves it, then this is considered consensus.

Imam Ahmed used to say: 'The consensus is the consensus of the companions and other than them are considered pursuant to them.

4. A statement of an individual companion which becomes popular or widespread and there is no one who disclaims the statement nor disproves it.

5. 'Qiyas': Is referring or returning an issue back to something which is parallel or equivalent to it, by using the justification which combines the fundamental aspect and the subsidiary aspect, if this is not possible then there is no 'qiyas'.

Imam Ahmed used to say: meaning: 'With 'qiyas' (is used) by the way of similarity and close relationship, until the issue manifests a correct justification to combine between the fundamental aspect and the subsidiary aspect.' He used to consider 'qiyas'-in the systematic approach of arranging the proofs and evidences-as the status of a dead animal in times of necessity, and dirt (tayamum) when lacking water. As for deducting and extracting proofs and evidences from 'qiyas' then this is considered impermissible in his view.'[1]

Ibnul Qayyim said: "Imam Ahmed's religious verdicts were based upon five fundamentals:

1. The authentic texts from the Quran and the Sunnah, if he came across a text then he would give his verdict in accordance with the text, and he wouldn't pay regard to anything nor anyone else. He would never give precedence to any action, saying, opinion, or 'qiyas', nor give precedence to a saying from one of the followers of the 'madth'hab', over an authentic narration, nor would he give precedence to not having knowledge of the opposition, which many people call 'consensus' and give this precedence over an authentic hadeeth. Indeed, Imam Ahmed viewed those who considered this to be 'consensus' as being liars, and he viewed it impermissible to give this precedence over an authentic narration.

2. The religious verdicts given by the companions, if he found that some of them gave a religious verdict, and he knew of no opposition from any of them, he would not consider anything else, nor would he say that it is 'consensus', this

---

[1] -Qitatu min Usool Madth'habuhu wa Mashrabuhu, by Abee Muhammad Rizqullah at Tameemee, printed at the end of 'Tabaqaat ibn Abee Ya'laa 2/283-285, with some summarization. Also the author narrated some strange statements attributing them to Imam Ahmed like his saying: My companions are like the stars'...

was because of his extreme piety in his statements in which he would say: 'I don't know of anything which can dismiss this statement.'

3. If the statements of the companions were numerous and differing he would select the statement that was closest to the Quran and the Sunnah, and he would not exceed their statements. If the suitability of one of the statements didn't become apparent to him or was not in accordance to the Quran and Sunnah, then he would mention that there is difference of opinion in the issue and he would not make a statement of absolute certainty.

Ishaaq ibn Ibrahim ibn Hani'[1] said in his 'Masaa'il': 'It was said to Abee Abdullah (Imam Ahmed): 'There is a man in a place and he asks about an issue in which there is a difference of opinion?, Imam Ahmed replied: 'He should give his verdict with that which is in accordance to the Quran and Sunnah, and whatever is not in accordance with the Quran and Sunnah then stay away from it', it was said to him: 'Are you worried or concerned about him? He replied: No."

4. Using and taking the 'mursal' and 'da'eef' (weak) ahadeeth, if there is nothing similar to it which can disprove it or falsify it. Imam Ahmed gave precedence to these over 'qiyas'. In addition, what is meant by 'da'eef' amongst Imam Ahmed is not the hadeeth which is falsehood nor a hadeeth which contains liars, or narrators who make frequent mistakes, whereas it is not permissible to use these hadeeth and act upon them. Rather the hadeeth 'da'eef' in his view is the opposite of a hadeeth 'saheeh' (authentic), and under the category of the 'hasan' (good) ahadeeth. Imam Ahmed didn't divide or categorize the ahadeeth into three categories (saheeh, hasan, da'eef) rather he would only consider them to be two categories-saheeh and da'eef. Furthermore, the 'da'eef' narrations are of different grades, if he didn't find a similar narration in opposition to the hadeeth, or a saying of one of the scholars, or consensus in opposition to the narration-then action upon the weak hadeeth would be given precedence over 'qiyas'. All the four scholars of 'fiqh' agreed with him-in general-regarding this fundamental. ..Then some of the issues in which Abu Haneefah, Malik and ash Shafi'ee gave precedence to ahadeeth 'da'eef' as evidence in were mentioned.

---

[1]-(TN)He is the sheikhul Islam the Muhaddith of Khurasaan, Muhammd ibn Ishaaq ibn Ibrahim ibn Mihraan al Khurasaani, Abul Abbaas as Siraaj. He was born in the year 216 hijri and died in the year 313 hijri. He was from the students of Ishaaq ibn Rahaway'ya and many others. Some of his students are Imam Al Bukhari, Imam Muslim, Abu Haatim ar Raazi, Abu Bakr ibn Abee Dunya, Abu Haatim al Bustee, Ibn Adee and others. He authored the 'Musnad al Kabeer' and is well known for his transmission of 'Masaa'il of Imam Ahmed'.

5. If Imam Ahmed didn't come across a text or a statement from the companions, even a statement from one of them, or a 'mursal' or 'da'eef' hadeeth, then he would resort to 'qiyas' which is the fifth and final fundamental that he would only use in extreme necessities.

It was mentioned in the book of 'al Khallal': 'I asked Imam ash Shafi'ee about 'qiyas' and he said: 'Only use it when it is necessary'...

And in another narration, of Abu Harith: 'What can you do with opinion and 'qiyas' while the hadeeth contains that which suffices you from using it?

In another narration, of Abdul Malik al Maymoonee: 'The one who speaks regarding 'fiqh' should avoid two things: abriged statements and 'qiyas'

These are the five fundamentals upon which Imam Ahmed's religious verdicts were based upon. Perhaps he may have hesitated in giving a verdict because of the incompatibility of some of the texts or evidences, or for the existence of differing statements amongst the companions, or for the lack of being familiar or coming across a narration or statement of one of the companions or 'tabi'een'. He extremely disliked and prohibited the passing of religious verdicts in any issue in which there did not exist a narration from the 'salaf'. He had mentioned to some of his students and companions: "Be warned/take heed, to speak about an issue in which you have no (Imam) one who preceded you in it."[1]

Imam Ahmed also viewed that the authentic narrations of the companions took precedence over weak ahadeeth.

Ibn Hani' said: 'I said to Abu Abdullah (Imam Ahmed): 'Is the narration mentioned from the Messenger of Allah ﷺ with trustworthy narrators[2] more beloved to you than the narration mentioned from the companions or the 'tabi'een' with a connected chain and trustworthy narrators? He replied: 'The narration from the companions is more beloved to me.'[3]

The four scholars of 'fiqh' always advised the people to take the proof and evidence and leave off their personal statements. Their statements are well

---

1- 'I'laam al Muwa'qaeen 1/29-33, verification of the texts done by Abdur Rahman al Wakeel and another copy of the book 2/50-60 which was verified by Mashoor Hasan al Salmaan, also see the book 'Usool al Imam Ahmed' by Dr. Abdullah ibn Abdul Muhsin at-Turkey
2- **(TN)** A narration which may have an unconnected chain of narration
3- 'Masaa'il Ishaaq ibn Ibrahim ibn Hani' 2/56

Al 'I'tibaa'a

known to all the world about abandoning their statements if they are in opposition to the proofs and evidences of the Quran and Sunnah.

Imam Abu Haneefah said: 'If I said something which is in opposition to the Quran and what the Messenger ﷺ informed us, then abandon my statement.'

And Imam Malik said: "There is no one after the Prophet Muhammad ﷺ except that his sayings are accepted and rejected –with the exception of the Prophet Muhammad ﷺ"

And he also said: "Truly I am only a mortal: I make mistakes (sometimes) and I am correct (sometimes). Therefore, study my opinions: all that agrees with the Book and the Sunnah, accept it; and all that does not agree with the Book and the Sunnah, ignore it."

Imam ash Shafi'ee said: "The Muslims are unanimously agreed that if a Sunnah of the Messenger of Allaah ﷺ is apparent to someone, then it is not permissible for him to leave it for the statement of anyone else.'

He also said: "'In every issue where the people of narration find a report from the Messenger of Allaah ﷺ to be authentic which is contrary to what I have said, then I take my saying back, whether during my life or after my death."

Similarly the statements of Imam Ahmed are numerous regarding adhering to and holding firmly unto the Sunnah, from his statements:

"Whoever rejects a statement of the Messenger of Allah ﷺ is on the brink of destruction"[1]

If the companions of Allah's Messenger ﷺ as well as the earlier scholars did not know nor recall a hadeeth from Allah's Messenger ﷺ, and issued a statement in opposition to it, they would withdraw and retract their statements immediately if they became familiar with a prophetic narration, and this is something which there is no differing or doubt about.

Abu Bakr as Sideeq, the most knowledgeable person after the Prophet Muhammad ﷺ, however he was not familiar with the amount of inheritance

---

[1]-See Introduction to The Prophet's Prayer Described, by al Albaani for all of these statements 45-53

legislated for the grandmother, then once he came to know, he immediately withdrew his statement.[1]

Abu Ubayd al Qasim ibn Sallaam narrated and from him Ibn Zanjawaya :

عَنْ طَارِقِ بْنِ شِهَابٍ، قَالَ: قَدِمَ وَفْدُ بُزَاخَةَ، مِنْ أَسَدٍ وَغَطَفَانَ، عَلَى أَبِي بَكْرٍ، يَسْأَلُونَهُ الصُّلْحَ، فَخَيَّرَهُمْ أَبُو بَكْرٍ بَيْنَ الْحَرْبِ الْمُجْلِيَةِ وَالسَّلْمِ الْمُخْزِيَةِ فَقَالُوا لَهُ: هَذِهِ الْحَرْبُ الْمُجْلِيَةُ قَدْ عَرَفْنَاهَا، فَمَا السَّلْمُ الْمُخْزِيَةُ؟ فَقَالَ: أَنْ تُنْزَعَ مِنْكُمُ الْحَلْقَةُ وَالْكُرَاعُ وَتَتْرُكُوا أَقْوَامًا تَتَّبِعُونَ أَذْنَابَ الْإِبِلِ، حَتَّى يُرِيَ اللهُ خَلِيفَةَ نَبِيِّهِ وَالْمُهَاجِرِينَ أَمْرًا يَعْذِرُونَكُمْ بِهِ، وَنَغْنَمُ مَا أَصَبْنَا مِنْكُمْ، وَتَرُدُّوا إِلَيْنَا مَا أَصَبْتُمْ مِنَّا، وَتَدُوا قَتْلَانَا، وَتَكُونُ قَتْلَاكُمْ فِي النَّارِ، فَقَامَ عُمَرُ، فَقَالَ: إِنَّكَ قَدْ رَأَيْتَ رَأْيًا وَسَنُشِيرُ عَلَيْكَ: أَمَّا مَا رَأَيْتَ أَنْ تَنْزِعَ مِنْهُمُ الْحَلْقَةَ وَالْكُرَاعَ، فَنِعْمَ مَا رَأَيْتَ، وَأَمَّا مَا ذَكَرْتَ أَنْ يُتْرَكُوا أَقْوَامًا يَتَّبِعُونَ أَذْنَابَ الْإِبِلِ حَتَّى يُرِيَ اللهُ خَلِيفَةَ نَبِيِّهِ وَالْمُهَاجِرِينَ أَمْرًا يَعْذِرُونَهُمْ بِهِ، فَنِعْمَ مَا رَأَيْتَ، وَأَمَّا مَا ذَكَرْتَ أَنْ نَغْنَمَ مَا أَصَبْنَا مِنْهُمْ وَيَرُدُّوا إِلَيْنَا مَا أَصَابُوا مِنَّا، فَنِعْمَ مَا رَأَيْتَ، وَأَمَّا مَا رَأَيْتَ أَنْ يَدُوا قَتْلَانَا وَتَكُونَ قَتْلَاهُمْ فِي النَّارِ، فَإِنَّ قَتْلَانَا قُتِلُوا عَلَى أَمْرِ اللهِ، أُجُورُهُمْ عَلَى اللهِ، لَيْسَتْ لَهُمْ دِيَاتٌ، قَالَ: فَتَابَعَ الْقَوْمُ عُمَرَ.

"On the authority of Tariq ibn Shihab who said: 'A caravan from Bazakhah[2] from Asad and Gatafaan[3] came to see Abu Bakr asking him to reconcile and make peace between them. So Abu Bakr gave them a choice between a devastating war in which you will be driven out or a disgraceful, humiliating peace treaty in which we will make conditions for you to abide by. They responded: 'We already know about the devastating war, but what is the humiliating peace treaty. Abu Bakr replied: it is that you remove from your brigades your cavalry and weapons, and you shall remain in your farms herding the camels and livestock until Allah makes you realize the status of the successor of the Prophet Muhammad ﷺ and the 'Muhaajireen' and you choose to remain here peacefully or be taken out forcefully. And we take possession of the war spoils which we gain from you and you must return to us everything you take from us. Also you must pay blood money for everyone whom you kill from amongst our people and your casualities will be in the hellfire.' So Umar ibn Al-Khattab stood up and said: 'Verily you have taken an opinion in which we would like to comment upon. As for what you said concerning removing their cavalry and weapons, this is a great view. As for what you said concerning

---

[1]-Abu Dawud, at Tirmidthi, Ibn Majah and others, but it is a weak narration, Ibnul Qayyim mentioned it in 'I'laam al Muwa'qaeen 4/19-20
[2]-**(TN)** Close to modern day Ha'il in Saudia Arabia
[3]-**(TN)** Two tribes who were hostile to Abu Bakr as Sideeq

Al 'I'tibaa'a

making them remain in their farms herding the camels and livestock until Allah makes them realize the status of the successor of the Prophet Muhammad ﷺ and the 'Muhaajireen' and they choose to remain here peacefully or be taken out forcefully, this is also a great view. As for what you mentioned concerning that we take possession of the war spoils and they return to us what they take from us, then this is also a great opinion. As for what you said concerning them paying blood money for our casualities and their casualities being in the hellfire, then verily our casualities fought and were killed for the sake of and by the will of Allah and there is no blood money concerning them.' Then the people followed Umar regarding the issue.'[1]

Another example is when Umar ibn al-Khattab was unfamiliar with the ruling regarding the permissibility of making 'tayummum' for the one who was sexually impure. So when he was informed about the narration from the Prophet ﷺ, he immediately followed it and recanted his previous statement.

As Imam Muslim narrated on the authority of Abdur Rahman ibn Abzaa that a man came to Umar and said to him:

عَنْ سَعِيدِ بْنِ عَبْدِ الرَّحْمَنِ بْنِ أَبْزَى، عَنْ أَبِيهِ، أَنَّ رَجُلًا أَتَى عُمَرَ، فَقَالَ: إِنِّي أَجْنَبْتُ فَلَمْ أَجِدْ مَاءً فَقَالَ: لَا تُصَلِّ. فَقَالَ عَمَّارٌ: أَمَا تَذْكُرُ يَا أَمِيرَ الْمُؤْمِنِينَ، إِذْ أَنَا وَأَنْتَ فِي سَرِيَّةٍ فَأَجْنَبْنَا فَلَمْ نَجِدْ مَاءً، فَأَمَّا أَنْتَ فَلَمْ تُصَلِّ، وَأَمَّا أَنَا فَتَمَعَّكْتُ فِي التُّرَابِ وَصَلَّيْتُ، فَقَالَ النَّبِيُّ صَلَّى اللهُ عَلَيْهِ وَسَلَّمَ: «إِنَّمَا كَانَ يَكْفِيكَ أَنْ تَضْرِبَ بِيَدَيْكَ الْأَرْضَ، ثُمَّ تَنْفُخَ، ثُمَّ تَمْسَحَ بِهِمَا وَجْهَكَ، وَكَفَّيْكَ» فَقَالَ عُمَرُ: "اتَّقِ اللهَ يَا عَمَّارُ قَالَ: إِنْ شِئْتَ لَمْ أُحَدِّثْ بِهِ" و في رواية: فَقَالَ عُمَرُ: نُوَلِّيكَ مَا تَوَلَّيْتَ.

'I became sexually impure and did not find any water to purify myself', Umar said: 'don't pray'. So then Amaar said to Umar: 'don't you remember O leader of the Believers, when you and I were with the army brigade, we became sexually impure and didn't find any water to make purification. As for you, well you didn't pray, but as for me than I rolled around in the dirt, then I prayed. Then when we told the Prophet ﷺ about it and he told us: 'Verily it would have been sufficient for you to tap your hands on the earth then blow the dust off then wipe your hand and face with them'. Then Umar said: 'Fear Allah O Amaar in what you say! He replied: 'If you view it beneficial, I will not mention

---

[1] -al Amwaal, by Abee Ubayd pg. 284, and al Amwaal, by ibn Zanjawaya 2/461 with an authentic chain of narration

Al 'I'tibaa'a

this incident.' In another narration: 'Umar said: 'We will hold you responsible and make you the official in that which you say.'[1]

Imam ash Shafi'ee mentioned in 'ar Risalah': If someone says: show me the incidents where Umar did something then abandoned it because of a narration from the Prophet Muhammad. Then verily ash Shafi'ee mentioned numerous occasions proving this, where Umar withdrew or recanted his statement or action after coming to know the narrations of the Prophet Muhammad ﷺ in opposition to his personal opinion.

Ibnul Qayyim mentioned in 'I'laam al Muwa'qaeen' numerous occasions also where Umar was not familiar with a Sunnah and then when coming to knowledge of it, he immediately abandoned his statement and followed the Sunnah.

Also Uthmaan ibn Affaan was unfamiliar with the minimum amount of time for pregnancy and giving birth until Ali ibn Abee Talib and Ibn Abbaas informed him of the ruling.

As Imam Malik mentioned in his 'Muwa'ta':

أَنَّ عُثْمَانَ بْنَ عَفَّانَ أُتِيَ بِامْرَأَةٍ قَدْ وَلَدَتْ فِي سِتَّةِ أَشْهُرٍ، فَأَمَرَ بِهَا أَنْ تُرْجَمَ، فَقَالَ لَهُ عَلِيُّ بْنُ أَبِي طَالِبٍ: لَيْسَ ذَلِكَ عَلَيْهَا، وقد قال اللهُ تَبَارَكَ وَتَعَالَى فِي كِتَابِهِ: ﴿وَحَمْلُهُ وَفِصَالُهُ ثَلَاثُونَ شَهْرًا﴾، وَقَالَ: ﴿وَفِصَالُهُ فِي عَامَيْنِ﴾ وقال: ﴿وَالْوَالِدَاتُ يُرْضِعْنَ أَوْلَادَهُنَّ حَوْلَيْنِ كَامِلَيْنِ﴾ قال: والرضاعة أربعة وعشرون شهراً والحمل ستة أشهر...

'That it reached him that a woman was brought to Uthmaan ibn Afaan, who had given birth after six months of pregnancy, so Uthmaan ordered that she be stoned. So Ali said to him: 'That is not necessary for her situation, for verily Allah has said in the Quran: 'And the bearing of him and the weaning of him is thirty months' (al Ahqaf 46:15), and Allah said: 'And his weaning is in two years' (Luqman 31:14) and Allah said: 'The mothers give suck (breastfeed) their children for two whole years' (al Baqarah 2:233).

---

[1] -Saheeh Muslim 1/280-281, Book of Menstruation, Chapter: Tayammum #368

Al 'I'tibaa'a

Then Ali said: 'So the period of breastfeeding is twenty-four months and the period of pregnancy is six months.'[1]

Also Abdur Razaaq narrated with an authentic chain of narration **on the authority of one of Ibn Abaas' generals who said:**

عَنْ قَائِدٍ، لِابْنِ عَبَّاسٍ قَالَ: كُنْتُ مَعَهُ فَأُتِيَ عُثْمَانُ بِامْرَأَةٍ وَضَعَتْ لِسِتَّةِ أَشْهُرٍ فَأَمَرَ عُثْمَانُ بِرَجْمِهَا، فَقَالَ لَهُ ابْنُ عَبَّاسٍ: "إِنْ خَاصَمْتُكُمْ بِكِتَابِ اللهِ فَخَصَمْتُكُمْ، قَالَ اللهُ عَزَّ وَجَلَّ: ﴿وَحَمْلُهُ وَفِصَالُهُ ثَلَاثُونَ شَهْرًا﴾ [الأحقاف: 15] فَالحُمْلُ سِتَّةُ أَشْهُرٍ وَالرَّضَاعُ سَنَتَانِ ". قَالَ: «فَدُرِئَ عَنْهَا»

'I was with Ibn Abaas when a woman who gave birth in six months was brought to Uthmaan, so Uthmaan ordered that she be stoned, so Ibn Abbaas said: If I was to contest you in your ruling with the Book of Allah than your opponent is Allah's saying:*'And the bearing of him and the weaning of him is thirty months'* (al Ahqaf 46:15).

Then he said: 'The period of pregnancy is six months and the period of breastfeeding is two years', then Uthmaan recanted his verdict.[2]

Also Abdullah ibn Mas'ud was unfamiliar with the ruling regarding 'tayammum' for the one who is sexually impure, as Imam Muslim narrated **on the authority of Shaqeeq, who said:**

عَنْ شَقِيقٍ، قَالَ: كُنْتُ جَالِسًا مَعَ عَبْدِ اللهِ، وَأَبِي مُوسَى، فَقَالَ أَبُو مُوسَى: يَا أَبَا عَبْدِ الرَّحْمَنِ أَرَأَيْتَ لَوْ أَنَّ رَجُلًا أَجْنَبَ فَلَمْ يَجِدِ المَاءَ شَهْرًا كَيْفَ يَصْنَعُ بِالصَّلَاةِ؟ فَقَالَ عَبْدُ اللهِ: لَا يَتَيَمَّمْ وَإِنْ لَمْ يَجِدِ المَاءَ شَهْرًا. فَقَالَ أَبُو مُوسَى: فَكَيْفَ بِهَذِهِ الآيَةِ فِي سُورَةِ المَائِدَةِ ﴿فَلَمْ تَجِدُوا مَاءً فَتَيَمَّمُوا صَعِيدًا طَيِّبًا﴾ [النساء: 43]. فَقَالَ عَبْدُ اللهِ: لَوْ رُخِّصَ لَهُمْ فِي هَذِهِ الآيَةِ لَأَوْشَكَ إِذَا بَرَدَ عَلَيْهِمُ المَاءُ أَنْ يَتَيَمَّمُوا بِالصَّعِيدِ...

'I was sitting with Abdullah and Abu Musa, when Abu Musa said: 'O Abu AbdurRahman! If a man becomes sexually impure and cannot find water for a month, what do you think he should do about offering the prayer? Abdullah said: 'He should not do 'tayammum' even if he doesn't find water for a month.

---

[1]-al Muwa'ta 2/825 #1763 in Abee Mus'ab az Zuhri's transmission of the Muwa'ta, and Ibn Abee Dthi'b mentioned it with a connected chain of narration in his 'Muwa'ta, also it was also mentioned in 'al Istidth'kaar' 24/37 and it was mentioned by Ibn Hajr in 'Muwafaqitil Khabr al Khabr 2/214

[2]-al Musanaf by Abdur Razaaq 7/351,# 13447

Al 'I'tibaa'a

Then Abu Musa said: 'What about this verse in surah al Ma'idah: *"and you find no water, then perform 'tayammum' with clean earth..."* (al Ma'idah 5:6)? **Abdullah said: 'If they were granted a concession because of this verse, soon they would resort to 'tayammum' with clean earth if the water was too cold...**[1]

Also al Khateeb al Baghdaadi mentioned a chapter heading in his book 'al Faqeeh wal Mutafaqih' **(Chapter: That which has been narrated about the companions taking back and withdrawing their opinions which they originally viewed and then following the ahadeeth of the Messenger of Allah after hearing the hadeeth or becoming familiar with it)**. Within this chapter he mentioned incidents about Umar, Ubay ibn Ka'b, Ibn Abbaas, and Ibn Umar and their abandoning of their opinions and interpretations and returning back to the hadeeth of the Prophet Muhammad ﷺ when it reached them.

Furthermore, Ibnul Qayyim mentioned in 'I'laam al Muwa'qaeen' a chapter regarding issues in which some of the companions were not familiar with the proofs. He mentioned incidents in which Abu Bakr, Umar, Uthmaan, Abu Musa, Ibn Abbaas, and Ibn Mas'ud weren't familiar with the prophetic narrations (Sunnah) regarding some issues, then their hastiness in recanting and withdrawing their statements once they came to know the Sunnah about the issue.

Then Ibnul Qayyim said: 'These incidents are numerous if we were to research and pursue them we could definitely compile a large book. So now we ask the different sects or groups who practice 'taqleed': 'Is it permissible or possible for the ones who you blindly follow (Imams) to be unfamiliar with some of the affairs related from the Prophet Muhammad ﷺ, as was the case with some of the best of people (companions of Allah's Messenger ﷺ) of the Muslim Nation? If they reply: 'No, it is impossible that something is unknown from their Imams and they know everything'-and even some things were unknown to the companions while living in the same generation of the Prophet Muhammed ﷺ'. The ones who say this have verily gone to extremes, to the point where they claim that their scholars are infallible. If they say: 'Yes it is permissible for them to be unfamiliar with and not have knowledge of some things', and this is the reality of it, and they are of different grades and levels, some few and some many. So we respond to them: 'We invite and implore all who within his heart and upon his tongue is: If Allah and His Messenger ﷺ passed a ruling in an issue in which the ones you blind follow are not familiar with or do not have

---

[1]-Saheeh Muslim 1/280, Book of Menstruation, Chapter: Tayammum #368

Al 'I'tibaa'a

knowledge of, does there remain an alternative for you to accept his saying or reject it, or are your alternatives non-existent? Likewise, do you deem it necessary to act upon what Allah and His Messenger ﷺ declared specifically while it is not permissible to do otherwise?? So prepare an answer for this question, and make sure it is a correct one.'[1]

The great Imam Malik, was unfamiliar with a Sunnah from the ablution of the Prophet Muhammad ﷺ, but when he became familiar with it he held unto it firmly. As al-Bayhaqi narrated in his 'Sunan' from Ibn Abee Haatim's chain of narration on the authority of Ahmed ibn Abdur Rahman ibn Wahb, who said: 'I heard my uncle say: 'I heard when Imam Malik was asked about cleaning between the toes during ablution. He said, 'The people do not have to do that.' So I left him until the crowd had lessened, then I said to him, 'We know of a Sunnah about that.' He said, 'What is it?' I said, 'Laith ibn Sa'd, Ibn Lahee'ah and 'Amr ibn al-Haarith narrated to us from Yazeed ibn 'Amr al-Ma'aafiri from Abu 'Abdur-Rahman al-Hubuli from Mustawrid ibn Shaddaad al-Qurashi who said, *'I saw the Messenger of Allah ﷺ rubbing between his toes with his little finger.'* Malik replied: 'This hadeeth is sound; I have not heard of it at all up until now.' Afterwards, I heard him being asked about the same thing, on which he ordered with the cleaning between the toes. Then my uncle said: 'It is rare that you find someone while making ablution that they rub between the crevice of the big toe and so whoever uses their little finger is safe from shortcomings in their ablution"[2]

Numerous narrations can be found in the compilations of Imam ash Shafi'e where one will find statements which are contingent upon the establishment of a hadeeth. This is only because he did not find or was not familiar with a hadeeth regarding the specific issue, or he found a hadeeth but the chain of narration was inauthentic or not established in his view.

Imam ash Shafi'ee said: 'I do not know of an obligatory 'ghusl' (bathing) except the 'ghusl taken for sexual impurity, in which the prayer will not be accepted without it.

The other type of bathing which proceeds the bathing of sexual impurity in emphasis, is the bathing of the deceased person. I do not prefer that it to be abandoned in any case, nor abandoning ablution conducive to touching the dead

---
[1]-I'laam al Muwa'qaeen 2/267-271
[2]-'Introduction of al Jarh wa Ta'deel' by Ibn Abee Haatim pgs.31-32 and al Bayhaqi narrated it in full in his 'Sunan' 1/76

person, then proceeding that in emphasis is bathing for the 'Jumu'ah prayer'. Verily the only thing which prohibited me from viewing the bathing of the deceased as being obligatory is the fact that there is a narrator in the chain of narration which I haven't come across anything which will convince me regarding his status (trustworthiness and preciseness) up until today. If I find someone who can convince me about his status than I would say that ablution is obligatory for the one who touches the dead person, for verily both issues are mentioned in one hadeeth.'[1]

He also said: 'It has been mentioned from the Prophet Muhammad ﷺ that he said regarding the grazing animals-sheep- if the hadeeth is authentic-that there is no 'zakat' (obligatory charity) for the non-grazing animals.'[2]

Imam ash Shafi'ee also said: 'Some of our companions said: 'It is no problem for the fasting person to do cupping and he does not break his fast by doing so.' As Imam Malik informed us on the authority of Ibn Umar that he used to do cupping while fasting, then he left it off. Also Malik ibn Hisham ibn Urwah on the authority of his father who mentioned that he never saw his father perform cupping while fasting, and this is the verdict of numerous scholars whom I have met.

And it has been narrated from the Prophet ﷺ that he said:

"أَفْطَرَ الحَاجِمُ وَالمَحْجُومُ"

'The one who does the cupping and receives the cupping have both broken their fast', and it also has been narrated that the Prophet ﷺ did cupping while fasting[3].

Then ash Shafi'ee said: 'I don't know that any of these two narrations are established, if one of them is established that it is from the Prophet Muhammad

---

[1]-al Umm 1/38
[2]-al Umm 2/23
[3]-Abu Dawud mentioned it in his Sunan, Book of Fasting, Chapter: The fasting person performing cupping, #2367 and it is authentic, also Ibn Majah #1681 and at Tirmidthi #774. The narration about the Prophet ﷺ doing cupping while fasting can be found in Abu Dawud also #2372 and it is also authentic.

then my statement would be in accordance to it, as the proof is within his statements.¹

As we previously confirmed regarding the methodology of ash Shafi'ee- rather, all of the four scholars of 'fiqh'- that if all of them came across a narration from the companions then they would never exceed it.

Ash Shafi'ee said:

قَالَ الشَّافِعِيُّ بَلَاغًا: عَنْ عَبَّادٍ، عَنْ عَاصِمٍ الْأَحْوَلِ، عَنْ قَزَعَةَ، عَنْ عَلِيٍّ رَضِيَ اللهُ عَنْهُ " أَنَّهُ صَلَّى فِي زَلْزَلَةٍ سِتَّ رَكَعَاتٍ، فِي أَرْبَعِ سَجَدَاتٍ خَمْسَ رَكَعَاتٍ، وَسَجْدَتَيْنِ فِي رَكْعَةٍ، وَرَكْعَةً وَسَجْدَتَيْنِ فِي رَكْعَةٍ"

'Abaad ibn Aasim al Ahwal said on the authority of Qaz'ah on the authority of Ali that he prayed six 'rak'at' (units) and four prostrations during an earthquake, and five 'rak'at' and two prostrations in one 'rak'at', and one 'rak'at' and two prostrations in a 'rak'at'.²

Then ash Shafi'ee said: 'We do not advocate this, but we say: 'There is no prayer for anything amongst the natural occurences or natural disasters except for the eclipse of the sun and the moon, and if this narration was established and authentic from Ali than verily we would advocate this statement.'³

He also said: 'Imam Malik informed us that it reached him that the crescent moon for Ramadan was seen in the evening in the time of Uthmaan ibn Afaan, so Uthmaan didn't break his fast until the sun disappeared, and he said: 'this is what we say: 'that if the crescent moon is not sighted, and no one bears witness that it was sighted in the evening, then the people will not break their fast for the sighting of the crescent moon during the day, and this occurred slightly before or after the sun's zenith, and it (crescent moon)-and Allah know's best- is the crescent moon for the following night.

Some of the people said: 'if the crescent moon is sighted after the sun's zenith than it is in agreement with our saying, and if it is sighted before the sun's zenith than the people should break their fast. And they said: 'Verily we are following a narration regarding this issue, and we have narrated it and it is not 'qiyas'. So we say: 'the narration is more deserving to be followed than 'qiyas', and if the

---

[1]-al Umm 2/97
[2]-Abdur Razzaq mentioned it in his Musanaf #4931 and Bayhaqi in his Sunan #6381
[3]-al Umm 7/167

narration is authentic and established then it takes precedence in being followed.'[1]

In 'al Mustadrak' of al Haakim he said: 'I heard Abu Abdullah Muhammad ibn Ya'qub al Hafith mention: it was said, I heard al Hasan ibn Sufyaan say: 'I heard Harmalah ibn Yahya say: 'I heard ash Shafi'ee say: 'If the hadeeth of Bir'wah' bint Washiq was authentic than I would speak in accordance to it.

Abu Abdullah (al Haakim) said: 'If I was present with ash Shafi'ee I would have stood up amongst his companions and said: 'the hadeeth is authentic, so take it and advocate it!'[2]

This is how the scholars of 'fiqh' throughout Islamic history used to suspend their statements or make conditions upon their statements based upon the establishment and authenticity of the narration, and this is obligatory upon every Muslim, and foremost upon the scholar and jurist.

Also Ibn Khuzaimah[3] mentioned many chapter headings in his 'Saheeh':

(Chapter: 'The cat's passing in front of someone praying, if the narration is authentic, with a connected chain, for there is something is my heart regarding its being raised to the Prophet)[4]

(Chapter: 'The desirability of reading Bani Israa'eel (surah Israa'a) and az Zumar every night, in adherence to the Prophet's Sunnah, if it is permissible to use Abu

---

[1]-al Umm 2/95
[2]-al Mustadrak 2/180

[3]-**(TN)** He is Muhammad bin Ishaaq bin Khuzaymah bin al-Mughirah bin Salih bin Bakr Al-Naysaboori; also known as Imam of the Imams. He met the companions of al-Shafi'e and learnt Fiqh from them. He was born in Naysabur; in the month of Safar 223 H. He travelled across many regions seeking the knowledge of Hadeeth; he travelled to Iraq, Shaam, Egypt and other countries. He entered the city of Gorgan (Jurjan) in the month of Rajab, in the year 300H; and he narrated Hadeeth there. He then headed to "Ribaat Dahistan" where he also narrated Hadeeth, and in the Old Masjid of the city, he narrated ahadeeths to others in order for them to be recorded. His two teachers; al-Bukhari and Muslim narrated from him in books other than their two Sahih books. He authored more than 140 books, besides the authored materials on specific topics which exceeds 100 parts; the Fiqh of the Hadeeth of Burairah is 3 parts and the paper of Hajj consists of 5 parts. He also authored the renowned book "Tawheed and Affirming the Attributes of the Lord" and "Sahih Ibn Khuzaymah."

[4]-Saheeh ibn Khuzaimah 2/20

Al 'I'tibaa'a

Lubabah's[1] narrations as evidence, for verily I do not know about his trustworthiness nor do I know of any criticism)[2]

(Chapter: 'The 'tasbeeh' prayer, if the narration is authentic, for verily there is something in my heart about the chain of narration)[3]

Ibn Khuzaimah also said in his book of 'Tawheed': (Chapter: Mention that the 'sideeqeen' (trustworthy ones) proceed the Prophet Muhammad ﷺ in the intercession on the Day of Resurrection, then the remaining Prophets proceed the 'sideeqeen', then the martyrs proceed the Prophets, if the hadeeth is authentic)[4]

The examples of this are many to be found within Ibn Khuzaimah's books, while they deserve to be gathered and researched in an individual compilation.

Yes, this is the 'fiqh' of the companions and the ones who followed them upon righteousness such as the great scholars of 'fiqh' who strictly adhered and followed the authentic and established proofs and evidences. Then after their era things changed, and the sickness of stagnant, rigid 'taqleed' became rampant and widespread throughout the following generations, until it reached a point where it was stated: 'Indeed it is not permissible for anyone except that they make 'taqleed' of one of the four Imams.'

In addition, whoever calls to taking and adhering directly to the proofs, then the scholar of the 'madthaa'hib' throw him out like an arrow from a bow.

Abu Shamah al Maqdisee mentioned regarding the 'fiqh' of the companions and their avoidance of asking about issues which did not occur, then he said: 'Then

---

[1]-(TN)He is Rafaa'ah ibnul Munthir ibn Zubayr ibn Zaid al Awsi al Ansaari, he witnessed the Aqabah Pledge and participated in the Battle of Uhud and the proceeding battles. He died in the time of the caliphate of Ali ibn Abee Taalib. He was one of the ones who was absent in the Battle of Tabuk, so after realizing the great sin he had committed he tied himself to one of the pillars of the Prophet's Masjid and denied himself of food and drink until Allah forgave him. He remained tied to one of the pillars and would be untied only for prayer and answering the call of nature. He eventually fainted after seven days and Allah the Most Merciful revealed His statement in surah Towbah, verse 102, as He says: *(And there are others who have acknowledged their sins, they have mixed a deed that was righteous with another that was evil. Perhaps Allah will forgive them. Verily Allah is the Oft Forgiving and Most Merciful.)* ,indicating Abu Lubaabah's forgiveness and the forgiveness of the ones who were absent in the Battle of Tabuk.
[2]-Saheeh ibn Khuzaimah 2/191
[3]-Saheeh ibn Khuzaimah 2/223
[4]-Book of Tawheed and the Establishment of Allah's Attributes pg.310

after that the occurrences, incidents and new issues came about and the companions, 'tabi'een' and their predecessors issued verdicts regarding some of the issues. Their verdicts were memorized, written down and compiled into books, and eventually reached those who proceeded them from amongst the scholars of 'fiqh'. Then they came along with their ramifications, subdivisions and subsidiary issues, using 'qiyas' and making 'ijtihaad' by adding on to and annexing other statements to these verdicts. So as the result of this, the issues related to 'fiqh' began to weaken and differing became more widespread and frequent.

It is said by some that: 'Differing amongst the Muslims is mercy'[1], this is only in regards to the fact that the texts of the Quran and the Sunnah imply and have capacity for various significances, purposes, standpoints of interpretation, and the various manners and techniques contained within the Arabic Language, for every saying there is a proof.

The knowledge of 'fiqh' continues to remain noble and honorable and the scholars inherit the knowledge of 'fiqh' solely depending upon the two main sources: The Quran and the Sunnah. Memorizing by heart the sayings of the 'salaf' with the correct understanding of them without making 'taqleed' of anyone. For verily Imam ash Shafi'ee prohibited people from making 'taqleed' of him, and making 'taqleed' of other than him, as we will mention in the next section.

The era of the four Imam's was filled with 'mujtahideen'[2] and everyone authored what he saw to be correct, and they all critiqued, commented on, and criticized each other based upon two principles, 1: The Quran and Sunnah, and 2: Giving precedence to the most strongest and preponderant statements from amongst the salaf.. The situation remained like this up until the authoring of the books of the 'madthaa'hib'. Subsequenty, only four of the 'madthaa'hib' became popular and widespread and the remaining 'madthaa'hib' were abandoned and forgotten. Then the attention and concern of the followers of these 'madthaa'hib' began to decrease except for a very few of them. So these loyal followers of the 'madthaa'hib' started to make 'taqleed' of the 'madthaa'hib' and they didn't consider, examine ,nor search for that which the earlier scholars

---

[1]-This statement has been taken from a fabricated hadeeth which has no foundation nor chain of narration

[2]-**(TN)**Those who diligently study, research and exerting all of their efforts into finding the truth regarding religious issues reaching the point where they can issue their 'ijtihaad'.

Al 'I'tibaa'a

did as related to deducting and extracting rulings and legislations from the main sources: from the Quran and Sunnah. Rather, the statements of their scholars were given the status of the Quran and Sunnah, and they accepted their statements uncontestedly without questioning or dispute. Then from there they built their rulings upon the statements of their scholars -ramifications, subdivisions, conditions, principles, hypothetical situations and subsidiary issues which led them to deduct rulings, judgments and religious verdicts from other than the Quran and Sunnah. This reached to the extent until there didn't remain anything for the followers of the 'madthaa'hib' to look into, study and research except the statements and views of their scholars. This led them to turn away from and abandon the knowledge of the Quran and the Sunnah so the 'mujtahideen' vanished and disappeared and the 'muqalidoon'[1] became predominant and gained the upper hand. Until it reached a point where 'muqalidoon' would be astonished by the one who aspired, desired and reached a status of 'ijtihaad' and at the same time they would despise, disrespect, belittle, and scorn him. In the meanwhile, bigotry and fanaticism to the 'madthaa'hib' became widespread and apparent while equity and justice became rare and insignificant. At this time many defects and shortcomings emerged, and the scorpions were creeping and crawling between them. So some of the 'muqalidoon' started issuing strange and unusual statements until it reached a stage of bigotry and fanaticism where if one of them became familiar with or came across something established and authentic from the Quran and the Sunnah in opposition to his 'madth'hab', he would exert himself in trying to repel, disprove, falsify it by interpreting it shrewdly with every way and means possible. This being done mainly for the purpose of aiding and advocating his scholars' statements and abandonment of what is obligatory upon him to follow and adhere to (Quran and Sunnah).

Where even if a text from the Quran or Sunnah reached the Imam which the bigoted one or 'muqallid' blindly follows, his Imam would accept it with esteem, respect and reverence, and would adhere to it if there were no opposing proofs or evidences.

Then the situation became worse and even more serious to the point where many of them held the opinion that it was better not to not busy themselves at all or even become engaged in knowledge of the Quran and the Sunnah. They used to criticize and find fault with the ones who concerned themselves and

---

[1] -(TN) plural of Muqallid: is one who follows another person's sayings whose sayings are not proofs in the religion

devoted themselves to the knowledge of the Quran and Sunnah. They viewed that the methodology they were treading upon was correct and should be given top priority over all things. Exhausting themselves in representing and defending the 'madthaa'hib' with personal opinions, disputes, debates and squabbles. Gatherings and sittings after more gatherings and sittings would conclude and not even a single verse from the Quran nor hadeeth from Allah's Messenger ﷺ would be mentioned or heard. If a hadeeth was mentioned then there would not exist anyone in the gathering who could distinguish between the authentic hadeeth and the ahadeeth with defects, nor would they quote it or cite it correctly, nor would they understand its meaning. The whole purpose behind them engaging in these sittings was to stifle, subdue and suppress their opponents, while abolishing and invalidating their opponents rulings and verdicts. In addition to their extreme lack of equity and justice in the affairs in which there were differences of opinions, while the injustice became more apparent especially when the religious endowments they were receiving were suspended and halted.[1]

Then other people emerged and it reached a point where their main concern was busying and engaging themselves with the issues and affairs of a particular 'madth'hab', like the main concern of those who busied themselves with the Quran and the Sunnah.

They used to view that precedence should be given specifically to studying and researching the points of differing which they invented and authored logical formalities and models, as a poet said:

$$\text{بِالمَنْطِقِ اشْتَغَلُوا فَقُلْتُ لِجَمْعِهِم - إِنَّ البَلاءَ مُوَكَّلٌ بِالمَنْطِقِ}$$

"They busied themselves with logic so I said to all of them-verily affliction is empowered by logic."

So they turned away and abandoned the amenities and named all those who busied themselves with knowledge of the 'madth'hab' to be great stallions. This is from the whisperings of the Satan, and signs of betrayal, and we seek refuge in Allah from this affliction, and the evil results of it, such as the wasting of time in arguing and debating. We ask Allah to make us firm in adhering to and

---

[1]-Meaning: they used to receive their salaries from the religious endowments which were designated and appropriated only for the followers of the 'madthaa'hib', and for this reason they were very eager and persistent in clinging to the madthaa'hib.

Al 'I'tibaa'a

depending upon the authentic narrations, and join us with the best of leaders and scholars, and we ask Allah to keep us far away from evil, ignorant, and foolish imbeciles.

Furthermore, other people were persuaded by the style and garb of the people of 'fiqh', and impressed by the crowing and shouting of the debaters and they used to say: 'why should we exhaust ourselves, when we are receiving income and earnings from the schools?[1]

Let it be known to all to fear Allah for verily He has placed an intellect in every human being, and has given him a good portion of knowledge after having sought it for some time. Allah has been gracious with the Muslim by blessing him with the understanding of the Book of Allah and the Sunnah of Allah's Messenger ﷺ, also by giving him understanding of the statements of the scholars of 'fiqh'. Allah has endowed him with success and the ability to distinguish between the preponderant and less preponderant issues and the ability to extract the truth from between the two. One should never make himself lowly or despicable, if he feels as though he is deficient or incapable in understanding than he should not give these feelings an open way to his heart which leads him to make 'taqleed' of a specific person in everything they say or do, without looking at, observing and taking into consideration that person's proofs and evidences.

Similarly one should fear Allah, and one should not be audacious nor courageous with Allah by giving religious verdicts without proofs or evidences, or without verifying the authentic narrations, for verily he will destroy his religion and his hereafter.

What is better than the beautiful advice of the great scholar Ibnul Qayyim regarding adhering to and following the texts of the Quran and Sunnah. If the jurist or 'mufti' were to ponder over this advice he would surely get goosebumps, shiver and the hairs on his head would stand up. Ibnul Qayyim said:

'In view of the fact that propagation and conveyance on behalf of Allah is dependent upon having knowledge of what is conveyed and truthfulness. In light of this, the scholar is truthful and honest in what he conveys, and he should always have a good approach and method while possessing a favorable history.

---

[1] -Introduction of 'al Kitab al Mu'amal lir rudd Ilaa al Amr al Awal' pg.99-102

Al 'I'tibaa'a

He should always be just and equitable in his actions and statements, while his public and private actions and affairs are similar. So if the status of an individual was an endorser on behalf of the kings and leaders in a matter which no one disapproves of, nor is ignorant of his ability, and this is the highest and most exalted of statuses. Then what is the situation regarding the endorsement on behalf of the Lord of the heavens and the earths.

It is most appropriate for the one whose status is so, to prepare his equipment and tools and gird up his loins and be prepared and ready for action, and truly understand the position and status he has been given. There should be no uneasiness or restraint within his heart from speaking the truth and declaring it openly to the people, for verily Allah is his aid, assistant, helper and the one who guides him. How is it when this is the rank and position which Allah has undertaken and assumed for Himself as He says:

﴿ وَيَسْتَفْتُونَكَ فِي ٱلنِّسَآءِ قُلِ ٱللَّهُ يُفْتِيكُمْ فِيهِنَّ وَمَا يُتْلَىٰ عَلَيْكُمْ فِي ٱلْكِتَبِ ﴾

"They ask you seeking a religious verdict or instruction concerning women, say: Allah instructs you about them and what is recited unto you in the Book..." (an Nisa'a 4:127)

And whatever Allah has taken up as His position and rank is sufficient for all as He also said:

﴿ يَسْتَفْتُونَكَ قُلِ ٱللَّهُ يُفْتِيكُمْ فِي ٱلْكَلَـٰلَةِ ﴾

"They ask you for a religious verdict, Say: Allah instructs (the following) about the one who doesn't have ascendents nor descendents..." (an Nisa'a 4:176)

So let the jurist and the 'mufti' know and understand who he represents (Allah) regarding the religious verdicts he gives, and that he will be held responsible tomorrow and stand before Allah.'[1]

Ibnul Qayyim also mentioned: 'Allah the Most High made it impermissible to speak about Him without knowledge while giving religious verdicts and such.

---

[1] -I'laam al Muwa'qaeen 2/17

Al 'I'tibaa'a

Allah has also deemed it to be one of the worst of the impermissible things, as Allah says:

﴿ قُلْ إِنَّمَا حَرَّمَ رَبِّيَ ٱلْفَوَٰحِشَ مَا ظَهَرَ مِنْهَا وَمَا بَطَنَ وَٱلْإِثْمَ وَٱلْبَغْىَ بِغَيْرِ ٱلْحَقِّ وَأَن تُشْرِكُوا۟ بِٱللَّهِ مَا لَمْ يُنَزِّلْ بِهِۦ سُلْطَٰنًا وَأَن تَقُولُوا۟ عَلَى ٱللَّهِ مَا لَا تَعْلَمُونَ ۝ ﴾

'Say O Muhammad: 'The things which my Lord has indeed forbidden are all great evil sins whether committed openly or secretly, sins of all kinds, unjust oppression, joining partners in worship with Allah for which He has given nor authority and saying things about Allah of which you have no knowledge.'' (al A'raaf 7:33)

Allah arranged these four impermissible things according to their severity, and started by mentioning the least of them, which is 'al Fawahish' (great, evil sins committed openly and secretly). Then mentioned secondly that which is more severe in its prohibition which are sins of all kinds and unjust oppression. Then mentioned thirdly that which is greater than it regarding its prohibition, which is polytheism. Then mentioned fourthly that which is the worst of all and most severe and dangerous of all these impermissible things, which is to speak about Allah or Islam without knowledge, and this is general regarding Allah's names and attributes, His actions, in His religion and in His legislations and rulings. Allah also said:

﴿ وَلَا تَقُولُوا۟ لِمَا تَصِفُ أَلْسِنَتُكُمُ ٱلْكَذِبَ هَٰذَا حَلَٰلٌ وَهَٰذَا حَرَامٌ لِّتَفْتَرُوا۟ عَلَى ٱللَّهِ ٱلْكَذِبَ إِنَّ ٱلَّذِينَ يَفْتَرُونَ عَلَى ٱللَّهِ ٱلْكَذِبَ لَا يُفْلِحُونَ ۝ مَتَٰعٌ قَلِيلٌ وَلَهُمْ عَذَابٌ أَلِيمٌ ﴾

"And do not say concerning that which your tongues pronounce falsely: 'This is lawful and this is forbidden", so as to invent lies upon Allah. Verily, those who invent lies upon Allah will never prosper-a passing brief enjoyment they will experience, but they will have a painful torment." (an Nahl 16:116-117)

Some of the 'salaf' said: 'Every one of you should fear saying: 'Allah has made this lawful and Allah has made this prohibited', so Allah will say to him: 'You lied, I didn't make this lawful and I didn't make this prohibited. So no one should speak about anything in which he doesn't know if the divine revelation has made it lawful or prohibited, or Allah has made it lawful or prohibited simply because of 'taqleed' or false interpretation.'[1]

---

[1]-I'laam al Muwa'qaeen 2/73-74

Al 'I'tibaa'a

Part Six

Seeking and giving religious verdicts and opinions[1]

Al Fatwa linguistically: as is mentioned in 'lisan ul Arab': Aftaa'hu fil amri- gave him a legal opinion, clarified or explained it to him.

Al'Futyaa, al Futwaa, and al Fatwaa: is that which a jurist gives as a legal opinion

Al istiftaa'a: means to seek or demand a 'fatwaa', as Allah says in the Quran:

$$ \text{﴿ يَسْتَفْتُونَكَ قُلِ اللَّهُ يُفْتِيكُمْ فِي الْكَلَالَةِ ﴾} $$

They ask you for a religious verdict, Say: Allah instructs (the following) about the one who doesn't have ascendents nor descendents..." (an Nisa'a 4:176)

Upon this the meaning of 'al istiftaa'a is: to seek clarification of a religious ruling from the one who can clarify the ruling with the proofs and evidences from the Quran and Sunnah.

Al Fatwa technically: clarification of a religious ruling with proofs for the one who seeks it.

The ruling of 'al istiftaa'a : it is obligatory upon every individual who needs or seeks clarification of an issue, because Allah says:

$$ \text{﴿ فَسْأَلُوا أَهْلَ الذِّكْرِ إِن كُنتُمْ لَا تَعْلَمُونَ ﴾} $$

"So ask the people of the reminder if you do not know" (al Anbiya 21:7)

And as the Prophet Muhammad ﷺ said from the narration of **Jabir ibn Abdullah who said:**

عَنْ جَابِرٍ قَالَ: خَرَجْنَا فِي سَفَرٍ فَأَصَابَ رَجُلًا مِنَّا حَجَرٌ فَشَجَّهُ فِي رَأْسِهِ، ثُمَّ احْتَلَمَ فَسَأَلَ أَصْحَابَهُ فَقَالَ: هَلْ تَجِدُونَ لِي رُخْصَةً فِي التَّيَمُّمِ؟ فَقَالُوا: مَا نَجِدُ لَكَ رُخْصَةً وَأَنْتَ تَقْدِرُ عَلَى الْمَاءِ فَاغْتَسَلَ فَمَاتَ، فَلَمَّا قَدِمْنَا عَلَى النَّبِيِّ صَلَّى اللهُ عَلَيْهِ وَسَلَّمَ أُخْبِرَ بِذَلِكَ فَقَالَ: «قَتَلُوهُ قَتَلَهُمُ اللهُ أَلَا سَأَلُوا إِذْ لَمْ يَعْلَمُوا فَإِنَّمَا شِفَاءُ الْعِيِّ السُّؤَالُ...

---

[1]-(TN)al Istiftaa'a: seeking a religious verdict, al Fatwa: giving a religious verdict

Al 'I'tibaa'a

'We were traveling and one of the men was hit with a stone which injured his head, then this man had a wet dream, so this man asked his companions: 'do any of you find a concession for me to make 'tayummum'? So they replied: 'We do not find any concession for you, and you have water.' So the man took a bath, then he died. So when these people came back to the Prophet they informed him what had occurred and the Prophet ﷺ replied: 'They killed him! May Allah kill them, if they only asked, for verily the cure for ignorance is asking questions.'[1]

Also the ruling of 'al Fatwa': It is a collective duty, it is obligatory that there exists someone from amongst the Muslims who gives religious verdicts concerning their issues and occurrences.

Allah says:

﴿ ۞ وَمَا كَانَ ٱلۡمُؤۡمِنُونَ لِیَنفِرُواْ كَآفَّةًۚ فَلَوۡلَا نَفَرَ مِن كُلِّ فِرۡقَةٍ مِّنۡهُمۡ طَآئِفَةٌ لِّیَتَفَقَّهُواْ فِی ٱلدِّینِ وَلِیُنذِرُواْ قَوۡمَهُمۡ إِذَا رَجَعُوٓاْ إِلَیۡهِمۡ لَعَلَّهُمۡ یَحۡذَرُونَ ۝ ﴾

'And it is not proper for the believers to go out to fight all together. Of every group of them, a party of them should go out, that they who are left behind may be taught their religion, and that they may warn their people when they return to them, so that they may beware of evil." (At Tawbah 9:122)

And Allah says:

﴿ وَإِذۡ أَخَذَ ٱللَّهُ مِیثَـٰقَ ٱلَّذِینَ أُوتُواْ ٱلۡكِتَـٰبَ لَتُبَیِّنُنَّهُۥ لِلنَّاسِ وَلَا تَكۡتُمُونَهُۥ فَنَبَذُوهُ وَرَآءَ ظُهُورِهِمۡ وَٱشۡتَرَوۡاْ بِهِۦ ثَمَنࣰا قَلِیلࣰاۖ فَبِئۡسَ مَا یَشۡتَرُونَ ۝ ﴾

'And remember when Allah took a covenant from those who were given the Scripture (Jews and Christians) to make the news of the coming of the Prophet Muhammad and religious knowledge known clear to mankind, and not to hide

---

[1] -Abu Dawud narrated this hadeeth on the authority of Ataa'a from Jabir pg 59-60 Book of Purification, Chapter: the injured one making tayummum. #336 , also Ibn Majah on the authority of Ataa'a from Ibn Abbaas pg.112-113 Chapter: Regarding the injured person who becomes sexually impure and who fears harm for himself if he bathes... and both of the chains of narration are 'Hasan'.

it, but they threw it away behind their backs, and purchased with it some miserable gain! And indeed what they bought is worse.'(al Imran 3:187)

Giving religious verdicts is very dangerous, if the jurist or one giving verdicts does not fulfill it's rights then his destruction is ominous, because verily he is-as previously mentioned by Ibnul Qayimm-signing or endorsing on behalf of Allah the Most Magnificent.

Muhammad ibn Munkadir said:

"إِنَّ الْعَالِمَ بَيْنَ اللهِ وَبَيْنَ خَلْقِهِ فَلْيَنْظُرْ كَيْفَ يَدْخُلُ بَيْنَهُمْ"

'Verily the scholar is between Allah and His creation, so he must observe as to how he interacts and goes between them.'[1]

Ibnus Salah said regarding 'Allah's saying:

﴿ وَلَا تَقُولُوا لِمَا تَصِفُ أَلْسِنَتُكُمُ ٱلْكَذِبَ هَٰذَا حَلَٰلٌ وَهَٰذَا حَرَامٌ لِّتَفْتَرُوا۟ عَلَى ٱللَّهِ ٱلْكَذِبَ ۚ إِنَّ ٱلَّذِينَ يَفْتَرُونَ عَلَى ٱللَّهِ ٱلْكَذِبَ لَا يُفْلِحُونَ ۝ مَتَٰعٌ قَلِيلٌ وَلَهُمْ عَذَابٌ أَلِيمٌ ۝ ﴾

"And do not say concerning that which your tongues pronounce falsely: 'This is lawful and this is forbidden, so as to invent lies upon Allah. Verily, those who invent lies upon Allah will never prosper-a passing brief enjoyment they will experience, but they will have a painful torment." (an Nahl 16:116-117)

"This is comprehensive, meaning that the one who deviates or strays in giving religious verdicts, saying that the prohibited things are permissible or the permissible things are prohibited and similar to that."[2]

---

[1]-ad Daramee 1/52 and 1/8 in another printing with an authentic chain of narration up until Muhammad ibn Munkadir, and Ibnus Salah mentioned it in 'Kitab al Fatwaa' pg.65
[2]-Kitab al Fatwaa by ibnus Salah pg.83

Part Seven

What is obligatory upon the one seeking a religious verdict

It is obligatory upon every Muslim to search for the truth in all affairs, religious as well as worldly. It is not permissible for him to follow falsehood if it becomes apparent to him as being so, even if it was from the worldly affairs. From the characteristics of the believers, as Allah says:

﴿ وَٱلَّذِينَ هُمْ عَنِ ٱللَّغْوِ مُعْرِضُونَ ۝ ﴾

'And those who turn away from evil vain talk, falsehood and all that Allah has forbidden' (al Mu' minoon 23:3)

Furthermore, it is necessary for the Muslim who seeks a religious verdict in an issue to ask the one who it is easy for him to ask from the people of knowledge. He should investigate, search diligently and work hard to find the most knowledgeable person in his area. If it so happens that the people differ regarding their methodologies and ideas then it is obligatory upon him to work hard in searching for the person who follows, adheres and continuously seeks the authentic texts and narrations (from the Quran and Sunnah). In addition, no one in specific is to be blindly followed or made 'taqleed' of-and this was the methodology of the companions of the Prophet Muhammad ﷺ and the 'tabi'oon' and those who proceeded them. After many of the deviants emerged and differing came about the people never used to seek religious verdicts from the 'Shia'a, Khawaarij, or the Nawasib' rather if they were mentioned, they were mentioned as well as their innovations.

From amongst the supplications of the Prophet Muhammad ﷺ when he got up to pray at night, he would start his prayer with the words:

"اللَّهُمَّ رَبَّ جِبْرِيلَ وَمِيكَائِيلَ وَإِسْرَافِيلَ فَاطِرَ السَّمَوَاتِ وَالأَرْضِ عَالِمَ الْغَيْبِ وَالشَّهَادَةِ أَنْتَ تَحْكُمُ بَيْنَ عِبَادِكَ فِيمَا كَانُوا فِيهِ يَخْتَلِفُونَ اهْدِنِي لِمَا اخْتُلِفَ فِيهِ مِنَ الْحَقِّ بِإِذْنِكَ إِنَّكَ تَهْدِى مَنْ تَشَاءُ إِلَى صِرَاطٍ مُسْتَقِيمٍ"

'O Allah, Lord of Jibreel, Mikaa'eel, and Isra'feel Originator of the heavens and the earth, knower of the unseen and the seen, you judge between your slaves concerning that wherein they differ. Guide me concerning that wherein they

Al 'I'tibaa'a

differ of truth by your leave, for you guide whomsoever you will to a straight path."[1]

It is obligatory upon the one who follows his Messenger ﷺ to always search for the truth, and there is no truth regarding the religious affairs except that which is from the Quran and the Sunnah of Allah's Messenger ﷺ. The truth is not in the opinions of men nor 'qiyas' based upon an incorrect foundation, for verily these things are dispraised.

It is obligatory upon the one seeking a religious verdict to:

1. Seek their religious verdict from the people of knowledge who are known by the people for their correct and authentic knowledge, knowledge of the Quran and the Sunnah. Indeed the Quran and Sunnah are what the Prophet ﷺ left for his nation as he said:

قَالَ رَسُولُ اللَّهِ صَلَّى اللهُ عَلَيْهِ وَسَلَّمَ: "إِنِّي قَدْ تَرَكْتُ فِيكُمْ شَيْئَيْنِ لَنْ تَضِلُّوا بَعْدَهُمَا: كِتَابَ اللَّهِ وَسُنَّتِي..."

'I have left for your two things, you will never be misguided after them, the Quran and my Sunnah...'[2]

2. It is not permissible to ask about a particular 'madth'hab' or about a statement of a specific scholar or jurist.

Sheikhul Islam ibn Taymiyyah said: 'If a mishap or incident occurs to the Muslim for verily he should seek a religious verdict from the one who he believes will answer him with Allah and His Messenger's ﷺ legislation (from the Quran and Sunnah) from any of the 'madtha' hib'. Furthermore, it is not obligatory upon any of the Muslims to make 'taqleed' or blindly follow anyone specifically from the scholars in everything that they say, nor is it obligatory upon any of the Muslims to strictly adhere to or follow a 'madth'hab' of a certain person other

---

[1] -Saheeh Muslim 1/534, Book of the Travelers prayer, chapter: Supplication in the night prayer, #771 from the hadeeth of Aishia

[2] -Al Haakim mentioned it in his Mustadrak, Book of Knowledge, Chapter: The Prophet's sermon in the farewell Hajj, #324, in this chain of narration is Salih ibn Musa at Talhee who is 'da'eef' (weak), however there are many other chains of narration, and the hadeeth itself is Saheeh. Imam Malik also mentioned it in his Mu'wa'ta, in the Book of Qadr #3, also Ibn Abdul Barr mentioned it in Jami' Bayaan al Ilm wa Fadlihi with other wordings #1389, 1866, and 2299, see Silsilah Ahadeeh Saheehah #1761 and al Mishkaat #186, also Saheeh al Jami' as Sageer 3/39, #2934

than the Prophet Muhammad ﷺ in everything he makes obligatory and informs us about.'[1]

Ibn Taymiyyah also said: 'As for the questioner seeking religious verdict and making 'taqleed' of the 'mufti', then the opinion of the four scholars of 'fiqh' and the remainder of the people of knowledge is that it is not obligatory nor permissible for him to bind oneself nor adhere to the statement of a specific person in everything he says is obligatory, impermissible or permissible except for the Prophet Muhammad ﷺ. However there are some of the people of knowledge who say: it is obligatory upon the one seeking religious verdict to make 'taqleed' of the most knowledgeable and most pious from amongst the people he can seek his verdict from. However, other scholars say: he should choose between the 'muftis'.

In addition, if the questioner possesses some kind of discernment, than it has been said that: he should follow the most preponderant of the two verdicts in his view, according to his discernment and distinction, for this takes precedence over unrestricted selection or choice.

It has also been said: 'One does not make 'ijtihaad' until he is considered to have the qualifications to make 'ijtihaad', and the previous statement is stronger then this.

So if one of the sayings of the 'muftis' is viewed as being stronger and preponderant by the questioner, either because of the stronger evidences or according to the questioner's discernment, or because one of the 'muftis' is more knowledgeable or pious- than this is no problem for the questioner, even if the verdict is in opposition to the 'madth'hab'.[2]

Al Asfahaani said in his commentary of the Quran: 'The duty of the one who is ignorant of the Quran and the Sunnah is that if there occurs a mishap, accident or new issue in which he doesn't know the answer, he must resort to and take refuge in a scholar of the Quran and Sunnah, and ask him about Allah and His Messenger's ﷺ decision or judgment in the issue.

So if the scholar informs him with Allah and His Messenger's ﷺ judgment regarding the issue, then the questioner should act upon it, adhering completely to the Quran and the Sunnah. Trusting the scholar of the Quran and Sunnah

---

[1]-Majmoo' Fatawaa ibn Taymiyyah 20/209
[2]-Majmoo' Fatawaa ibn Taymiyyah 33/168

Al 'I'tibaa'a

completely in what he informed him, even if the questioner does not know the meaning or significance of the proofs and evidences, so he does not become a 'muqallid' with this amount of knowledge. Don't you see that if it becomes apparent to the questioner that what the scholar told him is in opposition to the Quran and the Sunnah, that he would immediately return back to the Quran and Sunnah and not become bigoted towards the one who informed him.

In opposition to the 'muqallid', for verily he does not ask about Allah and His Messenger's ﷺ decision or judgment. For indeed the 'muqallid' asks about the 'madth'hab' of his Imam, and if it became apparent to him that the 'madth'hab' of his Imam is in opposition to the Quran and Sunnah he would not return back to the Quran and Sunnah. And the 'mutabi' is the one who asks about Allah and His Messenger's ﷺ decision and judgement, and he doesn't ask about the opinions of others nor their 'madth'hab'. If there occurred another mishap or accident in which he didn't know the ruling regarding it, it is not compulsory upon him to ask the first scholar who he asked previously. Rather he may ask any scholar that he meets, and it is not obligatory upon him to be devoted to the first opinion, whereas he does not listen to any other opinion other than the first scholar's opinion. In which he aids and advocates the first opinion to the point where if he knows that the text from the Quran and the Sunnah is in opposition to the opinion which he was given, then he disregards it and abandons it. This is the difference between 'taqleed' which the later generations were adhering to and between 'al iti'baa'a 'which the righteous predecessors were upon.'[1]

It is also obligatory upon the layman seeking religious verdicts to work hard and search diligently to find a scholar of the Quran and the Sunnah, just as it is obligatory upon him to search for lawful provisions while knowing that there are some provisions which are earned by the way of prohibited means. This is what Ibn Hazm affirmed, as he said: 'If someone says: 'What does the layman do if there occurs a mishap, accident or issue in which he doesn't know what to do? Ibn Hazm said: The answer -'with Allah is all success- Verily we have completely clarified Allah's prohibition of 'taqleed', and Allah did not specify this for the layman nor for the scholar, nor did Allah distinguish or make distinction between the two. Indeed, Allah's speech is directed towards all people, so 'taqleed' is prohibited upon the slave imported from his country, prohibited for the layman, prohibited for the virgin in her quarters, prohibited for the shepard between the

---

[1]-Taken from 'Eeqathu Himam U'lil Ab'saar pg.40-41

mountains, just as it is prohibited for the wise, knowledgeable scholar, there is no difference.

'Ijtihaad' in seeking Allah and His Messenger's judgment and decision in everything which concerns a person regarding his religion is obligatory upon all people just as it is obligatory upon the wise, knowledgeable scholar and there is no difference. So whoever makes 'taqleed' from amongst the people has verily disobeyed Allah and has sinned. However the manner, method and type of 'ijtihaad' differs amongst the people. It is not obligatory upon the person except to the extent of his ability, because of Allah's statement:

$$\lewline \text{﴿ لَا يُكَلِّفُ ٱللَّهُ نَفْسًا إِلَّا وُسْعَهَا ﴾}$$

'*Allah does not burden a person beyond his ability...*' (al Baqarah 2:286) And Allah says:

$$\text{﴿ فَٱتَّقُوا۟ ٱللَّهَ مَا ٱسْتَطَعْتُمْ ﴾}$$

'*So keep your duty to Allah and fear Him as much as you can...*' (at Taghabun 64:16)

Complete fear of Allah is acting upon everything Allah made obligatory in the religion. In addition, Allah did not command us with anything from the religion except that which we have the ability to do so. Indeed, Allah does not hold us responsible for the things which we do not have the ability to do. This is clear-cut, decisive evidence proving that it is only obligatory upon people to search for the answers, rulings, judgments, and decisions concerning the mishaps, accidents or new issues according to his ability. So everyone has their share of 'ijtihaad', and personal ability and faculty.

The 'ijtihaad' of the layman , if he asked a scholar about the affairs of his religion and asked the scholar should ask: 'This is what Allah and His Messenger decreed?, if the scholar replies: 'Yes', than his statement is taken, and it is not obligatory upon him to search for more than this.

But if the scholar says: 'no', or says: 'this is my statement', or says to him: 'this is Imam Malik's statement or Ibnul Qasim, Abu Haneefah, Abu Yusuf, ash Shafi'ee, Ahmed, Dawud, or named someone from the companions or tabi'een, or someone inferior to the Prophet Muhammad or reprimanded him or

Al 'I'tibaa'a

remained silent about it, then it is prohibited upon the questioner to take the 'muftis' religious verdict. It is also compulsory upon the questioner to ask another scholar and seek the answer to the issue wherever he finds a scholar. End of quote from Ibn Hazm.[1]

I say in clarification of Ibn Hazm's final statement: If the scholar answers the questioner with his personal opinion or the opinion of others and says to him: I do not know Allah and His Messenger's ﷺ judgment in this issue and this is the 'ijtihaad' of our scholars. If the scholar gives his religious verdict in accordance to what he sees to be the preponderant statement of one of the scholars of 'fiqh' and closest to the Quran and Sunnah while not restricting or limiting himself to a particular 'madth'hab' in the religious verdicts he conveys in these situations, then it is obligatory upon the layman to take this verdict if the issue is a state of emergency or one which needs an immediate answer. Likewise, if the issue is not a state of emergency and does not call for an immediate answer then he should be patient and search for another scholar who perhaps may have knowledge of the Quran and the Sunnah, and Allah knows best.

Furthermore, Ibn Hazm's statement regarding 'not accepting the statement of a companion'-is correct if he intended by this meaning, being contrary to the texts from the Quran and the Sunnah. However if he intended by this: not accepting the statements of the companions with the absence of texts from the Quran and the Sunnah, than this statement is not accepted from him. Verily this is because all of the 'fiqh' scholars have agreed upon the fact that statements of the companions are accepted if they do not oppose statements of other companions. If one finds the statements are in opposition, then the 'mufti' chooses the statement he wills and he doesn't exceed the statements of the companions.

Abul Waleed al Bajee Sulayman ibn Khalaf [2] said: 'It is obligatory upon the layman to ask about the one he wants to seek a religious verdict from. If the layman is informed about the one he wants to ask as being a pious scholar then he can take the scholar's verdict. Similarly, it is not permissible for the layman to ask

---

[1] -al Ihkaam fee Usool il Ahkaam pg. 862 , also see the statement of Ibnus Salah similar to this statement in his 'Kitab al Fatwaa' well known as 'Adaabul Mufti wal Mustaftee', pg.280

[2] -(TN)He is Abul Waleed Sulaymaan ibn Khalaf ibn Ayuub ibn Warith at Tajeebee al Bajee, the Spaniard, Maliki jurist. He was born in 403 hijri and he died in 474 hijri.

someone who is not known to be from the scholars who gives religious verdicts.'[1]

An Nawawi said in 'Faslu Adaabil Mustafee': 'It is absolutely obligatory upon the layman to search for that which will give him knowledge of the qualifications of the one which he wants to seek religious verdict from. If he does not know the scholars qualifications than it is not permissible for him to seek a religious verdict from one who ascribes himself to knowledge, or is a teacher or reads to the people, or other than these from the positions of the scholars solely because of his affiliation or position. For this reason it is permissible for him to seek religious verdict from the one who is well known for being qualified to give religious verdicts.'[2]

However, we do not find within both of the previous statements declaration of the required tools which give one sufficient qualifications as we find within the statements of Ibn Hazm and Ibn Taymiyyah. As for the question in a world in which 'taqleed' and bigotry have become widespread, while there are people who study, search for and try to know and ascertain the religious verdicts from the Quran and the Sunnah, then it is obligatory to ask the scholar of the Quran and Sunnah, as Imam Ahmed mentioned.

Ash Shaatibee[3] said: 'If the person is an absolute layman then perhaps some problems may become apparent to him when he sees the different opinions amongst the scholars of Islamic laws. So it is necessary for the laymen in this situation to return back to making 'taqleed' of some of them, as it is not possible for him to make 'taqleed' of those with different opinions in the same issue at the same time, solely because this is impossible and the breaching of consensus. Either there exists possibility to reconcile between the different opinions by acting upon them both or there is no possibility. If there is no possibility of reconciling between them then acting upon them both is impossible. And if it was possible then one's actions would not be in accordance to either of the two opinions, rather a third opinion which no one has ever mentioned would be

---

[1] -Ahkaamul Fusool Ahkaamul Usool' pg. 729, by al Bajee Abee Waleed al Malikee, verification of the book done by Abdul Majeed Turkey, Darul Garb, Beruit 1407
2-al Majmoo' 1/54

[3] -**(TN)** He is the great Imam, faqeeh Abu Ishaaq ibn Ibrahim ibn Musa ibn Muhammad al Lakhmee ash Shaatibee. The scholar and author of many important books. He died in the year 790 hijri. From amongst his compilations: 'al I'tisaam' (considered one of the main resources for researching religious innovations) also 'al Muwafaqaat' (which contains fundamentals and principles of 'fiqh' and much more)

made. What supports this is that we don't find any form of this action being acted upon amongst the earlier scholars from the righteous predecessors, so it is in opposition to consensus.

If it is established that one doesn't make 'taqleed' of anyone except one of them, and every one of them claim that they are the closer to the truth than their rivals, and for this reason he opposed them, and if it wasn't for this he wouldn't have opposed them. As for the layman who is ignorant of the situations in which to use 'ijtihaad', then it is necessary that he is guided to the one who is closest to the truth from amongst the scholars. So this is established for the layman in general because he will give precedence according to who the more knowledgeable scholar is. This is apparent by observing the majority of the scholars and those similar to them and this fact is well known to them, solely because the scholar being more knowledge than the other is a factor which overwhelms the layman's thinking which leads him to believe that the one possessing this knowledge is closer to the truth of The Judge (Allah), and not from any other aspect. So he should not make 'taqleed' except considering the fact that the scholar is a judge with knowledge of The Judge (Allah).'[1]

Ash Shaatibee also went on to say: 'Here is clarification of what is intended by the previous statement: 'If the scholar is one whom the people have not bore witness to his knowledge, or he is certain that he doesn't have knowledge or he has doubts . So choosing to be audacious and daring in these two situations is truly the following of one's desires. The scholar should have sought a verdict from someone else regarding the issue and didn't do so, so it is more deserving that he does not come forward in this issue except if someone else precedes him, who in all actuality didn't precede him.

Sheikh Muhammad Naasirud Deen al-Albaani mentioned this and authenticated it, and commented on this saying: 'This is the advice of Imam ash Shatibee to the scholar whom it is possible for him to place himself in front of the people with some type knowledge. Ash Shaatibee advises the scholar not to place himself in front of the people until the scholars bare witness or testify to his ability to do so, this being for fear of him being one of the people of desires. So what would you think if some of those people who are clinging to or associated with this

---

[1]-al I'tisaam 2/345

Al 'I'tibaa'a

Islamic knowledge of our time, no doubt that he would say: 'this is not your field so go on your way, is there anyone who will take heed from this?'[1]

If someone from amongst the laymen asked a scholar, after diligently searching, then it is not permissible for him to ask about a particular 'madth'hab' nor a specific opinion, rather the wording of his question should be: 'What is the Islamic ruling in this issue in light of the proofs and evidences from the Quran and the Sunnah?

Also it is not permissible for the layman, at any time to ask: 'What is Imam so and so's saying or view in the issue? Because it is obligatory upon the questioner to diligently search for the truth and then follow it, so the correct wording for his question should be: What is the Islamic ruling in this issue?

Imam ash Showkaani said: 'As for what was mentioned in regards to excluding the ones whose understanding of the Islamic texts is deficient or negligent and making this justification for them to make' taqleed', then the issue is not as they have mentioned. For there exists an intermediary between 'ijtihaad' and 'taqleed'. Indeed, it is the question put forth by the ignorant person directed towards the Islamic scholar according to his knowledge, not according to his outright opinion, nor his 'ijtihaad'. This is in accordance to the actions of the companions, the 'tabi'oon' and those who proceeded them.'[2]

Furthermore, Salih al Fulaani [3]mentioned on the authority of al Asfahaani from his commentary of the Quran which was mentioned from Ibn Daqeequl Eid what is a summarization of his statement: 'Indeed the 'ijtihaad' of the layman, amongst the scholars who have this opinion, is that if the layman asks in these times -in which verdicts based upon the selections of infallible human beings have become predominant-he asks the 'mufti': "Is this what Allah and His Messenger ﷺ have decided? If the scholar answers: yes, then the questioner takes his answer and it is not necessary for the questioner to do any more searching than this. It is also not necessary for the 'mufti' to mention to the questioner the Quranic verse or hadeeth and the legality, while extracting the ruling from the correct fundamentals and principles.

---

[1]-Silsilatul Ahadeeth Saheehah 2/713
[2]-'Irshaadul Fuhool' pg.268
[3]-**(TN)**He is Salih ibn Muhammad ibn Nuh ibn Abdullah al Umaree al Fulaani, scholar of hadeeth and a mujtahid, he was a Maliki jurist from al Madinah. He was born and raised in Sudan then moved to Al Madinah until he died in the year 1218 hijri. He is the author of the book 'Eeqath himam U'lel Absaar lil'Iqtidaa'a bi sayid al Muhaajireen wal Ansaar'

Al 'I'tibaa'a

However if the 'mufti' replies: 'this is my saying, my opinion, or the opinion of so and so or a particular 'madth'hab of the scholars of 'fiqh' or reprimands the questioner or remains silent, then the questioner can ask another scholar as long as he answers him with the judgment and decision of Allah's book and the Sunnah of His Messenger ﷺ, and answers him with what is obligatory within the religion of Islam regarding that particular issue. Whoever ponders and contemplates over the statements of the salaf and the four scholars of 'fiqh' regarding the encouragement of the people not to seek the answer to a religious issue except from a scholar of the Quran and Sunnah, in accordance to what we mentioned here.'[1]

Abdullah ibn Imam Ahmed said: "I asked my father about a man who wants to ask about an issue regarding his religion which he is afflicted by making various vows related to divorce and other issues as well, and within his city are the people of 'ray'e' opinions, and also the people of hadeeth-who from amongst them they do not recall nor memorize the narrations, nor do they distinguish between the authentic and inauthentic texts, and chains of narration. Who should I ask, the people of opinions or the people of hadeeth with what little they possess of knowledge?

Imam Ahmed replied: 'Ask the people of hadeeth, and don't ask the people of opinions, for the 'da'eef' hadeeth is better than the opinion of Abu Haneefah.'[2]

Imam Ahmed permitted seeking religious verdicts from the jurists of the people of hadeeth, and the companions of Imam Malik, and referred people to them. He would prohibit the people from seeking religious verdicts from all those who turn away from and abandon the hadeeth and do not build or base their 'madth'hab' upon the ahadeeth. He would also not permit acting upon their religious verdicts.'[3]

The Most Important Obligations Upon the one Seeking Religious Verdicts:

If a mistake from the first 'mufti' becomes apparent, then the questioner must return back to the correct statement. This is because, as it has been clarified that it is not obligatory upon the questioner to limit himself to one statement in

---

[1] -Eeqath Himam U'lel Absaar pg39
[2] -Masaa'il Abdullah ibn Ahmed ibn Hanbal pg.438. also the meaning of 'da'eef' here mentioned by Imam Ahmed is equivalent to 'hasan' amongst the later scholars, refer to footnote #226
[3] -I'laamul Muwa'qaeen 2/60 and Eeqathu Himam Uleel Absaar pg.39

particular, rather he is only obliged and ordered to act upon that which is correct based upon Allah's statement:

$$\text{﴿ ٱلَّذِينَ يَسْتَمِعُونَ ٱلْقَوْلَ فَيَتَّبِعُونَ أَحْسَنَهُ أُوْلَٰٓئِكَ ٱلَّذِينَ هَدَىٰهُمُ ٱللَّهُ وَأُوْلَٰٓئِكَ هُمْ أُوْلُواْ ٱلْأَلْبَٰبِ ﴾}$$

'Those who listen to the good advice (Islamic Monotheism) and follow the best thereof...' (az Zumar 39:18) and this is what the scholars have mentioned.

Ash Shaatibee said: 'With all respect, if some mistakes become apparent to him in various issues, and he was incorrect in relation to the correct knowledge of the Judge (Allah) then he should not take sides with his followers nor encroach upon them in regards to the issues which his mistakes are apparent. Verily his taking sides will lead to that which is contrary to the Islamic Laws, and secondly he will differ with his followers.'[1]

The summarization of this section is that it is obligatory upon the Muslim who is seeking a religious verdict to search for a scholar of the Quran and Sunnah, just as the sick person who is afflicted and overcome by illness would search for the best doctor or specialist to cure his sickness. Furthermore, it is obvious to the human being in his worldy affairs that he is bound to experience hardships, and under these circumstances he diligently searches for someone to cure him, and he will only accept the view or treatment of the best of doctors. So similarly it is obligatory upon him to search and exert himself in finding and knowing the best people of Islamic knowledge. Just as if he needed something in his worldy affairs, even if it was trivial, he would consult the specialists of that field, and ask the people who have the most knowledge of that subject. Similarly it is obligatory upon him to search diligently for the learned scholar who is well versed about the Quran, Sunnah and statements of the scholars, and ask him. So how does one know who is a scholar?

The answer: 'He knows him by the testimony of the scholars and students of knowledge bearing witness that he possesses knowledge of the Quran and Sunnah, perhaps the one who is in opposition to him will not testify to this nor consider him to be from the scholars, especially from those who view that the religion of Islam is that which the 'madthaa'hib' came with, and Allah is the Great Aider.

---

[1]-al I'tisaam 2/345, also see what Sheikhul Islam Ibnu Taymiyyah said in his 'Fatawaa' and also Ibnul Qayyim said in his compilations especially 'I'laam al Muwa'qaeen'.

Part Eight

Obligation of the Mufti to give verdicts with the strongest and most preponderant view along with evidences

It is compulsory for the 'mufti' to search diligently for the ruling in any issue: from the Quran, Sunnah, narrations of the companions, and the statements of the scholars of 'fiqh' and other then them in this order as was previously mentioned in the section about 'fiqh' of the companions and the scholars of 'fiqh'.

Indeed, the consensus of the companions, 'tabi'een' and those within the first three generations from the scholars of the righteous predecessors has taken place regarding the impermissibility of making 'taqleed' of anyone in specific. This is solely because it is not possible that one human being possesses all of the truth except if he is a Prophet and Messenger sent from the Creator of the heavens and earths. The truth which is guaranteed is that contained within the clear proofs contained in the Quran, Sunnah, narrations of the companions, consensus. As for the 'qiyas' and 'ijtihaad' of our scholars than within these there exists a possibility to be correct or incorrect.

We previously mentioned the statements of the companions regarding the ordinal arrangement of the proofs and evidences which one uses when giving religious verdicts. I would like to say that indeed consensus took place regarding this issue, and I do not know what is the excuse for those who made the statements of their 'fiqh' scholars-who proceeded the companions-a fundamental in their religion. Isn't this clear and outright opposition to the consensus which took place in the first three generations!? By Allah, of course it is! This is clear opposition to the consensus which took place in which there is no stronger nor better consensus which took place on the face of the earth.

No doubt that the ones responsible for this will be questioned in front of Allah, then in front of the Messenger ﷺ, then be questioned in front of the believers about the confirmation and establishment of 'taqleed' of one specific person. The ones responsible are the scholars who direct and lead the Muslims, and they are the ones who adorned this for the people and make it obligatory and compulsory upon them to make 'taqleed' of the 'madthaa'hib' (or a specific person).

Al 'I'tibaa'a

Let us listen to the advice of Imam ash Shaatibee who said: 'The 'mufti' has a position similar to that of the Prophet, as the 'mufti' is his successor and inheritor, as it came in a hadeeth: 'The scholars are inheritors of the Prophets..'[1] The scholar is the Prophet's deputy and agent in conveying the religious legislations and rulings, by teaching the people and warning them so that they may take heed. The scholar is also- in addition to being a conveyer of what has been transmitted from Allah and His Messenger ﷺ -holds the position of one who may institute rulings from that which he derived and extracted from the evidences according to his 'ijtihaad' and research. From this aspect he is a legislator whom it is obligatory to follow and act upon what he says, and this in all actuality is the true caliphate or successorship.[2]

So let the scholar closely observe, ponder and contemplate his position and status. Will his inheritance of the Prophet ﷺ be the taking of statements of the scholars, especially the statements which oppose the sayings of the Prophet ﷺ? Also, is it permissible for him to speak about religious issues with the opinions of people, or with the opinions of those whose opinions are not traced back nor based upon proofs from the Quran and Sunnah? The one whom the scholars inherit from (the Prophet) didn't used to speak nor pronounce a single word except after receiving revelation. If he was asked about something he would not respond to the questioner except after knowing and receiving revelation from Allah. Just as the Prophet ﷺ conveys on Allah's behalf, the scholar also conveys on Allah's behalf.

Listen to the beautiful statement of Ibnul Qayyim: 'In light of the fact that propagation and conveyance on behalf of Allah is dependent upon having knowledge of what is conveyed, as well as sincerity and honesty; so the scholar is truthful, honest, and sincere in what he conveys. He should be well-versed, sincere, and honest in what he is conveying. He should always have a good approach and method while possessing a favorable history, being just and equitable in his actions and statements, while his actions in public and private are simiar. So if one held the position of endorsing something on behalf of the kings and leaders in a matter which no one disapproves of nor is ignorant of his power, and this is the highest and most exalted of statuses; then what is the

---

[1] -Part of an authentic hadeeth wich Abu Dawud narrates in his Sunan pg.551, Book of Knowledge, Chapter: The encouragement of seeking knowledge #3641, from the hadeeth of Abu ad Dardaa'a

[2] -Taken from 'al Fatwaa Makaantuhaa, Mazaaliquhaa, Manhajuhaa as Saheeh' by Alaa'a Deen Za'taree 2/1

situation regarding the endorsing something on behalf of the Lord of the heavens and the earths.

It is most appropriate for the one whose status is a scholar, to prepare his equipment (himself and his knowledge) , and gird up his loins and be prepared and be ready for action, and truly understand the position and rank he has been given. There should be no uneasiness or restraint within his heart from speaking the truth and declaring it openly to the people, for verily Allah is his aid, assistant, helper and the one who guides him.

How is it when this is the rank and position which Allah has undertaken and assumed for Himself as He says:

﴿ وَيَسْتَفْتُونَكَ فِى ٱلنِّسَآءِ ۖ قُلِ ٱللَّهُ يُفْتِيكُمْ فِيهِنَّ وَمَا يُتْلَىٰ عَلَيْكُمْ فِى ٱلْكِتَٰبِ ﴾

"They ask you seeking a religious verdict or instruction concerning women, say: Allah instructs you about them and what is recited unto you in the Book..." (an Nisa'a 4:127)

And whatever Allah has taken up as His position and rank is sufficient for all as He also said:

﴿ يَسْتَفْتُونَكَ قُلِ ٱللَّهُ يُفْتِيكُمْ فِى ٱلْكَلَٰلَةِ ۚ ﴾

"They ask you for a religious verdict, Say: Allah instructs (the following) about the one who doesn't have ascendents nor descendants..." (an Nisa'a 4:176)

So let the jurist and the one giving religious verdicts know and understand who he represents regarding the religious verdicts he gives, and that he will be held responsible tomorrow and stand before Allah.'[1]

So what is more dangerous than giving religious verdicts and the responsibility of the 'mufti'?! Ibn Wahb said: 'I heard Imam Malik ibn Anas say: 'The Messenger of Allah ﷺ was the leader of the Muslims and the best person in creation, he

---

[1]-I'laam al Muwa'qaeen 2/17

would be asked about something and not respond until revelation came to him from the heavens.'¹

Ibnul Qayyim mentioned this statement then commented saying: 'So if the Lord of Creation's Messenger ﷺ didn't used to respond or answer questions except with revelation, so what great amount of audacity, courage, and bravery of the one who answers or gives verdicts from his personal opinions, 'qiyas', or makes 'taqleed' of someone who he thinks good about. What audacity of the one who responds with a custom, tradition, politics, taste or inner-feeling, or a claimed unveiling of the unseen, dream or even a conjecture or deeming of something to be good or appropriate, and Allah is the Aider and upon Him do we put our trust.'²

Furthermore, the scholars who have influenced and convinced the masses that it is obligatory to make 'taqleed' of one of the four scholars of 'fiqh' in specific need to sincerely look, observe and ponder over what these four scholars of 'fiqh' advised their students with and all those who proceeded them. Indeed they all said: 'If the hadeeth is authentic than that is my 'madth'hab, and abandon my statement for the narration of the Prophet ﷺ, everyone's statement is accepted or rejected except for the Prophet Muhammad ﷺ, if a narration comes from the Prophet Muhammad ﷺ then it is taken on the 'head and the eye'³, it is not permissible for anyone to take our statements except after knowing where we took them from, it is prohibited for the one who doesn't know my proofs and evidences to give verdicts with my statements, verily we are only mortals we may say something today and tomorrow we may withdraw that statement...', as these statements were previously mentioned.

This is what the scholars of 'fiqh' considered to be obligatory upon themselves. This being because the Quran, Sunnah and authentic narrations were the most important thing to them and the most exalted thing within their hearts, and they reached the highest pinnacle of piety, humility and fear of Allah. But we don't know, will those 'scholars' who say that 'taqleed' is obligatory be convinced as those who they make 'taqleed' of were convinced??? Rather, they will not be convinced, considering the fact that they have facilitated and made it very easy

---

¹-Ibn Hazm mentioned it in 'Ihkaam' 8/35 from the narration of Ibn Wahb and Ibn Abdul Barr in 'Jami Bayaanil Ilm wa fadhlihi' pg. 839
²-I'laam al Muwa'qaeen 2/470
³-**(TN)** This is an Arabic expression used to mean that something is given top priority, utmost importance, emphasis

for themselves to abandon and turn away from the creed of the scholars of 'fiqh', so whatever proceeds that is even more easier to abandon and less significant. It is a small minority of the later generation Muslims who are not following the creed of the 'Ash'ariyyah' or the other misguided ideologies. Similarly, it is also very rare that you will find someone who is not attached to the innovated ways, beliefs, ideas of the 'Soofiyyah' which have no proof, reference, or source from the religion of Allah which was revealed to the final Messenger Muhammad ﷺ.

Furthermore, let those people ponder and contemplate: 'with what intellect, logic, correct reasoning, and religion do they deem the ones who adhere to the Sunnah and strive to revive it throughout the Muslim lands, as being misguided and innovators!!???

With what intellect, logic and religion do they make enmity towards and harm those who are symbols of how to correctly adhere and follow Allah's religion while opposing the innovations and innovators. While they are the ones who are rectifying and correcting what the people have corrupted. Why do they provoke, antagonize, oppress, and show enmity towards their masaajid and schools.

With what proofs and evidences do they oblige the people with something that Allah did not oblige upon them?? Is this not considered aggression, enmity and showing hostility to Allah and His Messenger ﷺ? Why do they spread dissension amongst the people and split them into groups and sects which end up showing enmity, aggression, and resort to deceiving each other?

Is this what we would consider as 'holding fast' which Allah intended for His worshippers? As Allah states:

$$ \text{﴿ وَٱعْتَصِمُوا۟ بِحَبْلِ ٱللَّهِ جَمِيعًا وَلَا تَفَرَّقُوا۟ ﴾} $$

'And hold fast, all of you together, to the Rope of Allah (Quran, Sunnah) and do not be divided amongst yourselves...' (ali Imraan 3:103) So what will they answer the day their Lord says to them:

$$ \text{﴿ وَقِفُوهُمْ ۖ إِنَّهُم مَّسْـُٔولُونَ ﴾} $$

'But stop them, verily they are to be questioned' (as Saffat 37:24)

Part Nine

The Mufti's knowledge of the different opinions

We have established with decisive proofs and evidences that it is necessary for the 'mufti' and the student of 'fiqh' in every era and especially this era, to look in the Quran and Sunnah and know that there is no opinion after the establishment of the Sunnah. Then the Quran and Sunnah are proceeded by the consensus of the companions. Which is proceeded by the individual narrations of the companions.[1] Then these are proceeded by the statements of the four 'fiqh' scholars and their 'ijtihaad'. Then the 'mufti' may give his verdict according to that which is the closest to the Quran, Sunnah and narrations of the companions as well as their religious verdicts, as well as giving precedence to the most preponderant and strongest narrations of the companions, as we mentioned previously. Qatadah ibn Du'aamah said:

عَنْ قَتَادَةَ قَالَ: «مَنْ لَمْ يَعْرِفِ الِاخْتِلَافَ لَمْ يَشُمَّ (رَائِحَةَ) الْفِقْهِ بِأَنْفِهِ»

'Whoever doesn't know the different opinions of the companions his nose will never smell the scent of 'fiqh'.[2]

Sa'eed ibnu Abee Uroobah said:

قال سَعِيدُ بْنُ أَبِي عَرُوبَةَ يَقُولُ: «مَنْ لَمْ يَسْمَعِ الِاخْتِلَافَ فَلَا تَعُدُّوهُ عَالِمًا»

'Whoever doesn't listen to the different opinions do not consider him a scholar.'[3]

---

[1]-(TN)The narrations of the companions which are in agreement are given precedence over the narrations which are contradictory or in opposition

[2]-(TN) Ibn Abdul Barr mentioned it in 'Jami' Bayaan al Ilm wa Fadlihi' #1520,1522 and the chain of narration is weak because of the narrator Sa'eed ibn Basheer al Azdee and Abu Aasim Rawaad ibnul Jaraah al Asqalaani. Khateeb al Baghdaadi mentioned it in 'Faqeeh wal Mutafaqih' #659

[3]-(TN) Ibn Abdul Barr mentioned in in the previous mentioned book #1521 with an authentic chain of narration.

Hisham ibn Ubaydillah ar Raazi said:

«مَنْ لَمْ يَعْرِفْ اخْتِلَافَ الْقُرَّاءِ فَلَيْسَ بِقَارِئٍ، وَمَنْ لَمْ يَعْرِفْ اخْتِلَافَ الْفُقَهَاءِ فَلَيْسَ بِفَقِيهٍ»

'Whoever doesn't know the different methods of Quranic recitation then he is not a reciter, and whoever doesn't know the different opinions of the jurists then he is not a jurist'[1]

Uthmaan ibn Ataa'a said on the authority of his father:

«لَا يَنْبَغِي لِأَحَدٍ أَنْ يُفْتِيَ النَّاسَ، حَتَّى يَكُونَ عَالِمًا بِاخْتِلَافِ النَّاسِ؛ فَإِنْ لَمْ يَكُنْ كَذَلِكَ رَدَّ مِنَ الْعِلْمِ مَا هُوَ أَوْثَقُ مِنَ الَّذِي (بعده) فِي يَدِهِ»

'No one should give religious verdicts to the people until he is well versed about the various opinions of the companions, and if he is not familiar with them then he will reject the knowledge which is stronger and more precise in exchange for the knowledge which (proceeds it) is in his hands, which is weaker.[2] Ayuub as Sikhtiyaani and Ibn Uyainah said:

"أَجْسَرُ النَّاسِ عَلَى الْفُتْيَا أَقَلُّهُمْ عِلْمًا بِاخْتِلَافِ الْعُلَمَاءِ"

'The most audacious of people in giving religious verdicts are the ones who have the least knowledge of the different opinions of the scholars.' Ayuub added on saying:

"وَأَمْسَكُ النَّاسِ عَنِ الْفُتْيَا أَعْلَمُهُمْ بِاخْتِلَافِ الْعُلَمَاءِ"

'And he who is the most abstaining from giving religious verdicts is the most knowledgeable of the different opinions of the scholars.'[3]

---

[1]-Ibn Abdul Barr mentioned it in 'Jami Bayaan al Ilm wa Fadlihi' #1523, in the chain of narration is Hisham ar Raazi, Imam adh Dhahabee said in Meezan al I'tidaal #923: Abu Haatim said he is 'Sudooq', I haven't seen anyone greater than him in Ar Ray'u." End of quote. Ibn Abee Haatim also said: 'he is trustworthy and he is someone whose narrations are good' see al Jarh wa Ta'deel for Ibn Abee Haatim ar Raazi #15911, vol.9/85.

[2]-'Jami Bayaan al Ilm wa Fadlihi #1524, in the chain of narration is Uthmaan ibn Ataa'a ibn Abee Muslim who is
'Da'eef' (weak)

[3]-'Jami Bayaan al Ilm wa Fadlihi #1525,1527, and al Khateeb Baghdaadi mentioned it in al Faqeeh wal Mutafaqih 2/350 #1079 with a similar meaning from the narration of Ishaq ibn Rahaway'yah on the authority of Sufyaan ibn Uyaynah with an authentic chain of narration.

Al 'I'tibaa'a

Imam Malik was asked:

سُئِلَ مَالِكٌ، قِيلَ لَهُ: لِمَنْ تَجُوزُ الْفَتْوَى؟ قَالَ: «لَا تَجُوزُ الْفَتْوَى إِلَّا لِمَنْ عَلِمَ مَا اخْتَلَفَ النَّاسُ فِيهِ» قِيلَ لَهُ: اخْتِلَافُ أَهْلِ الرَّأْيِ؟ قَالَ: «لَا، اخْتِلَافُ أَصْحَابِ مُحَمَّدٍ صَلَّى اللهُ عَلَيْهِ وَسَلَّمَ وَعِلْمُ النَّاسِخِ وَالْمَنْسُوخِ مِنَ الْقُرْآنِ وَمِنْ حَدِيثِ رَسُولِ اللهِ صَلَّى اللهُ عَلَيْهِ وَسَلَّمَ وَكَذَلِكَ يُفْتِي»

'For who is it permissible to give religious verdicts?', he replied: 'It is not permissible to give religious verdicts except for the one who knows what the people differ in', then it was said to him: 'Differences amongst the people of opinions?', Imam Malik replied: no, the different opinions amongst the companions of Allah's Messenger ﷺ, and knowledge of the 'nasikh' and 'mansookh' texts from the Quran and the hadeeth of Allah's Messenger ﷺ, this is how he gives religious verdicts...'[1] Also Abdullah ibnul Mubaarak was asked:

مَتَى يَسَعُ الرَّجُلَ أَنْ يُفْتِيَ؟ قَالَ: «إِذَا كَانَ عَالِمًا بِالْأَثَرِ بَصِيرًا بِالرَّأْيِ»

'When is it permissible for a person to give religious verdicts? He replied: 'If he is knowledgeable and well versed regarding the narrations and discerning about opinions.'[2]

Yahyaa ibn Salaam said:

وَقَالَ يَحْيَى بْنُ سَلَامٍ: "لَا يَنْبَغِي لِمَنْ لَا يَعْرِفُ الِاخْتِلَافَ أَنْ يُفْتِيَ، وَلَا يَجُوزُ لِمَنْ لَا يَعْلَمُ الْأَقَاوِيلَ أَنْ يَقُولَ: هَذَا أَحَبُّ إِلَيَّ"

'The one who doesn't know the different opinions should not give religious verdicts, and it is not permissible for the one who doesn't know the statements of the salaf to say: I prefer this statement or that one...'[3]

---

[1]-Jami' Bayaan al Ilm wa Fadlihi #1529
[2]-previous reference #1532
[3]-Jami' Bayaan al Ilm wa Fadhlihi #1534 with a 'Hasan' good chain of narration.

Al 'I'tibaa'a

Part Ten

The actions of the Mufti regarding the affairs in which the religious opinions differ

Imam Malik, ash Shafi'ee and their contemporaries who tread upon their path, as well as Laith ibn Sa'd, al Awzaa'ee, Abee Thowr and a group of the scholars of opinions said: 'In the issues which opinions differ then there is a correct opinion and an incorrect opinion. When the scholars differ it is obligatory to seek the proofs and evidences from the Quran, Sunnah, Consensus, and the correct 'qiyas' based upon these sources, and this is what is necessary. However, if it so happens that the proofs are similar or corresponding than it is obligatory to lean towards that which is closest to the Quran and Sunnah. If this does not become clear to the person then he should cease in making any ruling or decision, and it is not permissible to assert anything except with complete certainty.

If the 'mufti' is forced or compelled to use these techniques specifically for himself, then it is permissible to make 'taqleed' as it is for the laymen. In times when the texts are similar and analogous; to an extent that he finds difficulty reconciling between them, and establishing the proofs for every statement, he should use the Prophet's ﷺ statement to remind him and assist him, as the Prophet ﷺ said:

»الْبِرُّ مَا اطْمَأَنَّتْ إِلَيْهِ النَّفْسُ وَالْإِثْمُ مَا حَاكَ فِي الصَّدْرِ فَدَعْ مَا يَرِيبُكَ إِلَى مَا لَا يَرِيبُكَ«

'Al Birr[1] is that which the soul is assured and at ease with, and al Ithm[2] is that which makes the heart restless, worried, troubled; so abandon that which

---

1-(TN) Al Birr has several meanings from them: 'dealing with the creation with goodness and righteousness, performing the obligatory duties apparent and inapparent, good manners, but in this hadeeth the meaning which is most appropriate is 'righteousness, obedience to Allah, goodness, piety and correctness' and Allah knows best.

2-(TN)al Ithm also has several meanings: disobedience to Allah, that which makes the persons heart uneasy, worried, confused, also they are the actions which if people see them being done they would disapprove of it, but in this hadeeth the appropriate meaning is that which is evil, bad, incorrect, sin, disobedience that which one feels bad or worried about in his heart, and Allah knows best.

causes you doubt for that which does not cause you doubt.'¹

This is the condition for the one who doesn't deeply ponder or contemplate and is weak in doing so. This is the condition of the laymen whom it is permissible for them to make 'taqleed' of their scholars who gave them religious verdicts in the new issues, mishaps, and incidents which occur. As for the 'muftis' than it is not permissible for them (and this is the opinion of everyone we mentioned previously) to give a religious verdict or ruling except after it becomes clear to him the significance, meaning and aspect of what he gives as a religious verdict from the Quran, Sunnah, or Consensus, or that which holds the meaning of these three.'²

Imam ash Shafi'ee mentioned in his book 'Adaabul Qudaah': 'It is not permissible for the judge nor the 'mufti' to give religious verdict or pass a judgement in an issue until he is well-versed and extremely knowledgeable of the Quran and what the scholars of Quranic commentary have said concerning it's explanation. He should also be well-versed and very knowledgeable of the Sunnah, and the narrations of the companions, and well-versed regarding the different opinions of the scholars. He should also possess good observation and study skills, wholesome provisions, while maintaining piety and devoutness and always consulting his peers when things are not clear to him'

All of this was mentioned in the 'madth'hab' of Imam Malik and the rest of the Muslim jurists worldwide. They all state that it is conditional and contingent upon the judge, 'mufti', and the 'muqallid' and not permissible for them to have anything except these mentioned characteristics.'³

Here is the advice of Ibn Abdul Barr which is rare and invaluable he said: 'O my brother it is necessary for you to memorize the fundamentals and show diligent concern and pay attention to them. Know that whoever devotes his attention and concern to memorizing the Sunan and the legislative texts in the Quran, while studying the statements of the scholars of 'fiqh'that studying these issues will aid him in his 'ijtihaad' and will act as a key to upon up the many doors of

---

[1]-(TN)Jami Bayaan al Ilm wa Fadlihi #1692 and it is authentic. This hadeeth has similar wording and meaning to other ahadeeth mentioned in Saheeh Muslim on the authority of an Nawaas ibn Sam'aan #2553, and at Tirmidthi #2379 and Bukhari mentioned it in al Adam al Mufrad (295,302). It is also narrated on the authority of Anas ibn Malik, al Hasan ibn Ali, Wabisah ibn Ma'bad and Ibn Umar.
[2]-Jami' Bayaanil Ilm 2/903-904
[3]-Jami' Bayaanil Ilm 2/908

perception, examination and consideration. That which also aids him in explaining and interpreting phrases and statements which have more than one possible meaning. None of them ever made 'taqleed'(the type that it is compulsory to submit to and comply to in every situation) without studying or contemplating the issue. Nor does he stray away from what the scholars did for themselves such as memorizing, contemplating, and understanding the sunan while at the same time taking them as examples and role models in their understanding, observations and research skills. One constantly thanks the scholars of 'fiqh' for their endeavors, benefits and observations which they pointed out to those who came after them. He also praises them for what was correct which is the majority of their statements, and he also does not say that they are free from mistakes, as they themselves did not even say this. So this is the student who is adherent to what the righteous predecessors were upon, and this is his good portion and the tool which he uses to scrutinize and examine so as to be guided, and to follow the Sunnah of the Prophet Muhammad ﷺ, and the guidance of the Prophet's ﷺ companions, and all those who followed them in goodness.

Whoever exempts himself from researching, contemplating and observing while abandoning and leaving off what we just mentioned and rejects the sunan with his opinions, and desires to refer the sunan back to his opinions and independent contemplations, then this person is misguided as well as one who misguides others. Whoever is ignorant of these things and engages courageously in giving religious verdicts with knowledge, for he is the most blind and the most misguided person. As is mentioned in Arabic poetry:

لَقَدْ أَسْمَعْتُ لَوْ نَادَيْتُ حَياً-وَ لَكِن لا حَيَاةَ لِمَنْ تُنَادِي

'I have called out to the people, the ones who are alive-but however the ones who you call out to are not living'

Verily I have come to know that I will never submit to an ignorant stubborn person who doesn't know. As is mentioned in Arabic poetry:

وَ لَسْتُ بِنَاجٍ مِنْ مَقَالَةِ طَاعِنٍ-وَ لَوْ كُنْتُ فِي غَارٍ عَلَى جَبَلٍ وَعِرٍ
وَ مَنْ ذَا الذِي يَنْجُو مِنَ النَّاسِ-وَ لَوْ غَابَ عَنْهُمْ بَيْنَ خَافَيْتَي نِسْرِ

'I cannot succeed from the statement of the criticizer, even if I was in a cave upon the most treacherous mountain. And who is the one who succeeds from the people, even if he was not present amongst the people, while being within the grasp of the eagle'[1]

Abu Usamah said: 'There are two issues: either supplication for a person, or the cursing, slandering and defaming of him. The supplication as well as the cursing, slandering and defaming of a person reaches him in his grave after his death. The scholar is resurrected upon the Sunnah and 'al it'ibaa'a' until the supplications of the righteous are supplications and the cursing, slandering and defamation of him by others is transformed into supplications for him, by the will of Allah. The Prophet Muhammad ﷺ said:

"مَنْ أَرْضَى النَّاسَ بِسَخَطِ اللهِ، وَكَلَهُ اللهُ إِلَى النَّاسِ، وَمَنْ أَسْخَطَ النَّاسَ بِرَضَا اللهِ كَفَاهُ اللهُ النَّاسَ"

'Whoever pleases the people with Allah's discontent then Allah entrusts him to the people, and whoever angers the people with Allah's pleasure, Allah will suffice him from the people.'[2]

So what is required- in every era and especially this time-is that the 'mufti' looks at, observes and studies the statements and 'ijtihaadat' of the scholars as well as their understandings of the proofs and evidences. After this he then gives his verdict according to the strongest and most preponderant proofs. One should also research this issue regarding the manners of the 'mufti' and the one seeking religious verdicts in the book 'I'laamul Muwa'qaeen' by Ibnul Qayyim specifically the fifth and sixth volume.

Ibnul Qayyim said: 'Whoever examines and compares the statements of the scholars with the texts (Quran, Sunnah) and weighs their statements with the Quran and Sunnah, and happens to find some statements in contradiction to the texts- no matter what the situation is this person will never find the statements of the scholars to be in vain, nor will he be unjust or unfair to them. Rather he would be taking after their example and emulating them, for indeed all of them ordered the people with this. So the one who truly follows the scholars of 'fiqh', is the one who adheres to and follows what they advised the people with and not the ones who opposed them. Opposing them in a statement of theirs which a clear-cut text came in opposition to it - is easier than opposing them in a general, all-comprehensive principle which they ordered the people with and

---

[1] -Jami' Bayaanil Ilm wa Fadhlihi 2/1139-1140
[2] -Saheehul Jami as Sagheer 5/238, also at Tirmidthi narrated it as well as Imam Ahmed in his 'Musnad' and other than them, from the hadeeth of Aishia

Al 'I'tibaa'a

called them to which is: <u>giving precedence to the texts of the Quran and Sunnah over their own statements.</u>

From this aspect the difference between making 'taqleed' of a scholar in everything he says and between utilization of his understanding and seeking enlightenment or insight by the light of his knowledge is made clear. The first type (taqleed) is the one who accepts and takes a statement without contemplating or looking into it, nor does he seek or demand the proofs and evidences from the Quran and Sunnah. Rather he makes the statement as the rope which is tied around his neck and is driven around everywhere, this is why it has been called 'taqleed'. This is in opposition to the one who seeks aid and help from the scholars understanding and seeks enlightenment or insight by the light of his knowledge in arriving to the Messenger of Allah ﷺ. For verily he makes the scholars as the first order of proofs, and if he arrives to what the Messenger of Allah ﷺ decided then he is content with this proof and leaves off the proofs of others.'[1]

Ibnul Qayyim also said: 'The 'mufti' should be warned-as he is the one who should fear Allah the most as regarding his position and status with Allah the Most High. Especially, about answering the questioner with a religious verdict from the questioners specific 'madth'hab' which he strictly adheres to, while knowing that another 'madth'hab'- in this issue in particular- takes precedence and it's proofs and evidences are stronger. One may find that the influence of leadership makes him engage courageously in giving religious verdicts which he knows that what is correct is in opposition to what he said. So in this case he is a betrayer, disloyal, and deceiver of Allah and His Messenger ﷺ, as well as the questioner, while cheating him at the same time. Allah does not guide those who are deceptive, disloyal, or betrayers; and Allah has prohibited the paradise from all of those whom He meets and they have cheated or betrayed Islam and the Muslims. Indeed, the religion is sincere advice and cheating is contrary to the religion, just as lying is contrary to truthfulness and truth is contrary to falsehood. Many occurences and issues have come to us which we believe are in opposition to the 'madthaa'hib'. So in turn, it is not permissible for us to give a verdict in opposition to what we believe. In this situation we mention the strongest and most preponderant 'madth'hab and we give this precedence over

---

[1] -ar Rooh by Ibnul Qayyim pg. 422-423

the others. We say: 'this is what is correct, and it's acceptance should be given priority over other statements, and with Allah is all success.'[1]

Ibnul Qayyim also said: 'It is not permissible for the 'mufti' to testify on behalf of Allah and His Messenger ﷺ that they have allowed this, prohibited that, or made this obligatory and that is disliked except when he is certain that the issue is as so, from what Allah and His Messenger ﷺ informed of in the authentic texts of the Quran and Sunnah regarding its legality, prohibition, obligation, or disliking.' As for what one finds in his book which he learned from (his sheikh) the one whom he makes 'taqleed' of in his religion, then it is not permissible for him to testify on behalf of Allah and His Messenger ﷺ with it and deceive the people with that, while he possesses no knowledge of Allah and His Messenger's ﷺ legislations. Many of the righteous predecessors used to say:

لِيَحْذَرْ أَحَدُكُمْ أَنْ يَقُولَ: أَحَلَّ اللهُ كَذَا، أَوْ حَرَّمَ اللهُ كَذَا، فَيَقُولُ اللهُ لَهُ: كَذَبْتَ، لَمْ أُحِلَّ كَذَا، وَلَمْ أُحَرِّمْهُ.

'You should take heed and be warned from saying: 'Allah permitted this and that, or Allah prohibited this and that, then Allah will say to him: You have lied, I did not permit this nor did I prohibit that.'[2]

---

[1] -I'laamul Muwa'qaeen 4/228
[2] -I'laamul Muwa'qaeen 4/225-226

Part Eleven

The Manners of the Mufti

From the manners of the 'mufti' is that he mentions the proofs and evidences for the issue at hand.

The 'mufti' should mention the proofs for the judgment or verdict he gives, and his approach in doing so if possible. He shouldn't mention these things to the naïve questioner who won't understand the proofs or the approach regarding how he came to his judgment, this is because of the layman's lack of knowledge and understanding. Whoever ponders over the religious verdicts of the Prophet Muhammad ﷺ which are proofs within themselves, one will definitely find them being comprised of a hint towards the wisdom behind the rulings, it's equivalent, and the aspect of its legality. This is made clear when the Prophet Muhammad ﷺ was asked about selling ripe dates for dried dates and he replied:

أَيَنْقُصُ الرُّطَبُ إذا جَفَّ"؟ قُلْنَا: "نَعَم فَنَهَى عنه"

'Do the ripe dates decrease in value if they dry? They replied: yes, so then the Prophet ﷺ prevented them from doing so.[1] As it is well known that the Prophet ﷺ knew very well about the decrease in value of the dates after drying, however he wanted to bring to their attention and remind them of the justification and reason of its prohibition.'[2]

---

[1]-Kanzul Omaal fee Sunanil Aqwaali wal Afaal, chapter: Usury and its ruling 4/191
[2]-I'laamul Muwa'qaeen 4/208

Closing Statements

Verily Allah created all of the people, they will be created until the Day of Resurrection solely for the purpose of worshipping Allah alone without partner. Allah also sent Messengers and Prophets to their nations before the Prophet Muhammad ﷺ, and made it obligatory upon the nations to follow their messengers. Allah also sent our Prophet and Messenger Muhammad ﷺ as the last of them which there is not Prophet or Messenger after him.

Everyone who lived in the era of the Prophet Muhammad ﷺ, and his message reached them, no matter what religion they followed, it was obligatory upon them to follow Muhammad ﷺ even if it was Musa as the Prophet ﷺ stated:

"لَوْ كَانَ مُوسَى حَيًّا بَيْنَ أَظْهُرِكُمْ، مَا حَلَّ لَهُ إِلَّا أَنْ يَتَّبِعَنِي"

'If Musa was alive amongst you all, he would have no choice except to follow me.'[1]

Just as Allah created the people to worship Him alone, similarly after the sending of the Prophet Muhammad ﷺ the reason for their creation was to be in complete obedience to Allah's Messenger ﷺ. So it is obligatory upon the Muslims that they do not give the status and rank of complete obedience to someone other than the Prophet Muhammad ﷺ, and every person's statements are accepted or rejected except for our noble Prophet and Messenger Muhammad ﷺ.

Allah praises are due to Allah and with His blessing and virtues, good actions and deeds are completed.

Dr. Wasiullah ibn Muhammad Abbaas

---

[1]-**(TN)** Imam Ahmed narrated it in his Musnad #14631, 15156, and others. Sheikh al Albaani said it is 'hasan' (good) narration in 'Irwaa'a al Ghaleel #1589

Al 'I'tibaa'a

Bibliography

1-Quran Kareem

2-Adaabu ash Shafi'ee wa Manaaqibuhu, by Ibn Abee Haatim Abdur Rahman ar Raazi (240-327 hijri), verification of the texts: Abdul Ghanee Abdul Khaliq, Dar ul Kitab

3-Al Ihsaan fee tarteeb Saheeh ibn Hibaan, by Ibn Bulbaan Alaa'a Deen al Farisee (675-739 hijri), verification : Shuayb al Ar'na'oot, Mu'as'sastur Risalah

4-Ahkaamul Janaa'iz wa Bidahiha, by Mumammad Naasirud Deen al Albaani, al Maktab al Islaamiyee, Beriut

5-Ihkaamul Fusool fee Ahkaamil Usool, by al Baajee, Abee al Waleed (died 447 hijri), verification: Abdul Majeed at Turkey, Darul Gharb, Beruit 1407 hijri

6-Al Ihkaam fee Usoolil Ahkaam, by Ibn Hazm, Abee Muhammad Ali (384-456 hijri), Mat'ba'atul Aasimah al Qahirah

7-Akhbaar Abee Haneefah wa As-habuhu, by al Saymeree, al Husein ibn Ali, (436 hijri), photocopied version by darul Kitab al Araabi by a Indian copy

8-Akhbaarul Qudaat, by Wakee' Muhammad ibn Khalf (306 hijri), Aalimul Kitab, Beruit

9-Irshaadul Fuhool, by ash Showkaani, Muhammad ibn Ali, (1255 hijri), photocopied version Darul Fikr

10-Al Istidthkaar, by Ibn Abdul Barr, Yusuf ibn Abdullah an Nimaree (463 hijri), Darul Kutubul Ilmiyyah distributions

11-Al I'tisaam, by ash Shaatibee, Ibrahim ibn Musa (790 hijri), photocopied version Darul Fikr from Riyadh al Hadeethah printers

12-I'laamul Muwa'qaeen, by Ibnul Qayyim, Shamsu Deen Muhammad ibn Abee Bakr (751 hijri), verification of texts and referencing by Mashoor ibn Hasan, Dar ibnul Jawzee, 1423

13-I'laamul Muwa'qaeen b Ibnul Qayyim, Shamsu Deen Muhammad ibn Abee Bakr (751 hijri), verification of texts by: Abdur Rahman al Wakeel 1389

14-Al Umm, by ash Shafi'ee, Muhammad ibn Idrees, the Imam, (150-204 hijri), verification: Muhammad Zuhri an Najjaar, Darul Ma'rifah, Beruit 1393

15-Al Amwaal, by Ibnu Zanjawee Humaid, (251 hijri), verification by Shakir Dheeb Fayaad, Markazul Malik Faisal for Research , 1406

Al 'I'tibaa'a

16-Al Amwaal, by Abee Ubayd al Qaasim ibn Salaam (157-224 hijri), verification by: Muhammad Khaleel Haraas, Darush Sharq, 1381

17-Inbaa'a ul Ghamar bi'anbaa'a al Umur, by Ibn Hajr Ahmed ibn Ali al Asqalaani (852 hijri), Da'iratul Ma'aarif, India, 1390

18-Intifaa'a fee fadaa'il ath Thalathatul Fuqahaa'a, by Ibn Abdul Barr, Yusuf ibn Abdullah (368-463 hijri), Darul Kitab al Ilmiyyah, Beruit

19-Eeqathu Himam Uleel Ab'saar, by Saleh ibn Muhammad al Umaree al Fulaani, (1196-1217 hijri), photocopied version, Dar Nashr al Kutub al Islaamiyyah, Pakistan

20-Al Bidayyah wan Nihiyyah, by Ismaa'eel ibn Umar ibn Kathir (701-774 hijri), verification: Abdullah ibn Abdul Muhsin at Turkey, Dar Hijr , 1418

21-Bidatul Ta'asub al Madth'habee, by Abaasee Muhammad Eid, Dar al Wa'ee al Arabee

22-At Tarikh, Yahya ibn Ma'een, ad Dowree's transmission, verification: Ahmed Nur Saif, Markaz al Bahth al Ilmee, Makkah 1399

23-Tarikh Ulamaa'a al Andulus, by Ibnul Fardee Abdulah ibn Muhammad al Azdee (403 hijri), ad Dar al Misreeyah lil Ta'leef wat Tarjamah, 1966 gregorian

24-Tuhfatul Ahwadthee, by al Mubaarakfuree, Muhammad ibn Abdur Rahman (1283-1353 hijri), photocopied Darul Kitab al Arabee from and Indian printing

25-Takhreej Ahaadeeth Mushkilatul Faqr, by Muhammad Naasirud Deen al Albaani, al Maktabul Islaamee 1405

26-Tafsir ibn Jarir-Jamiul Bayaan, by Ibn Jarir at Tabari Muhammad ibn Jarir (died 310 hijri), Darul Ma'rifah, Beruit

27-Tafsir Ibn Kathir-Tafsirul Quranul Adtheem, by Ismaa'eel ibn Umar ad Damishqee, Ibn Kathir (701-774 hijri) Darud Daleel al Athariyyah

28-Tafsir as Sa'dee, Tayseerul Kareemul Rahman, by Abdur Rahman ibn Naasir as'Sa'dee (1307-1376 hijri) Mu'as'sa'satur Risalah

29-Taqdumatul Jarh wa Ta'deel, by Ibn Abee Haatim Abdur Rahman (240-327 hijri) , Da'iratul Ma'aarif, Hyder Aabaad, India

30-At Tawheed, by Ibn Khuzaimah, Muhammad ibn Ishaaq, (223-311 hijri), comments: Muhammad Khaleel Haraas, Darul Baaz, Makkah

31-Al Jami'us Saheeh ma'a Fathul Baari, by Muhammad ibn Ismaa'eel al Bukhari (193-256 hijri) Mat'ba'atul Salifiyyah , Egypt

Al 'I'tibaa'a

32-Al Jami'us Saheeh, by Muslim ibnul Hujaaj an Naysaabooree (206-261 hijri) numbering by Fu'aad Abdul Baaqi, Isa al Baabi al Halabee, 1374

33-Hujjatullahi al Baligah, by Shah Waliullah ad Dahlawee, Darut Turath, Cairo, 1355 hijri

34-Hilyatul Aw'liyyaah, by Abee Nu'aym al Asbahaani, Ahmed ibn Abdullah (336-430 hijri), Darul Kitab al Araabee, Lebanon 1387

35-Khutbatul Kitab al Mu'amal, by Abu Shamah Abdur Rahman ibn Ismaa'eel al Maqdasee (599-665 hijri), commentary: Jamaal Azoon, Adwaas Salaf, 1424

36-Ad Daleel Alaa Butlaan at Tahleel, by Ibn Taymiyyah, Ahmed ibn Abdul Haleem (661-728 hijri), verification: Hamdee Abdul Majeed as Salafi, al Maktabul Islaamee, 1418

37-Rahmatul lil Alaameen, by al Qaadi Sulaymaan al Mansoorfooree, Dar as Salaam, Riyadh

38-Risalatul al Ash'ariyyah Ilaa Ahlul Thagr, by Imam Abeel Hasan al Ash'aree, (260-326 hijri), Maktabatul Uloom wal Hikam

39-Ar Risaalah, by Muhammad ibn Idrees ash Shafi'ee (150-204 hijri), verification: Ahmed Shakir, 1358

40-Ar Risaalah, by Muhammad ibn Idrees ash Shafi'ee (150-204 hijri), Darul Fath, Ash Shariqah

41-Ar Rooh, by Ibnul Qayyim (690-751 hijri), verification: Salih Ahmed ash Shaami

42-Silsilatul Ahaadeeth as Saheehah, by Muhammad Naasirud Deen al Albaani (1332-1420 hijri), al Maktabul Islaamee, and Maktabatul Ma'aarif

43-Silsilatul Ahaadeeth ad Da'eefah, by previous author

44-As Sunnah, by Ibn Abee Aasim, (287 hijri), verification: Muhammad Naasirud Deen al Albaani, al Maktabul Islaamee, 1400

45-As Sunan, by Abee Dawud Sulaymaan ibn Ash'ath as Sijistaani, (202-275 hijri), checking the texts: Mashoor Hasan, Maktabatul Ma'aarif, Riyadh

46-As Sunan, by Ibn Majah, Muhammad ibn Yazeed al Qazweenee, (209-273 hijri), checking the texts: Mashoor Hasan, Maktabatul Ma'aarif, Riyadh

47-As Sunanul Kubraa, by Abee Bakr Ahmed ibn Husein al Bayhaqee, (384-458 hijri), Da'iratul Ma'aarif, HyderAabaad, India

Al 'I'tibaa'a

48-As Sunan, by Muhammad ibn Isa ibn Surah at Tirmidthi (died 279 hijri), checking by: Mashoor Hasan, Maktabatul Ma'aarif, Riyadh

49-As Sunan, by Abdullah ibn Abdur Rahman ad Daaramee (181-255 hijri), Dar Ihyaa'as Sunnah an Nabawiyyah

50-As Sunan, by Ahmed ibn Shuayb an Nisaa'ee (210-303 hijri), checking: Mashoor Hasan, Maktabatul Ma'aarif, Riyadh

51-Su'aalaat Abee Dawud, Sulaymaan ibn Ash'ath (202-275 hijri), verification: Dr. Ziyaad Muhammad Mansoor, Maktabatul Uloom wal Hikam, 1414

52-Seer A'laamun Nubalaa'a, by Muhammad ibn Ahmed ibn Uthmaan adh Dhahabee (673—747 hijri), Mu'as'sa'satur Risaalah

53-Sharh Sunan ibn Majah, by Abeel Husein Nurud Deen as Sindee, (died 1138 hijri), Darul Ma'rifah, Beruit, Lebanon

54-Sharhul Aqeedatut Tahaawiyyah, by Ibn Abee Izz al Hanafee (731-792 hijri), hadeeth referencing by: Sheikh al Albaani, al Maktabul Islaamee

55-Shifaa'ul Garaam bi Akhbaaril Baladil Haraam, by Taqiud Deen al Faasee, (775-832 hijri), photocopied Darul Kutubul Ilmiyyah

56-Saheehul Jami' as Sagheer, by al Albaani, al Maktabul Islaamee, 1399 hijri

57-As Saheeh, by Ibn Khuzaimah, Abee Bakr Muhammad ibn Ishaaq, verification: Muhammad Mustafaa al' A'thamee, al Maktabul Islaamee, Beruit, 1395

58-Tabaqaat al Hanabilah, by Ibn Abee Ya'laa Muhammad ibn Muhammad ibnul Husein, (451-526 hijri) Darul Ma'rifah, Lebanon

59-Illalul Hadeth, by Ibn Abee Haatim Muhammad ibn Abdur Rahman, (240-327 hijri) verification: Team of researchers, Muta'bi'ul Humaydee, second version of the book printed by Maktabatul Muthanaa, Baghdaad, 1343

60-Al Uloow lil Alee'il Gaffaar, by Shamsud Deed adh Dhahabee, (673-747 hijri) Mat'ba'atul Aasimah, Cairo 1380

61-Al Awaasim minal Qawaasim, by al Qaadi Abee Bakr ibnul Arabee, (468-543 hijri)

62-Kitabul Fatwaa, by Ibnus Salah Uthmaan ibn Abdur Rahman (died 643) verification: Mustafaa Mahmood, Dar Ibnul Qayyim

63-Fusoolul Ahkaam, by Qaadi Abeel Waleed al Bajee Salman ibn Khalf (403-474 hijri), verification: Muhammad Abul Ajfaan, Maktabatut Towbah, Dar ibn Hazm, 1422

Al 'I'tibaa'a

64-Al Faqeehu wal Mutafaqih, by Abee Bakr Ahmed ibn Alee al Khateeb al Baghdaadi (391-463 hijri), correction of the texts: Ismaa'eel al Ansaari, Muta'bi'ul Qaseem, 1389

65-Lisaanul Arab, by Ibn Manthoor al Ifreeqee, (603-711 hijri), Dar Sadir, Beruit

66-Al Majmoo' Sharhul Muhadthab, by Yahyaa ibn Sharaf an Nawawi (631-676 hijri), al Maktabatus Salifiyyah in al Medinah

67-Majmoo' Fataawaa Sheikhul Islaam Ibn Taymiyyah, (661-728 hijri), texts gathered by: Abdur Rahman ibn Muhammad ibn Qaasim

68-Mukhtasir at Tahaawee, Ahmed ibn Muhammad ibn Salaamah (died 321), verification: Abul Wafaa al Afghaani, Dar Ihyaa'ail Uloom, Beruit

69-Mukhtasir al Uloow lil Aleeil Gaffaar, by al Albaani, al Maktabul Islaamee, 1413

70-Al Madkhal ilaa Sunan by al Bayhaqee, verification: Di'yaa'a ar Rahman, Darul Khulafaa'a lil Kitabil Islaamee

71-Masaa'il Imam Ahmed, Abdullah ibn Ahmed's transmission, verification: Zuhair ash Shawees, al Maktabul Islaamee, 1401

72-Masaa'il Imam Ahmed, Ibn Hani' Ishaaq ibn Ibrahim, (died 275) verification: Zuhair ash Shawees, al Maktabul Islaamee, 1400

73-Masaa'il Imam ahmed, Abu Dawud as Sijistaani Sulaymaan ibn Ash'ath (died 275), Muhammad Ameen Damaj

74-Al Mustadrak, by al Haakim Abee Abdullah (321-405 hijri), photocopied from a Indian printing, Halb

75-Al Masjidul Haraam Tarikhuhu wa Ahkaamuhu, by Wasiullah ibn Muhammad Abbaas, 1413

76-Al Musnad by Imam Ahmed ibn Hanbal (164-241 hijri) copied from an Egyptian copy, al Maktabul Islaamee, Beruit

77-Al Musnad by Abee Dawud Sulaymaan ibn Dawud at Tayaalasee (203 hijri), Da'iratul Ma'aarif, India, 1321

78-Al Musannaf, by Abdur Razaaq as Sanaanee, (126-211 hijri), verification: Habeebu Rahman al A'thamee, Darul Qalam, Beruit, 1390

79-Al Mu'jam al Kabeer, by Sulaymaan ibn Ahmed at Tabaraani, (260-360 hijri), verification: Hamdee Abdul Majeed as Salafee, Baghdaad, 1978

Al 'I'tibaa'a

80-Maqaalaat al Islaamiyeen, by Abeel Hasan al Ash'aree (260-326 hijri), verification: Retar, 1400

81-Manaazil al A'immah by al Sulmaasee, Yahyaa ibn Ibrahim, verification: Mahmood ibn Abdur Rahman Qadh, al Jamiatul Islaamiyyah

82-Manaaqib ash Shafi'ee, by al Bayhaqee, Ahmed ibnul Husein (384-458 hijri), verification: as Sayid Ahmed Saqar, Darut Turath, 1391

83-Mawaaridu Tham'aan bi Zawaaid Saheeh ibn Hibaan, by Nurud Deen al Haythamee, (735-807 hijri)

84-Al Muwaafaqaat fi Usoolish Sharee'ah, by Ibrahim ibn Musa Abee Ishaaq ash Shaatibee, (died 790), photocopied Abbaas Ahmed al Baaz, from the Abdullah Diraz version of the book

85-Muwafaqitul Khabar al Khabar, by Ibn Hajr, Ali ibn Ahmed al Asqalaani, (773-850 hijri), verification: Abdul Majeed as Salafee, Maktabatur Rushd, Riyadh

86-Al Muwa'ta'a, by Imam Malik ibn Anas (95-179 hijri), Mustafaa al Halabee, 1370

87-Al Hidaayah fi Sharhil Bidaayah, by al Margaynaanee, Alee ibn Abee Bakr (530-593 hijri) with 'al Binaayah' by Badrud Deen Mahmood ibn Ahmed al Aynee, (762-855 hijri), Darul Fikr

Al 'I'tibaa'a

Glossary of Terms

1-al-I'tibaa'a: This Arabic word has several meanings in English such as: observance, adherence to, imitation, copying, following the example of. What is intended in this compilation is clarifying how to follow, imitate and strictly adhere to the Prophet's Sunnah as done by the noble companions and the earlier scholars of 'fiqh'.

2-'at Taqleed: This Arabic word is similar in meaning to al-I'tibaa'a, as it means: imitation, copying, mimicry. Technically it means: acting upon a saying or action from someone whose sayings and actions are not authoritative sources or evidences in the religion.

3-Madth'hab, plural 'Madthaa'hib': School of 'fiqh' thought, also the word may be used to refer to a certain way, belief or ideology which is followed.

4-'makrooh' (disliked). The usage of this word amongst the salaf and earlier generation scholars mean something 'impermissible'. The later generation scholars understood it to mean 'disliked'

5- 'al ijtihaad': The scholar or jurist exerting all of his efforts and doing everything in his ability to know a religious ruling which contains no text, by the way of deductive and inferential reasoning.

6-Tayammum: To strike the earth with the hands and then blow the dust off and pass the palm of each hand over the other and then to pass them over the face. This is performed in the absence of water or/and when water is not available.

7- 'Madth'hab'/ Plural: Madthaa'hib: School of 'fiqh' thought, also the word may be used to refer to a certain way, belief or ideology which is followed.

8-Sunnah: Linguistically means way or path. Sunnah has different definitions according to the specific field of knowledge. Amongst the scholars of hadeeth, Sunnah means: any saying, action, approval, or attribute whether physical or moral which can be ascribed to the Prophet Muhammad. Amongst the scholars of 'Usoolul Fiqh' (principles of 'fiqh') Sunnah denote a saying, action, approval related from the Prophet other than the Quran. Amongst the scholar of 'Fiqh' Sunnah means: that which is firmly established as being demanded from one in the religion but not being obligatory.

9-Faqeeh, plural Fuqaahaa'a: a Jurist or scholar of 'fiqh'

10-Mu'tazilah: A deviant sect whose beliefs centre around five fundamentals: negating Allah's attributes, rejecting 'al Qadaa and al Qadr', believing that whoever commits a

Al 'I'tibaa'a

major sin is doomed to the hellfire, and that such a person is considered as not being a disbeliever nor a believer but between the two, also they believe that it is permissible to rebel against Muslim rulers.

11-Jahmiyyah: The Jahmiyya claimed that disbelief in Allah is but ignorance of Allah. This doctrine is attributed to Jahm ibn Safwan. The Jahmiyya claimed that if a person receives knowledge, then disavows it with his tongue, he does not commit disbelief with such a disavowal. They claim that belief (*eeman*) is indivisible and that its subscribers are all in one-and-the-same category. They claim that belief and disbelief can only be in the heart at the exclusion of any other member of the body ... What Jahm alone said is that Paradise and the Fire shall pass away and become extinct; that belief is only knowledge of Allah and nothing else; that disbelief is but ignorance of Allah and nothing else; that no act is anyone's doing in reality, other than Allah's alone, and that it is His doing. [This is the core of the belief of the Jabriyya] ... Jahm used to profess the ordering of good and the forbidding of indecency ... He used to say that Allah's knowledge is brought to be (*muhdath*). This is what they related from him. He also used to say that the Qur'an is created and that it must not be said that Allah has always been cognizant of things before they take place. [This is also what the Qadariyya and Mu`tazila professed.] (Al-Ash`ari, "Maqalat al-Islamiyyin wa Ikhtilaf al-Musallin" (1/214, 338).The Jahmiyya were considered to be disbelievers, and it is related that al-Bukhari said: "I hold as ignorant whoever does not declare the Jahmiyya to be disbelievers." This was also the Hanbali position as shown in many places of Ibn Abi Ya`la's "Tabaqat al-Hanabila" and the books of `Abd Allah ibn Ahmad ibn Hanbal, Abu Bakr al-Khallal, and `Uthman Abu Sa`id al-Darimi. Ibn Abi Ya`la relates from the Hanbali Abu Muhammad al-Barbahari:Some of the scholars, among them Ahmad ibn Hanbal, said that the Jahmi is a disbeliever (al-Jahmee kafir), he is not of the People of the Qibla, and his blood is licit to shed. He neither inherits nor is inherited-from. This is because they say that there is no jum`a prayer, nor congregational (jama`a) prayer, nor `Eid prayer; they say that whoever does not say that the Qur'an is created is a disbeliever; they consider licit the use of the sword against the Community of the Prophet (saw); they contravene all those who came before them; they investigate people with something which the Prophet (saw) never said, nor any of his Companions (ra); they try to close down mosques, humiliate Islam, and get rid of jihad; they strive toward disunity; they contradict the narrations of the Prophet (saw) and the Companions they speak on the basis of abrogated (*mansukh*) texts; they use ambiguous (mutashabih) texts as proofs; they instill doubt in the people concerning their Religion; they argue concerning their Lord [i.e., they deny His Attributes]; they say that there is no punishment in the grave, nor Basin (*hawd*), nor intercession, and that neither Paradise nor the Fire are yet created; and they deny much of what the Prophet (saw) said. (Abu Muhammad al-Barbahari, "Sharh Kitab al-Sunna," in Ibn Abi Ya`la's "Tabaqat al-Hanabila" (2:30))

Al 'I'tibaa'a

12- The People of al Qadr or Qadarriyah: This innovation came chronologically from the following people: Al-Jahm ibn Safwan to Al-Ja'd ibn Dirham toBayan ibnSam'an toTaloot to Labeed ibn Al-A'sam. Among them Taloot was the nephew of Labeed ibn Al-A'sam who himself was a magician and had a Jewish root. Some Jewish sects have extreme Qadar ideology.

Al-Jahm ibn Safwan (and his wife) introduced three concepts among the Muslims which are very deadly for the whole religion. These concepts destroy the belief of Muslims.

a) Al-Jabriyyah: This says that everything that we do is done by Allah.We have no free will and are like feathers scattered by the wind without any sort of control. Meaning we won't be held responsible for anything.

b) Al-Tajahhum: This says that Allah has no names. This will mean that Allah doesn't exist.

c). Al-'Erjiya': Faith is knowledge in the heart. So no need for actions.

Al-Qadariyyah, who went to extremes in denying Al-Qadar. The innovators: Ghaylan Ad-Dimishqee (105 A.H.) Ma'bad Al-Juhanee (80 A.H.)Seesawayh (a.k.a Sinsawayh Al-Baqqal and Sawsan). Seesawayh was Christian monk. This view was also spread by Wasil ibn 'Ata (131 A.H.) and 'Amr ibn Ubaid (134 A.H.). Bishr ibn Mu'tamir Al-Koofee, and Shams Ad-Deen Ja'far Al-Bahloolee Az-Zaidee (573 A.H.).al-Qadariyyah became more popular and was adopted by the Al-Mu'tazilah who in turn convinced the 'Abbasid khalifah al-Ma'mun to spread it in Baghdad, and this belief was especially popular in Kufa.

13-Tawheed: Islamic monotheism

14-Aqeedah: creed

15-'fiqh' : linguistically means 'understanding'. Technically it means "fiqh"

16-Maturiddiyyah: The Maturidiyyah are a faction amongst the factions of Ilm al-Kalaam, sharing with the Jahmiyyah, Mu'tazilah, Kullaabiyyah and Ash'ariyyah in the foundations of their approach (i.e. Ilm ul-Kalaam) but differing with them on subsidiary matters following on from those kalaamist foundations. There was no immediate faction known as the Maturidiyyah after the death of its founder, Abu Mansur al-Maturidi (d. 333H), but the sect and its creed became formalized and codified a few centuries later. The founder of the Maturidiyyah is Abu Mansur Muhammad bin Muhammad bin Mahmood al-Maturidi as-Samarqandi, an ascription to Maturid, a place near to Samarqand, beyond the river, in what is today Uzbekistan. There is not a great deal of biographical accounts present for him and his upbringing, who he took knowledge from, his learning and influences. The teachers mentioned for him are Abu Nasr Ahmad al-Iyaadee, Naseer bin Yahyaa al-Balkhee, Muhammad bin Muqaatil ar-Raazee, Abu Bakr Ahmad al-Jawzjaanee. He is held in veneration and respect by the Maturidiyyah who give him lofty titles such as the "Imaam of the Mutakallimeen". He was a contemporary of Abu al-Hasan al-Ash'ari (d. 324H), but it is not established that they met. What is common to them both is that they were present in a time in which there were battles between the people of the Sunnah and and the innovators, the Jahmiyyah and Mu'tazilah. The Jahmiyyah and Mu'tazilah were the pioneers of Ilm ul-Kalaam, and through that they entered much deviation amongst the Muslims. The Kullaabiyyah, Maturidiyyah and Ash'ariyyah were also Ahl ul-Kalaam, and thus their doctrinal positions represented an attempt to reconcile between what was laid down by their predecessors in certain affairs, especially in the subject of al-Asmaa was-Sifaat, and between the madhhab of the Salaf. The Maturidiyyah stemmed out of the Hanafiyyah and the Ash'ariyyah stemmed out of the Kullaabiyyah in the midst of these conflicts. The result was that they tried to tread a middle path between the Mu'tazilah Jahmiyyah and the people of Hadeeth, using kalaamist principles fundamentally. They rejected the sifaat fi'liyyah (actions tied to Allaah's will and power), considering them to be "hawaadith" (events, occurrences). This was in order to maintain an intellectual proof they share with the Jahmiyyah and Mu'tazilah which was used to demonstrate the universe is created to the atheists, using the language, classification and terminologies of the atheists themselves in that regard. For this reason, the Kullaabi-Ashari creed is very similar to the Maturidi creed, as its roots and foundations are the same. These roots and foundations were acquired from the Jahmiyyah and Mu'tazilah, as they were its predecessors, even if the Kullaabiyah, Asha'riyyah, Maturidiyyah differed on issues with their fellow Mutakallimeen. Abu Mansur al-Maturidi died in 333H, and he had a number of works, amongst them "Ta'weelaat Ahl is-Sunnah" in which he gathered together many ta'weels whose origins lay with the Jahmiyyah and Mu'tazilah, in their ta'weels of the verses pertaining to the Attributes. He also has a book, "Kitaab ut-Tawheed", based upon the way and path of the Jahmiyyah and Mu'tazilah in affirming Allaah's Ruboobiyyah through ilm al-kalaam whilst negating and figuratively explaining away the attributes, opposing the way of the Salaf in that, differing only with the Jahmiyyah and Mu'tazilah in what can and cannot be negated or denied for Allaah without invalidating their devised rational proof for His existence. He also had refutations of the Mu'tazilah, the Raafidah, and the Qaraamitah. The creeds of the Kullaabiyyah, Ash'ariyyah and Maturidiyyah are all approximate to each other in that they are all based upon the negation of what they call "hawaadith" (events, occurrences) from Allaah - which is a term used to refer to actions of Allaah that are tied to His will and power. As they perceive the universe to be nothing but a collection of events (hawaadith), then whatever gives the presumption of an event in the revealed texts, must be explained away. Thus, their ta'weel of istiwaa (ascent), and nuzool (descent) and ghadab (anger), mahabbah (love), ridhaa (pleasure) and so on. In their debates with the Mu'tazilah, they were not able to free themselves completely of the doubts and arguments of the Mu'tazilah against them in this regard, whilst they did manage to argue rationally for the affirmation of the attributes. Thus, the creed of these factions became settled upon affirming the Names and some of the Attributes whilst rejecting the Sifaat Fi'liyyah. And all of these factions are in opposition to the creed of the Salaf, the people of Hadeeth, Aathaar and Sunnah, whose creed was to affirm for Allaah whatever Allaah and His Messenger (sallallaahu alayhi wasallam) affirmed for Him whilst negating takyeef and tashbeeh from all of that, and sticking to the revealed texts in both affirmation and negation of attributes for Allaah, and shunning ambiguous, or new terms not found in the revealed texts and nor used by the Salaf.

17- The Ash'arees are the followers of Abul Hasan Al-Ash'aree (d.324). Abul Hasan Al-Ash'aree was a student of [forgot his name] who was a student of Jahm Ibn Safwaan, who was a student of Ja'd Ibn Dirham, (who was executed because of his deviant beliefs), who took his doctrine from Bayan ibn Sam'an, who took his doctrine from Talut, who was the nephew and son-in-law of Labid ibn A'sam (the Jew), who once cast a spell on the Prophet (saw). So the Asharees have their roots from Jewish beliefs, as the Jews were the first ones to proclaim such beliefs (that Allaah does not have such "human-like" (as they claim!) attributes).The Jahmiyyahs (misguided sect) deny all of Allaah's Attributes, whereas the Ash'arees deny all except 7, and they make ta'weel (figurative interpretations) in the Attributes of Allaah. For example, the change the meanings of the Attributes from their apparent meanings (i.e, to say Allaah's Hand means Allaah's power).The seven attributes they (the Ash'arees) affirm for Allaah are; Living, Knowing, Speech, Will, Hearing, Seeing and Ability (Power).Both, the Jahmiyyah and the Ash'arees perform Ta'weel (an interpretation not in accordance with the way of the Salaf) with the attributes they deny. Examples of such ta'weel is saying Allaah's Hand means power, Allaah's Face means reward, or Allaah's Eyes to mean knowledge, or His Pleasure to mean His rewards etc. Other deviations of the Ash'arees are: they claim that Allaah will not be seen in the hereafter, they claim that one cannot point up when being asked where Allaah is, they claim that the speech of Allaah is without sound and is an internal speech, and many other misguided beliefs which are contrary to what the Prophet and his companions believed.The Ash'arees are found amongst more muslims than one thinks. The Hanafees, Maalikees, And Shaafi'ees are mostly devided into being Ash'arees and Maatureedees in their 'aqeedah. The same istrue for many of the "scholars" of Al-Azhar (in Egypt), the deobandees, Brelwees, Soofees.The Ash'arees are under the umbrella of the people of theological rhetoric (Ahlul Kalaam). The works of the Greek Philosophy over time was translated into Arabic as was the philosophical works from Indian and Persian philosophers. This, in turn, effected the Ummah, and caused much deviation to occur, and they themselves are considered one of the misguided groups and not from Ahlus Sunnah.

18-Saheeh: In the science of hadeeth means: a hadeeth which has a continuous chain of narration, made up of trustworthy reliable narrators, who narrate from similar trustworthy narrators, which is free from defects and irregularities. There are five conditions for a hadeeth to be 'Saheeh': 1. Connected chain of transmitters, 2. Integrity

Al 'I'tibaa'a

of the narrator, 3. Accuracy and preciseness of the narrator, 4. Conformity, 5. Absence of hidden defects.

19-Hasan: In the science of hadeeth means: a hadeeth which is transmitted by upstanding narrators with a continuous chain of narration, free from any hidden defects or conflict with superior texts. Except that it contains a narrator or narrators whose accuracy is inferior and less than the narrators of 'saheeh' ahadeeth.

20-Da'eef: In the science of hadeeth means: a hadeeth in which any one of the five conditions of 'Saheeh' have not been met. They are of many grades and types, but there are two main factors which cause a hadeeth to be 'Da'eef' or rejected: 1. A break in the chain of narration, 2. A defect in the narrator.

21. Mursal: In the science of hadeeth means: a hadeeth in which the companion is omitted from the chain of narration, and the successor of the companion (tabi'ee) narrates it from the Prophet Muhammad.

22. Mufti: One who gives religious verdicts

www.ingramcontent.com/pod-product-compliance
Lightning Source LLC
LaVergne TN
LVHW011934070526
838202LV00054B/4635